MUSIC IN CUBA

CULTURAL STUDIES OF THE AMERICAS

Edited by George Yúdice, Jean Franco, and Juan Flores

MUSIC IN CUBA

Alejo Carpentier

EDITED AND WITH AN INTRODUCTION BY

Timothy Brennan

Translated by Alan West-Durán

CULTURAL STUDIES OF THE AMERICAS, VOLUME 5

University of Minnesota Press
Minneapolis • London

The University of Minnesota Press gratefully acknowledges the assistance provided for the publication of this book by the McKnight Foundation.

The University of Minnesota Press appreciates the assistance of Timothy Brennan and Richard Swartz in the translation of this book.

Published by the University of Minnesota Press
111 Third Avenue South, Suite 290
Minneapolis, MN 55401-2520
http://www.upress.umn.edu

Library of Congress Cataloging-in-Publication Data

Carpentier, Alejo, 1904–1980
    [Música en Cuba. English]
    Music in Cuba / Alejo Carpentier ; edited and with an introduction by
Timothy Brennan ; translated by Alan West-Durán.
        p.   cm. — (Cultural studies of the Americas ; v. 5)
    Translation of: Música en Cuba.
    ISBN 0-8166-3229-4 (hardcover)
    1. Music—Cuba—History and criticism.   I. Brennan, Timothy.
II. Title.   III. Series.
    ML207.C8 C313 2001
    780'.97291—dc21   00-011171

Printed in the United States of America on acid-free paper

The University of Minnesota is an equal-opportunity educator and employer.

12 11 10 09 08 07 06 05 04 03 02 01   10 9 8 7 6 5 4 3 2 1

A true tradition is not the witnessing of a past closed and finished; it is a living force which animates and informs the present.

– IGOR STRAVINSKY

Contents

Introduction to the English Edition

Timothy Brennan

Music in Cuba, written by chance in the early 1940s, is among the most plagiarized masterpieces of the New World canon. The Cuban *son* of the late nineteenth century, which later became "salsa" in the commercial studios of New York in the 1970s, had its first real panegyrist in Alejo Carpentier (1904–80). He was first to see its full importance and first to prophesy its future. As the author of *Music in Cuba*, he was also the prototype for those street philosophers and musical savants who crept onto the scene with the rock invasions of the 1960s. Musicians in New York were borrowing Caribbean rhythms for years, following a tradition laid down in Cuba by U.S. composers such as the mid-nineteenth-century pianist Louis Moreau Gottschalk, or later Cole Porter, George Gershwin, and others who "knew a good thing." Carpentier saw the implications of all that first, and recorded it in this book.

As the largest island of the Antilles, and the customary port of departure for homebound Spanish galleons throughout the age of empire, Cuba had been from early times the "little Europe" of the New World. Its classical music had flourished for centuries through the work of accomplished performers of the ballet, the opera, and the symphony. By the late nineteenth century following the abolition of slavery, the central place of working-class, urban African music was becoming clearer to almost everyone. It crowded in upon the world of the artistic elite, drifting up into the concert halls from the streets and the *cabildos*. The *cabildos* — the black mutual-aid societies set up to control slaves by keeping distinct African ethnicities separate — also served as clearing houses for Afro-Caribbean art and religion following slavery's repeal.

1

This unique setting conspired to make Cuban musicians model popularizers. Traveling to New York, Mexico City, Miami, and Paris, they colloquialized traditional symphonic music by blending it with African rhythms and rural Spanish riffs. Unimpressed by the supposedly rigid boundaries between high and low culture, they brought Cuban music to global prominence. In *Music in Cuba*, Carpentier attempts to drive home the significance of this transgression: "Today the Cuban composer has eliminated this erroneous notion by which one posits a difference between popular and elite music."[1] Steering clear of the crudely anthropological approach of his predecessors, Carpentier studied Afro-Caribbean music with impeccable classical credentials. His work is where European classical music and black national-popular styles live in a permanent productive tension.

Contemporary attempts to continue that unsettling mix of the classical with the popular have been eloquent but uneven. Salsa never enjoyed the reverence shown reggae in Britain, for example, or rock and jazz in the United States — at least in the big music markets. This divergence in the respect paid various African-based New World musics is with us still. One can see it vividly in the high production finish of the CD retrospectives, or in the tone of awe accompanying television documentaries on Peter Tosh, the Rolling Stones, Bob Dylan, or John Coltrane. The music of MTV or BET, the music dubbed in basements and sold in New York cassette stalls — all the music, in other words, that finds its way to us without our having to look for it — has lately, and for a variety of reasons, been the subject of serious books. Most of them speak of mass culture as a socially important thing. Rap particularly is considered (rightly) to be a subject worthy of scholars.[2]

Carpentier pioneered that sort of discussion in 1946. And so it is something of a paradox that Latin music has been comparatively ignored in recent studies of pop. There are a variety of reasons for the neglect, but the elusive aura of "old-fashioned" Latin America is part of it. Not as hip as our contemporaries, nor as joyfully sociopathic as the Dionysian punksters of a later era, *Music in Cuba* has some of that languorous solemnity of Havana's Doric columns and the Old World charm of Carpentier's novels from the 1950s. Yet the book managed to popularize (or better, colloquialize) a story that had until then been imprisoned in ethnography of a technical sort.

Far from being simply a journalist, Carpentier managed in *Music in Cuba* to build a narrative around the ponderous fieldwork of the brilliant Cuban sociologists Fernando Ortiz and (later) Lydia Cabrera. With a great deal more depth and literary flair than non-Cuban musicologists such as Nicholas Slonimsky (one of the few North Americans who paid attention early to Latin American forms), Carpentier nevertheless wrote with some of Slonimsky's goals in mind. Like Slonimsky's, his work is, among many other things, a straight, technical history of musical forms, encyclopedically laid out. But Carpentier did not limit his story to the genre of brief musical appreciation as found in the work of practicing musicians such as Eduardo Sánchez de Fuentes. Some of Ortiz's famous studies on *lucumí* religion and the Afro-Cuban musical practices preceded Carpentier's, but while they were fantastically detailed, innovative, and theoretically brilliant, they were also basically monographs. Carpentier, by contrast, offers a limber dance among several genres. In Latin musical criticism at least, nothing like it existed before.

Leaving Cuba for Paris in 1928, Carpentier fled a country as suffocated by the United States as it had earlier been by Spain. His friends and colleagues on the island were all radicals of various sorts — toiling in the studios and salons when not in the streets. They represented the paradigmatic situation of all colonial intellectuals: breaking down social barriers, finding ways to outrage the creole bourgeoisie, manufacturing a nationally specific cultural uniqueness, building a nation independent of outside (in this case, Yankee) control. The malcontents of the national movement in those years took their lead from the champions of Afro-Cuba. Their movement was *negrismo* — largely, although not exclusively, led by white intellectuals in the 1920s and 1930s, and similar to the Harlem Renaissance but more socially conscious. Disgusted by the blind prejudice that surrounded them, the *negrismo* intellectuals set out for the first time in Cuban history to document the cultural and demographic centrality of "blackness" to Cuban identity. Their undertaking was not merely cultural but political and strategic in an island colony where the binds of color and class were rigid and unforgiving.

Making his living in Paris as a chronicler for the upwardly mobile back home, Carpentier might have looked back upon the time as an inevitable preparation for the book. If his newspaper employers in Cuba were primarily interested in uplifting accounts of the European salon and concert scene—and this is what he primarily produced for them—Carpentier would also witness another, unexpected transformation. "There is nothing more contemporary, nothing more *now* in Paris these days," he wrote in 1922, "than the abrupt and unexpected triumph of Cuban music."[3] Several of his dispatches broke with custom, then, by offering testimony that could only have pleased his audience, particularly because the testimony was true. These reports excitedly described the *"cubanismos"* then invading Europe under the sign of *"rumba"*: Julio Cuevas, Rogelio Barba, the Tres Hermanos Barreto, and Fernando Collazo performed in such Parisian clubs as La Coupole and Melody's Bar. With a certain amusement, Carpentier bore witness to the parade of celebrities and intellectuals who found their way into the nightclubs: Charles Chaplin, Buster Keaton, Jacques Rivière, André Schaeffner. Even "the pallid daughters of Albion forget for a moment their Pre-Raphaelite poses by burying themselves in the sonorous sortilege of the Antilles," he snickered.[4] Writing in the so-called Jazz Age, Carpentier insisted it was also the age of the Cuban *son*. Few were telling that story, and no one as successfully as he.

And yet, had it not been for a trip to Haiti with his wife Lilia and Louis Jouvet in 1943, he might have amounted to little more than another Cuban hanger-on in Paris—and there was no small number of those. As one of the products of that trip, *Music in Cuba* set the stage for everything in his career that followed: it "trained [him]" in his own words, "to write the later novels."[5] Considered by his friends and contemporaries at the time as a journalist and radio producer, as the author of a few "Afro-Cuban" poems and a failed novel, Carpentier began to compose the fiction that made him famous only after the trip to Haiti, and the musical investigation it inspired.

Music in Cuba was, in that sense, a fortunate accident. On the other hand, it had to be written, and all of his life up to that point dictated that it would be. His first tentative assaults on the project probably date from before his wanderings in Haiti in his first full year back in Cuba. In that year (1939), he stumbled upon the lost scores of Esteban Salas y Castro, the eighteenth-century Cuban composer. Some of the scholarly legwork was probably done in a haphazard fashion over the next few years. When he found himself in the offices of the Fondo de Cultura Económica while returning from Haiti to Havana via Mexico in 1943 (some friends had casually invited him to accompany them), the idea for the book must already have been in his head. The Fondo's director, Daniel Cosío Villegas, chided him for wasting his talents on radio, and ended up commissioning him to write a history of Cuban music that was to be part of a general encyclopedia on Latin America. "That suits me fine," said Carpentier. "How much time do I have?" Eleven months, came the reply. "It was monstrous," Carpentier later recalled.[6]

Three years after the publication of *Music in Cuba*, Carpentier announced that he had "usurped" the title of musicologist. He admitted once again that the book's genesis was not the accident it seemed — more a well-prepared venture, long in the making:

> As often happens in our America, one is anxiously driven to be many-sided.... There are so many jobs waiting to be done...
> I, for example, set about writing music criticism when I saw that the young Cuban composers of my generation — Amadeo Roldán, Alejandro García Caturla — staged their innovative works before an uncomprehending public. They had to suffer the hostility of critics who still hadn't gotten past Wagner.... In 1924, Jorge Mañach, who had just finished writing an outline for a history of Cuban painting, asked me why there was no parallel in Cuban music. My answer came in 1939, when I returned to Cuba after eleven years of European life. Seeing that no one had decided to do it, I took the burden on my own shoulders. I turned myself into a scholar, a library rat, a paleographer, a midget historian and, in 1946, the book was published.[7]

It had taken eleven months, working "from six in the morning un-til five in the afternoon," traveling the whole length of Cuba to gather primary sources. *Music in Cuba* had opened a door on a vast new field of investigation, not because no one had written about Cuban music before, but because the history had never been nar-rated like this.

The originality of the book consists in its combination. Books on Cuban music had certainly preceded Carpentier's, as he him-self remarks in his Preface. And there are others he did not men-tion — among them, Emilio Grenet's *Música popular cubana* (1939). This work, which is primarily a compendium of musical scores, opens with a forty-page study of the basic genres of Cuban music, divided between those "bordering on the Spanish" and those "bor-dering on the African." But it never delves deeper than this super-ficial categorization. A much more important precursor was, of course, Ortiz in his groundbreaking studies on Afro-Cuban cul-ture — a subject that confronted the twin, inseparable, aspects of black Caribbean life: religion and music (*palo monte* and *rumba/ candomblé* and *son*). Before Carpentier's book, Ortiz had already written *La clave xilofónica de la música cubana: ensayo etnográfico* (The xylophonic *clave* of Cuban music: an ethnographic essay, 1935) and *De la música afrocubana: un estímulo para su estudio* (On Afro-Cuban music: a stimulus for further study, 1934). But, as their ti-tles suggest, these were either specialist monographs or appeals to future work. They were in that respect an invitation that Carpen-tier accepted.

Traveling all of Cuba in search of primary sources (the most important were found in the cathedral of Santiago more than 450 miles from Havana on the far eastern tip of the island), Carpentier grew proud of his achievement.[8] He later claimed that *Music in Cuba* had prompted an entirely new set of questions. By 1974, however, he was more retiring: "Others have ... surpassed my work." A few years later: "The book deserves a complete revision and expan-sion."[9]

If assembling the documents for *Music in Cuba* gave him the his-torical repertoire for his later fiction, that fiction itself was struc-turally, and anecdotally, musical. Carpentier's novels would eventually change the international scope of the genre by articulating concepts that helped to show the Latin novelists of the "boom" how to reach North American and European readers with portraits of a *political* (rather than merely racial) other. The runaway success of Latin American fiction in U.S. and European translation throughout the 1970s had much to do with its portrayal of the political subject formulated in Carpentier's generation. If Carpentier managed to transform an exoticized "homo tropicalis" into a political actor in a history that happened (the Haitian revolution, the revolts of early colonial Guadeloupe, and so on), he also helped overcome the U.S. prejudice against the dramatization of politics itself, which is what tended to make Caribbean fiction, in American eyes, all the more foreign. The thrill of making new connections in the music project, at any rate — and a good deal of the material that project unearthed — found its way into the series of novels known as "The American Cycle." Indeed, music is integral to all of his novels, from the musician antihero of *Los pasos perdidos* (The lost steps, 1953), who sets off on a journey to the upper Orinoco to discover the origins of "primitive" music, to *El acoso* (Manhunt, 1956), whose major character might be said to be Beethoven's Fifth Symphony. In *El concierto barroco* (The baroque concert, 1974), one finds an imaginary convocation of Handel, Scarlatti, and Vivaldi; and again in *El arpo y la sombra* (The harp and the shadow, 1979), a depiction of the dangerous sensuality that was imported to Spain with Caribbean rhythms. Even his Marxist novel-memoir of interwar Europe — the great, late, unfinished work he wrote while serving in Castro's government, *La consagración de la primavera* (1987) — begins by invoking its namesake, Igor Stravinsky's *Rite of Spring.*

Music in Cuba, then, is much more than a simple chronicle of an island's musical past. Positioned between socialism and capitalism, Latin France and Latin America, the book theorizes the political role of music in the Caribbean as a whole, not only Cuba, and includes significant passages on influences from the French colonies (especially Haiti), the southern United States, Mexico, and Venezuela as well. Moreover, it clarifies the role of Latin intellectuals in Europe. Apart from that, it turns on its head the usual view of interwar Marxist approaches to African diasporic culture. *Music in*

Cuba declares that Cuba played a leading role in the field of popular music. But, like all the cultural worlds that found their origins in slavery, the Afro-Latin sound typically hovers like an indistinct echo, a sort of "background music" simultaneously highbrow and lowbrow, rarefied and pop. One hears it often (in Hollywood film-scores, for example) without knowing where it came from.

Now Cuban music is once again sweeping through Hollywood, luring the stars out to clubs and spawning films just as it did in the time of Rudolph Valentino, and then again in the mambo craze of the 1940s and 1950s, just as Frank Sinatra popularized bossa nova in the 1960s (Sinatra, the David Byrne of his day, was instrumental as a conduit for Brazilian pop). "Albita," an exile from 1993 who came to the United States via Mexico, has a following at the Centro Vasco in Miami's Little Havana, where Angelica Huston, Liza Minelli, Bob Rafelson, and Madonna flock to hear her perform. Andy Garcia recently made a documentary on the seventy-six-year-old mambo master, Israel "Cachao" López. Garcia took him personally to the trendy House of Blues on LA's Sunset Strip. Meanwhile, in the woolly field of "world music," a new city youth culture takes its Latin music straight, learning cha-cha-chá steps at the local dance halls, paying money to bring in the living legends ("Chucho" Valdés, Los Van Van, Rubén González, and others). Latin music has always been here—a staple of orchestral film music, of Broadway, and of jazz from Tommy Dorsey to Dizzy Gillespie. The point of *Music in Cuba* is, among other things, to describe where it came from.

DOWN AND IN—PARIS AND AFTER

Heralded as the inventor of "magical realism," honored by contemporaries such as Edith Sitwell and Roger Caillois as the greatest novelist of the century, Alejo Carpentier was, in his own mind at least, primarily a music critic. The only one of his major works ignored in this country—untranslated if not unknown—is *Music in Cuba*. Living a little more than a decade in Paris between the wars, Carpentier spent his years of apprenticeship in the avant-garde circles of the Deux Magots, experimenting with the art of radio, and composing enough music reviews to fill more than four volumes.

Brought up on Balzac, Zola, and Flaubert, Carpentier—although born and raised in Cuba—had studied in Paris at the Lycée Jeanson de Sailly before he was sixteen, and spoke Spanish throughout his life with a French accent. He also spent key parts of his youth and early teens on a small ranch in "El Lucero" on the outskirts of Havana, purchased by his architect father in 1915. There he lived among the chickens and geese he would later describe in the last chapter of *The Kingdom of This World*.

In 1922, at the age of eighteen, Carpentier launched his column "Obras famosas" (Great works) for the small Havana weekly *La Discusión*—a publication he later dismissed as an uneventful literary broadsheet. The articles, nevertheless, represented a flurry of highbrow treatments of European classics that also considered work ranging from H. G. Wells and Gogol to the little-known early plays of Georges Bataille. Apart from giving us a map of Carpentier's remarkably broad early interests, the column prefigured his later program on "great figures" for a Havana radio station during World War II, betraying his eagerness to be part of the mainstream by showing some of the flair for publicity he would display at Radio Luxembourg and Poste Parisien between the wars. The early journalism also demonstrates that Carpentier—already in 1927, well before many of the musical studies of Ortiz—was writing on the "possibilities of Afro-Cuban music" for the small Havana journal *Musicalia*.[10]

Journalist and reviewer, Carpentier cut his life down the middle. He had returned from the lycée, in his own words, "an acceptable pianist" and clearly had more designs as a librettist than a novelist in early life: "At the age of seven, I was playing the Preludes of Chopin. And I knew Debussy perfectly.... I soon succeeded at becoming a tremendous improviser [*repentista*] (I think the word has disappeared from the dictionaries): that is to say, I used to play everything anyone put in front of me."[11] His father, a French émigré and a distinguished cellist, had studied with Pablo Casals; his grandmother had been a distinguished protégée of César Franck. His own noteworthy musical career began with the study of composition while attending a secondary school in Havana, where he displayed modernist sympathies from the start. Speaking of a slightly later period, he remarked: "I passed without any difficulty to Stravinsky and Schoenberg and — for that reason (we're talking about 1924) — to the discovery of jazz and the return to Bach. Whoever lived during that time knows what I'm talking about."[12]

By 1927, he had written a one-act ballet with Amadeo Roldán, and, later in the same year, two Afro-Cuban poems for voice and piano, with music by Alejandro García Caturla. Over the next few years came public success. Shortly after arriving in Paris, his fragment of a future novel — *Yamba-O* — was performed at the Théâtre Beriza, a burlesque tragedy with music by Marius François Gaillard (the novel ¡*Ecué-Yamba-Ó!*, which he had written in Machado's prisons, would not be published until 1933 in Madrid). Having staked out a role as interpreter of the minor ballet form, he went on to compose two choreographic poems, *Mata-Cangrejo* (Killer crab) and *Azúcar* (Sugar), which were both reviewed favorably. Meanwhile, with the waters well tested in France, he allowed his Afro-Cuban fantasy, *La rebambaramba*, to be staged in Cuba by the Orquesta Filarmónica de La Habana in 1928, with music by Roldán. Similar collaborations with European masters of more international reputation followed — Edgar Varèse, for example, and Darius Milhaud — all performed publicly, and to surprisingly large acclaim. By 1937, departing from the role of librettist, he played his hand as a musician proper, composing the incidental music for a production of Miguel Cervantes's *Numancia* at the Théâtre Antoine, directed by Jean-Louis Barrault.

None of these successes had been foreseeable. Carpentier had written these pieces opportunistically, and with a similar intention. By profession, his job was that of instructing a provincial Cuba on recent artistic developments in France. By disposition, his role became more and more adamantly the opposite: simply explaining to the French public what made Cuba artistically matter. Against the grain of his cultural training, he was playing a political role, and he knew it. While still living in Havana in his late teens and early twenties writing artsy pieces for magazines such as *Carteles*,

Chic, and *Social*, he had joined the "Movement of Veterans and Patriots," organized against the government of Alfredo Zayas. As the world of politics opened up before him, he traveled to Mexico in 1926, tracking down the famous *muralistas* whose legends had already spread throughout Latin America. He returned with memories of fleeting encounters, ready to try his hand at social change. By joining the Grupo Minorista a year later, he embraced its famous manifesto calling for "the revision of all false and wasteful values, for a vernacular art and . . . for Cuba's economic independence." He put his name to the document, and for that act was imprisoned by Machado in 1927.

While contributing his editorial and writing skills to the Minorista's journal, *Revista de Avance*, Carpentier made friends with Julio Antonio Mella, Rubén Martínez Villena, and Juan Marinello in 1923 (two years later Mella and Martínez Villena founded the Cuban Communist Party). To understand *Music in Cuba*, one has to imagine something of this dissident mind-set among relatively privileged intellectuals living under colonial conditions. In accounts of Carpentier's life, the *Revista de Avance* has often been called simply "avant-garde." But despite the journal's title, this is a misunderstanding. The journal was really a forum for cultural internationalism, rudimentary party organization, and a more generalized intellectual hunger — combative, sociological, and eminently practical. The *Revista de Avance*'s points of departure were its own, and it reads today as if it were written yesterday. Its articles urgently demanded independence for Puerto Rico, and provided a superb analysis of cosmopolitanism ("la pretensión ecuménica") in an essay titled "Spanish Universalism" (1927).[13]

In its pages, the black question was raised loudly, but not exotically. The Minoristas saw black culture as an important way of simply saying "No." Its attractions stemmed, as Carpentier put it, from an "intense desire to recuperate all the traditions depreciated by the bourgeoisie."[14] In 1929, one finds an unsentimental piece of political strategy, "The Negro Question," followed by dignified outbursts against Southern U.S. lynch-mob justice and the Havana Yacht Club ("Civility and Skin Color," 1930); articles on the rights of workers and the cruel counsel offered the poor and the hungry;

a historical and somewhat theoretical analysis of "Vanguardism" (1927); articles on the topic "Capitalism and Intelligence" (undated); on "Proletarian Russian Theater" (1927) as well as the Havana Exhibition of new art in 1927. There is a long translation of an essay by Bertrand Russell on the new philosophy (language philosophy, pluralism, pragmatism) (1927) and a favorable piece on feminism.

Carpentier, it might be said, came to Afro-Cuban music through two doors. He entered first of all as a proponent of the new music of Stravinsky and the Second Viennese School of Arnold Schoenberg, Alban Berg, and Anton Webern, as well as the experimentalist composers who drew on the folkloric strategies of musical nationalism (Glinka, Prokofiev, Villa-Lobos, and others); second, as a left nationalist who befriended the future founders of Cuban socialism. His music criticism primarily covered European composers — Dvořák, Poulenc, Weber, Strauss — but long looks at jazz, rock and roll, and the popular Cuban sound are interspersed. Both of Carpentier's musical enterprises are part of one complex liberatory desire.

Although in the Western intellectual imagination, the black had been alternately figured as the forbidden, the despised, and the longed-for, it has to be appreciated that in Cuba — unlike, say, in France or Zurich — blackness was not primarily an image. Slavery continued to exist in Cuba until the end of the nineteenth century (shortly before *negrismo* began) in spite of the fact that black military leaders, national heroes, and musicians played the role (as Carpentier puts it in the text) of "political men," filling the pages of Cuban history. Being despised and envied at once — not unlike in Europe of the Jazz Age — they were nevertheless the ignored material factor of Cuban national identity: a sign of Cuba's ownership abroad, and a force for ending that ownership. Much more than a symbolic yearning, "blackness" was a strategic and demographic force in a way that it simply could not be in Europe.

Carpentier's prologue to *La rebambaramba* is one of the better places to discover how experimentalism combines with the creole intellectual's attempt to politicize blackness. Most of his libretti of the 1930s had a common rationale:

Everything in our present climate can be transcribed in gestures, refrains, verses, and rhythms. The past as well as the present. The comic as well as the dramatic. . . . The libretto of *La rebambaramba* (1927) came to me while poring over a recording by Milhaud based on some *comparsas* [carnival bands] from the Día de Reyes festivals. . . . In *Manita en el suelo* [Hand in the soil] (1930)—a farce for puppets and actors written for the composer Alejandro Caturla—I set in motion characters such as la Virgen de la Caridad del Cobre, el Capitán General de España, Juan Odio, Juan Indio y Juan Esclavo, el Chine de la Characa, Candita la Loca, El Gallo Motoriongo, and Papá Montero, who presided as master of ceremonies. . . . In *El milagro de Anaquillé* [The miracle of Anaquillé] (1927), I used the choreography of traditional Afro-Cuban initiation ceremonies without changing a thing. In the next ballet, *Azúcar,* I tried by way of dynamic action to express the fearful life of a sugar factory, the rhythms of the harvest, the sweat of workers, and the blind activity of the machines.[15]

Figures from Afro-Cuban religion and popular legend were accompanied here by all the signs of modernity, seen, for example, in the characters' names in *El milagro de Anaquillé:* the Businessman, the Sailor, the Flapper, the Little Devil. The feeling was a quasi-futurist, rather than a surrealist, one: the buzz of the machine found itself in the company of social types from Constructivist theater or the early Bertolt Brecht. There was, in other words, an intentionally harsh, almost sociological iconography to this brand of vanguardism—a realist sublime that foreshadows *"lo real"* of Carpentier's later "marvelous reality."

Although the story of Carpentier's departure from Cuba for Paris in 1928 has sometimes been explained as his fleeing the Machado dictatorship, he was not really forced to leave. It is true that he had spent the previous seven months in prison, but he left the country because it was simply too hard for him to make a living there. The antiquated social customs combined with the exigencies of tyranny to make life intolerable for left intellectuals of his stripe. Carpentier was compelled to register with the authorities, and so he naturally complained of the government's ludicrous stupidities: "Gerardo Machado, overthrown by a general strike, died without ever knowing the difference between 'anarchism,' 'communism,' and 'vanguardism': so he once closed down as subversive an exposition on modern painting."[16] To be fair, Machado was not alone, and his particular confusion continues to plague aesthetic theory today. What is more, the years 1925–26 in Latin America were alive with talk of revolution, sprouting in many colors from a variety of plots. The enormous cultural and aesthetic influence of the Soviet experiment on all of Europe (and, indeed, the world), was the major reason for the prevailing mood, but it was not the only one. The Mexican revolution, which preceded the Russian Revolution, had still not run its course by the time Carpentier arrived in Paris. In fact, Carpentier protested in retrospect that it was to Mexico, not France, that he desired to go after he escaped the cultural purgatory of Machado's Cuba. And he would have, had Robert Desnos not swept him away.

WARS OF THE AVANT-GARDE: RADIO

Surrealism was at its height between 1924 and 1930. In October 1923, the first European radio program aired in Germany. In Europe at least, the rise of surrealism and the rise of radio were simultaneous.

The overlap had consequences for Carpentier's career and for the story of popular music. So let us begin with his career in radio. The Cuban author landed in Paris precisely at the point of surrealism's first serious internal crises, when many of the movement's former stalwarts were turning on its grandiloquent founder, André Breton. Although welcoming surrealism's refusal to rest with an academic or apolitical art — and spending long passages in his memoirs describing the freedom it gave his generation — Carpentier soon joined a chorus of reaction against Breton and surrealism's major currents. It was a time of extraordinary artistic activity, much of it propelled by ex-surrealists such as Georges Bataille, who labeled Breton a "eunuch pope." The German Marxist theorist Walter Benjamin also spoke disparagingly of surrealism as work for "down-at-heel dowagers," while the Peruvian poet, César Vallejo (like Carpentier, a journalist in Europe at the time), spoke of its pompous "parlor games" and "abracadabra method."[17]

It was one of these dissidents of 1928 who brought Carpentier to Paris — the surrealist poet Robert Desnos. On March 4, 1928, while attending a press congress in Havana, Desnos grew bored by the official ceremonies and set out to wander the city's streets. As a young journalist fluent in French, Carpentier played the role of guide. Havana impressed Desnos deeply. In a preface to a later article by Carpentier on Cuban music, Desnos wrote:

> I've never forgotten the poor village close to Havana where
> Alejo Carpentier (whom I had just met for the first time) led me
> the very night of my arrival. Two deafening orchestras dueled
> in grand style. Above it all, an immense plaintive wail of
> trombones passed over a sonic background of strange
> instruments and the drone of the sea.[18]

Showing an obsessive love of Latin America from then on, Desnos gave free rein to his passions for music, preferring popular song, café concerts, and jazz to the works of Bach or Stravinsky. As it turned out, Desnos returned from Cuba with an important collection of records: *rumbas, danzones, sones,* all of which "filled the sounds of the night in his atelier."[19] Once again, under Carpentier's guiding hand, Desnos "more or less regularly sampled the wares displayed in several record catalogs, ending up with an important record collection." Desnos eventually put the young journalist on the ship *España* bound for Paris, giving him his own transit papers and passport. Carpentier arrived in Paris under the name "Robert Desnos."[20]

In his first year there, Carpentier immediately began collaborating on the breakaway surrealist journal *Documents,* edited by Bataille, as well as on the journal *Bifur.* Overwhelmed in some respects by the theoretical accomplishments of the surrealists (since the movement had already done so much of what he himself had wanted to do), Carpentier threw himself into "America," setting out to gain an education in his own continent's history and traditions. In these years, he devoured the letters of Columbus, the writings of Inca Garcilaso, and the Latin American authors of the eighteenth century. For eight years, or so he boasted, he read nothing but New World texts. Invited by Breton to take part in the journal *Révolution Surréaliste*, he declined; but he did come to know Louis Aragon, Tristan Tzara, Paul Éluard, Georges Sadoul, Benjamin Peret, and such painters as Giorgio de Chirico, Ives Tanguy, and Picasso. He wrote his first essay in French, "The Cardinal Points of the Latin American Novel" (1928), and made friends with "the greatest composer the Americas have produced," Heitor Villa-Lobos.

But there was a restless side to Carpentier throughout this stage. From his editorship of various magazines (*Imán* in 1931, *Tiempo Nuevo* in 1940) to his position as *homme d'affaires* for the Cuban government after 1959, he was always a promoter and educator. His short, lively dispatches from Paris were written with an advertiser's flair, bulging with rhetorical questions, terse humor, set scenes, and always an appeal to fame, the star, the "phenomenon." One of Carpentier's major objectives in these terse essays was to brag to his brethren at home about the power Latin American culture had over European audiences. A typical example is "Mexico as Seen by One European Film":

> After a period of various centuries, during which France has lived folded in upon itself, without opening its eyes to the varied and multiple spectacle of the rest of the universe, its literature, its art, its ideas have suddenly been seen to be influenced by great currents that have arrived from every corner of the world, even the most backward. The vogue for black art; Martinican music; admiration for the wisdom of Asiatic saints, such as Milarepa; the success enjoyed by translations of the books of Güiraldes, Martín Guzmán, Azuela, and of the North American novelists; the furor over books of travel literature. . . . The most demanding editors open their arms to young poets such as Michaux, who returns from Ecuador, or Malraux, who comes back from Indochina, inviting them to tell their stories. . . . Nevertheless, an old tradition dictates that the French are the people least able to open their eyes to the spectacle of their own planet. With a few exceptions, Parisians have always traveled badly and pretentiously, and

when they have wanted to create an image of the countries that surround them, have committed the most laughable errors.[21]

In spite of such comments, the flow of information went unequally in the other direction. It was, as we said, Carpentier's job to keep Cuba up to date. Upon returning to Cuba, he held conferences on the "unexplored zones of sound" in 1939 at the Hispano-Cuban Institute of Culture in Havana; there was an illustration of *"musique concrète"* where he arranged for twenty-six pianos to be played simultaneously.[22] He gave his Cuban listeners a short course on Byron, Hugo, and others in his popular radio program on "famous persons" and taught courses on the history of music at the National Conservatory. He organized the first exposition of the paintings of Picasso at the Lyceum Lawn Tennis Club in 1942. These decades of apprenticeship culminated after 1959, when he became administrator general for the state publishing house, cultural minister for the revolutionary government, and vice president of the National Union of Writers and Artists (UNEAC).

What struck Carpentier immediately about Europe between the wars was its multiculturalism, including that of surrealism itself. This had been the result, ultimately, of colonial contacts. The 1926 rebellion in Morocco had been only one of the focal points of an emerging colonial consciousness among European intellectuals. Even the famed early experimentalism of Cubism had been primarily the product of Europe's Spanish periphery (Picasso, Miró, Dalí), which was more in touch with Latin American sources than its French, English, or East European counterparts. American jazz performers, Mexican muralists such as Diego Rivera, and Caribbean student intellectuals were resident, and active, in Europe throughout the interwar period. Surrealism itself (both its dissidents and its loyalists) was an essentially international movement. Looking back from the vantage point of 1945, the late convert to surrealism, Pierre Mabille (the French psychologist who would bring Breton to Haiti in the final stages of World War II) wrote of Paris already at the time of the International Exposition of 1900 that "Cubans and Americans of every persuasion . . . knew the streets of the Madeleine district better than the provinces of their own country"[23] — a phenomenon that would continue throughout the interwar period and into the Latin boom, as seen, for example, in the novels of Julio Cortázar.

Carpentier's views on surrealism — which are crucial and defining, not least because *Music in Cuba* represented his final departure from its spell — were always complicated. Recent fashions tend to exaggerate surrealism's hold on the intellectuals whose fame and influence live on (the portraits of Benjamin as a German surrealist are particularly false in this regard). But despite his angry break, Carpentier could wax lyrical as well:

> They were fantastic... [They established] solid relations with the "delirious" arts of early painting, with the primitives and mystics, with the poetry of the fantastic from all eras and places — African and Oceanic art, Bosch, Hogarth, Elizabethan theater, black novels in English, Blake, Lautréamont, Hölderlin, and so on — and found in the past a tangible testament to an eagerness to evade reality that has appeared sporadically throughout the history of art."[24]

But almost from the start, he was convinced that surrealism — laboriously constructed in the urban centers of Europe — already existed in the Americas, or at least that everything essential to it did. He describes the altars of a *lucumí* priest, arguing that everything visually associated with surrealist discovery can already be found there. "In America, surrealism turns out to be quotidian, current, habitual; it beats and breathes in the heart of the home, in the simple flowering of a mushroom."[25] But he does not want to make the movement seem less than what it is. It had "twenty years of indisputable vitality giving us all a manner of seeing, of feeling and interpreting, that depended on contrasting dissimilar objects, establishing a determinate hierarchy among images, and advertising the sheer surprise to be found in various manifestations of popular culture." The only problem is that it had "becom[e] a propaganda cartel, a mere shop window." It provided all the leads for New York and Mexican fashion. By 1945, he thought people who talked about it spoke too reverentially, with an air of dramatic pretension. He would later lampoon surrealism mercilessly in *The Lost Steps*.

There remains a great need for a general study of the role played by non-European intellectuals in the creation, as well as promotion, of interwar intellectual life. We know something of the pivotal role played by the Cuban artist Wifredo Lam, the painter to whom Breton dedicated a chapter of his *Surrealism and Painting*. But one could well counter that Lam spent the years of surrealism's formation in Madrid, not Paris, or that his return to the Caribbean (where he met up with Breton during the latter's visit to Haiti) occurred at a relatively late date. We know what surrealism owes to its Dadist predecessors; and although Francis Picabia, the painter and filmmaker of Cuban origin, is a legend among them, few are aware that Picabia built on Cuban leads and sources.[26] (He is referenced in Maurice Nadeau's history of surrealism, for example, as a "Spanish painter," whereas the *Pequeño Larousse* and the biographical dictionaries predictably refer to him as a "French painter.") The Cuban *choteo* ("poking fun") — for Picabia at least — found expression in Dada's celebrated acts of embarrassing the consumers of art. The "independence, violence, and verbal play" of Picabia were for Carpentier one of Latin America's signal contributions to the interwar avant-gardes, however much they have been smoothed over into a nondescript Europeanness.[27]

Although extensively covered in writings on the avant-garde, Dada is unknown territory as Carpentier describes it. The movement had been many things, of course, but above all, as Carpentier reminds us, "it was a fever, a spiritual reflex of turbulent years in which conventional values crumbled away in the boom of the canons [of World War I]."[28] In the disgust and anguish produced by the war, as Marcel Duchamp and Man Ray pulled poems out of Tzara's hat, Dada (we can now see) was largely about cutting Europe down to size with leads taken from the global periphery. The "peripheral" intellectuals, rather than the avant-garde's official historians, have seen this colonial borrowing most clearly. In Carpentier's report, Dada's aftermath produced an intellectual situation that strangely echoed the *Revista de Avance*'s: "I arrive in Paris, in Montparnasse, and what do I find? In the very moment I think I'm falling into full-blown surrealism, into poetry, everyone's talking about revolution. Everyone's saying: either sell out, or don't sell out; either commit yourself, or don't; you have to choose. I enlisted myself in the excision of surrealism."[29] But the flow went two ways. Aimé Césaire's *Tropiques* would later absorb surrealism, using the movement to cloak its own strident demands for a nationalist revolution with the artifice of a French verbal play forged in France by an international cast of characters.

In the sounds of the New World, a different kind of rebellion seemed possible to many of the avant-garde intellectuals of Europe. The Americas were political in a much more dangerous sense than Breton's oneirism. Like Bataille—with whom Carpentier collaborated on *Documents*—the European avant-garde discovered in Latin America both a politics and an art, and they were surprised at times by their own belatedness. Tristan Tzara, the founder of Dada, had an extensive collection of rumba records; Robert Desnos found in Cuban music "a new accent but one which spoke a language familiar to me, more human than any other." Nino Frank was even more blunt: "If one day the Soviet experiment is destroyed by the forces of reaction, only one thing will stand in the way of old bourgeois civilization: Latin America." And Carpentier had fostered some of these views as editor in chief of the short-lived journal *Imán*, published in Spanish in Paris in 1931. The rise in the same year of the journal *Légitime Défense* through the efforts of Martinican students at the Sorbonne points again to the often obscured reality that the artistic movements of the interwar period were not merely conjured from the idea of the so-called primitive (as it was then called): third-world artists and activists were physically there, collaborating—among them René Menil, Jules Monnerot, Pierre and Simone Yoyotte, Étienne Léro.[30] And although Cuban musicians and writers were prominent in Paris from the early part of the century, one will look hard to find Carpentier's name mentioned in accounts of surrealism. And yet he was at its very center and, like Picabia, he was so on European terrain.

This turning away from Europe, as we know—particularly as Dada gave way to surrealism—was part of an unromantic attrac-

tion to the colonies inspired by Arthur Rimbaud, who in his hallu-
cinogenic poetry wrote of the "third world" in a fatal and cynical
way by evoking his role as exploiter in Africa. By the early 1920s,
the scandal of Bolshevism on Europe's eastern fringe provided further weaponry. One could say that an attempt to account for surrealism without acknowledging its immersion in the domestic and
colonial politics of the Third International is impossible. Under its
influence, Rimbaud gave way to the uprisings in China, to the Italian campaigns in Ethiopia, and to the New World, where the very
literalness of what before had been romantic flight (the African
nonsense poems of Richard Huelsenbeck, for example) paradoxically enriched the imagery of surrealist unreason. The active participation of Caribbean intellectuals resident in Europe, as well as the
later travel of several of surrealism's members (Desnos, Leiris, Mabille, Breton) to the Caribbean, transformed surrealism from within.
Some of that spirit comes through in Carpentier's account, for
Cuban audiences, of the Colonial Exposition:

> In 1931, speed has shrunk the dimensions of our planet and
> reduced the human scale. Modern novelists permit themselves
> such wanderings that the voyages of Loti through Morocco
> seem utterly without interest. The European people, infected
> with imperialism, go out to meddle in the lives of those who
> never before cared about "civilization"; by way of monopolies,
> customs agents, substantial impositions, they are brought into a
> problematic "happiness" represented by highways, railroads,
> serums, canned foods, and more or less clumsy hymns. In the
> epoch of electricity and television, the epoch in which antipodean
> existence assumes an unsuspected importance, only a Colonial
> Exposition would have been able to seem current during the
> Exposition of 1900 . . . And it is that exposition we are seeing
> right now in Paris.[31]

We may forget that antisurrealist polemics were practically a
cottage industry in these years. The famous examples are early
Georges Bataille, Walter Benjamin, and César Vallejo, but, again,
attempts to revise surrealism went much deeper, and looked specifically to the colonies. Take, for example, the comments of Philippe

Soupault in 1931: "I am not afraid to assert that the spectacle Europe offers today is one of decadence. By my writings, my words, my actions, I'm steeling myself to warn of the death, not a little ignominious, that this useless peninsula of ours deserves, and to prepare a nice burial for it. . . . What I want to emphasize is that Latin America has got to stop turning to the European continent, which still retains in its eyes an incomprehensible prestige."[32] Or that of Michel Leiris: "the historic mission of Latin America is to counterpose itself to the rationalizing influence of the United States in the world." Or that of Robert Desnos: "[Latin America] will be the theater of astounding events in the evolution of world society. . . . What interests us is the destiny of the Cuban cane cutter, the Brazilian coffee picker, and the Argentinian workers on cattle farms. . . . Fewer phrases, less lyricism."[33]

The demur of these circles toward surrealism, on the other hand, was not directed against the entire ambience of the movement, but only Breton's ecstatic and narrowly psychological brand. Breton's notorious distaste for music was a typically modernist rejection of the publicizing or popularizing gestures implicit in the uses of radio. Thus, in his essay "Silence Is Golden," Breton is merely repeating a famous Weimar-era debate over the unacceptable vulgarization of art heard in radio broadcasts of opera into the homes of the millions. Written in 1944, the essay is in a sense still in the world of Rimbaud, holding on to the idea that "physical and mental representations" are one, and that they are dissociated only by abandoning the *"primitive single faculty . . . found in* savages and children."[34] To prohibit the collaboration of musician and poet would, he argues, "save us from all those *poems set to music* (that make us prefer they were left between the closed covers of a book) and would rid us of the silly nonsense of opera librettos." The "inner word" of surrealist automatism was intimately linked for him to an "inner music" that music itself only blunted. Inspired by such notions, the great Martinican poet Aimé Césaire later exclaimed that "the search for music is a crime against poetic music which can only be the breaking of a mental wave against the rock of the world."[35]

Thus the splits in surrealism were occasioned by disagreements about music as well as politics, and both were expressed as matters of *publicity* (should surrealism reach ordinary people?). The rise of radio brought all three issues together. From the mid-1920s, radio played a crucial part in the debate over surrealism. It was against this background that Carpentier began his career at the private radio station of Poste Parisien; Radio Luxembourg was the regional broadcast network to which the station belonged. Approached in 1932 by Paul Deharme, a young businessman with surrealist sympathies, Desnos recruited Carpentier as musical director of what the latter would call "an experimental laboratory for the radio."[36] Within days, Carpentier was given carte blanche with "an electric organ, a symphony orchestra, a chorus, various soloists, a declaimer, and a speaker," all housed in an immense auditorium at the Poste Parisien. Three months later he had "organized, blended, and directed more than forty-two broadcasts."

It is amazing how little explored are the investments of interwar intellectuals in radio. One only has to think how much time such unlikely modernists as Walter Benjamin, George Orwell, Antonin Artaud, and Bertolt Brecht spent on the airwaves, and then consider the relatively scant attention paid in the voluminous biographies they have prompted.[37] As a radio intellectual and artist, Carpentier has a certain special claim to attention in these circles. Leaving alone random appearances, Carpentier spent twenty-seven consecutive years (1932–59) as a director of radio programs in three different countries, and was deeply involved in all the technical aspects of the medium. The employment was not only practical. It had theoretical implications; for it is more difficult than it seems to determine whether surrealism is as well known as it is because of the ability of a commercial technology like radio to advertise it, or, by contrast, whether radio "took off" so confidently because of the efforts of surrealist technique to make the technology aesthetically interesting. In any event, radio work supported the literary careers of many poets of the surrealist movement.

From the start, radio was also the vehicle through which New World African musics conquered European popular culture. It was, in the words of some commentators, "thanks to the radio [that] . . . jazz fever spread across the republic like wildfire."[38] In 1926, Kurt Weill proclaimed: with its "liberated rhythm and improvised humor . . . a certain kind of dance music so completely expresses the spirit of our times that it has even been able to achieve a temporary influence over a certain part of serious art music. The rhythm of our time is jazz."[39]

For interwar European intellectuals, however, the term *jazz* was flexible and ill-defined, as anyone familiar with Theodor Adorno's well-known essays on the subject knows. It was an amalgam of musics ranging from "hot" performances of show tunes by white bands to the rawer underground sound of vintage Dixieland. For our purposes it is important to remark that it also included Afro-Caribbean arrangements and rhythms that would eventually be known as *mambo*. It was not, in other words, only the well-known "jazz" clubs—Le Grand Duc or Bricktop's in Montmartre—that attracted the likes of Bataille and Leiris in the 1920s, but a specifically New World complex of musical styles whose cross-border intricacies were first traced with accuracy in *Music in Cuba*. In Parisian clubs, one found performers such as Moisés Simons and Eliseo Grenet, the percussion virtuoso Frontela, and others: together, they constituted what Carpentier at the time described as a virtual "military offensive of our rhythms" in Paris placed "at the service of our most authentic creole traditions."[40]

To Carpentier's mind, these musicians were bold cultural innovators rather than merely entertainers. His fondness for Rita Montaner, the Cuban opera star of the early 1920s, took the form of comparing her to Josephine Baker, whose career resembled Montaner's after the latter switched to the popular stage. Montaner had acted alongside Baker in a production of 1928, although her most famous performance was in the zarzuela *Niña Rita*, where she sang the tango congo "Mama Inés." Leaving a profitable career as "serious" vocalist, she gave up (in Carpentier's words) "the satin curtains for the smoky underground in order to place her talents at the service of Cuban popular music."[41] If the Afro-Cuban, he pointed out, "had been scorned until then by musicians whose mission it was to disparage indigenous practices, Rita Montaner contributed much to destroying that absurd prejudice."

As a radio broadcaster, Carpentier was in effect the arranger. His job was to know acoustics, the capacities of the orchestra, and the tonal quality of the voices. What interested him most was exploring the possibilities of setting texts to music, just as he had done earlier in his career. Among his projects was a series of improvisational wordplays by Jacques Prévert and Desnos, called *Get Going,* which sought to simulate automatic writing; selections from Paul Claudel's novel *Christopher Columbus;* and poetry recitals by Paul Éluard, Langston Hughes, and Nicolás Guillén. He experimented in the sound room by playing simple themes on the piano, recording them, superimposing them on other themes played later, until he achieved a collage of melodies no pianist could perform by normal means.

In describing his aesthetic principles, he displays some of Deharme's complicated desire to *publicize* surrealist technique without betraying its principles:

> A radio "audition" excludes all visual elements. In the same
> way that music is made for the ear — the sensory medium that
> transmits music to the conscious emotive centers — we need
> to create a theater, a poetry, in a word, a *spectacle* for the ear,
> endowed with the maximum of intelligibility. One shouldn't
> be ordered by the listener who sits there comfortably in an easy
> chair by the fire, exerting very little imagination. The point
> is rather to utilize direct images, in a simple language that
> expresses an idea with the greatest clarity. Mobilize, if possible,
> an *interpellative style,* always speaking to the listener in the
> *present indicative:* I enter, *you* are, *he* says.[42]

Winging it, as many early radio artists did, the twenty-nine-year old Carpentier tried to make the best of a rough opportunity, turning the commercial into the demotic. He had company. Erik Satie's "musique d'ameublement" (furniture music) was a similar attempt, although earlier, and more ironic. Satie was part of a group called "Les Six" that included Francis Poulenc and Darius Milhaud; Carpentier later collaborated with Milhaud on *Invocations*, a cantata for male voices, in 1938. Carpentier's work for the radio, though, looked more to Bertolt Brecht than the ironies of Satie. Like Brecht's *Gebrauchslyrik* (poetry for use)—a term echoed in the composer Paul Hindemith's *Gebrauchsmusik*—it set out to deflate aesthetic pretensions by copping the popularity of commercial culture. Rather than flaunting a modernist disdain for the masses, it sought popularity on behalf of progressive politics and experimental form. As part of a general (and often ignored or repressed) enthusiasm among 1930s European intellectuals for the Soviet avant-garde, Carpentier's radio theory had affinities to Russian Futurism's love of "noise":

> Every radio "audition" ought to be carried out in a rapid rhythm, evading silence.... Dialogue is anti-radiophonic.... The role of the speaker ought to be analogous to the dragoman of the classical farce, or that of the cicerone of early film.... He should dehumanize his voice as far as possible, adopting a neutral tone, uniform, one that stands out over the rest as a sort of talking machine.... It works especially well when his text is composed of short rhythmic verses, such that their form—the form of biblical parables—contributes to fixing the ideas in the mind of the listener, by way of an agile repetition of phrases.... I don't want to be understood as arguing for that stupid system of *melopoiea*, consisting of someone declaiming verses while a violin performs the *Serenata* of Toselli. But accompanied by rhythms and melodies, or simple chords, the word takes on an extraordinary poetic heightening. (393)

The actual techniques used in a program that featured a ballad by Paul Fort sounded, on Carpentier's account, like the stuff of commercial television:

> I put together a basic sound composed of a sustained low note played on a sixteen-foot organ pedal; blurred, repeated notes in the horn registers could be heard over it. A tom-tom, vibrating continuously, helped to make the contours of sound still vaguer, creating a shadowy atmosphere, without definite tonality. On the word *bell*, a sorrowful tap of the drum could be heard. And, over the verse "behind him singing," two artists, seated three

> meters from the microphone, covered their mouths with their
> hands and sang a brutal theme without articulating the
> words . . . These latter intervene in the monologue, comment on
> it, debate it, giving *the sensation of a dialogue that does not exist,*
> and creating, in this way, a new theatrical form, adapted to the
> psychological demands and materials of broadcast art. (394)

By far the trio's biggest success was the now legendary broadcast, *La Grande Complainte de Fantomas* (1933) (Fantomas's complaint). Based on a feuilleton by Marcel Allain *(Si c'était Fantomas!),* it was broadcast in prime time over all France and the neighboring countries reached by Radio Luxembourg. Dubbed by its creators "an unedited radiophonic suite" featuring the famous criminal Fantomas ("the master of terror, the man for whom nothing criminal is alien," according to the ads), the text was written by Desnos, with original music by Kurt Weill.[43] The young and unknown Antonin Artaud was dramatic director (and played the part of Fantomas himself), with musical direction by Carpentier.

Other broadcasts included *Salut au monde* (Hello world) and *La Clef des songes* (The key to dreams). The latter was a radio-montage based on themes solicited each week from the audience's actual dreams, its secret desires. The former, a dramatic rendering of Walt Whitman's poem, tried to evoke a countryless place of mind, an "imaginary disorientation." This broadcast on July 4, 1936, was, according to Germaine Blondin, admired for its "sonorous fresco of sound . . . a montage where the culture and intelligence of the professional competes with a poetic sensibility . . . Here one finds one of the very greatest acts of sonorous imagery, which permits us to see what radio art can truly be."[44]

While making these broadcasts, both Carpentier and Desnos were busy advertising a French pharmaceutical firm — their chief sponsor — floating commercials for "Le Vin de frileuse." In spite of Paul Valéry's quip that advertising was one of the great curses of the modern age — "insulting our sight, falsifying our speech, polluting the countryside, and corrupting the critical mind" — Radio Luxembourg was wholly dependent on advertising from the start, receiving no money from listeners or government agencies. Desnos was one of the pioneers of the advertising department, and Deharme was not shy in stating that he intended to offer "programs made to the measure of advertisements."[45] Desnos was more direct. He saw radio as a way of completing his break with surrealism, which had become in his eyes more occult, a mode of selective initiation and alchemy. What is often thought of as a kind of renegacy from art was seen by these artists as an expansion into a more challenging experimentalism. All of this is recalled in *Music in Cuba*'s claim that the exportation of a form of Cuban musical entertainment had a way of reorienting the minds of foreign listeners. Cuba's international influence in culture had, as it were, the imprimatur of a flagrant commercial viability.

Commercials weren't the only compromise of the interwar years. Between February and May of 1939, Desnos and Carpentier made fifteen broadcasts dedicated to "Songs of the French Empire." The songs were accompanied by "light fanfare" and recalled "victorious moments from our history like the conquest of Algeria" and like that of "Ma Tonkinoise" expressing the "Parisian vision of the colonies."[46] When Carpentier returned to Cuba, he again directed radio programs professionally; by 1945, he had moved on to Caracas, where he became director of the radio station Publicidad Ars, working there until 1959. During that time, he wrote three novels and a collection of stories, *Guerra del tiempo* (War of time, 1958). Carpentier's principal fiction was written while he worked in radio, and lived in Venezuela.

THE PRIMITIVES

Like Desnos, Carpentier would part ways with the renegades of *Documents*. While his former associates—Michel Leiris, Bataille, Roger Caillois—were rummaging around in the sacral illuminations of interwar primitivism and its *crise de couleur,* Carpentier was already leaving that orbit with a sharp anticolonial parting glance. *Music in Cuba,* among other things, marks his own transformation from effete reviewer to historian of cultural disruption.

More than a decade before *Music in Cuba,* Carpentier had been able to nose out many of the pretensions of interwar Europe's rage for blackness. He set out repeatedly to undercut his own earlier positions—even in the pages of *Music in Cuba* itself. There he takes himself to task for the embarrassing language of some of his own earlier statements. But some of the book's casual exoticism, it must be said, seems almost to ape a tourist brochure as in Carpentier's approving quotation of one of Ortiz's more egregious passages: "But another race spilled forth their passions, pleasures, and arts, from the heat of the equatorial jungles, in the ebullitions that were Seville and Havana. For centuries, from both shores of the Atlantic controlled by whites, muscular strength and spiritual impetuosity were drawn from within the marrow of Africa, traits that both here and there gave greater ardor to the soul and sensitivity to the flesh." The writing of "progressive" France simmered with that sort of imagery. Precisely because Cuba's investment in race was immediate and urgent in a political sense, he was able to work his way out of this hyperbole and suspect longing. On the other hand, being Cuban also meant suffering under the burden of cultural dependency. Thus, even in a discussion of an Afro-Cuban song of the nineteenth century in *Music in Cuba*, Carpentier feels he must draw comparisons to Stravinsky's *Les Noces*!

In a similar vein, *Music in Cuba* offers a weak portrayal of the so-called *bufo* in chapter 13 (not to be confused with the European "opera buffa"). Carpentier shrewdly observes that, whatever its downsides, the genre provided a platform for the public dissemination of Afro-Cuban speech (the "argot of the slave barracks"), and educated the elite in black popular legends ("slum and lowlife mythology").[47] When Desi Arnaz tells Lucille Ball that he, unlike her, knows the meaning of *babalú*, he is alluding, among other things, to the training he would have received in the vernacular theater of *bufo*. But Carpentier gives a very poor sense of the *bufo*'s racial dynamics.[48] He calls Francisco Covarrubias a "caricaturist," for example, even though it was not simply caricature — nor humor — that made the form popular. The *bufo* was a form of blackface minstrelsy. It is rather puzzling that Carpentier does not comment more directly on the grotesque quality of such performances regardless of their historical importance. His portrait here is uncharacteristically muffled. It hardly matters that the theatrical companies of touring comedians or performers of *zarzuela* included many black performers as well.

If *Music in Cuba* is guilty at times of racial insensitivity, it was also critical. Carpentier complains that "the Afro-Cuban tendency often remained superficial and peripheral, with its romanticized evocations of the 'black man under palm trees, drunk on the sun.'" Elsewhere, he laments the "false conception of the 'national' that those in my generation had in those years," and calls his *¡Ecué-Yamba-Ó!* "overblown, an abominable example of futurist bad taste." Recalling his friendship with Roldán, he went even further:

> Roldán and I, along with others of like mind, went through a period of "infantile disorder" in regard to Afro-Cubanism. We devoured the books of Fernando Ortiz, and sought out rhythms with the points of our pencils. Papá Montero and María de la O became living figures and provoked in us an admiration analogous to Siegfried and Brünehilde in the mind of Catulle Mendes and Elemir Bourges.[49]

Carpentier's posthumous novel-memoir *La consagración de la primavera* (The rite of spring) continues this sort of self-criticism. The book shows a revolutionary artist's retrospective recognition of the inadequacies of mere art: "I analyzed the characteristic devices of rejection that intellectuals used to dodge the imperatives that hovered over them, obliging them to participate in history (History, in this case) that took place between 1937 and 1961."[50] His complex relationship with surrealism became more attenuated as he moved in the harsher world of policy and government. As Carpentier matured, he found his way to a political understanding of race that abandoned the mystifications of his earlier writing: "'Afro-Cuban' is an absurd term, and to use it today [1974] in Cuba is equivalent to speaking about the existence of what used to be called '*negritude*.' Under the growing influence of the United States, a discrimination that separated one part of the people and its culture from the body of the nation has developed in Cuba." The point, he said, was to "eliminate this discrimination" (218).

Characteristically in his divided life, part of Carpentier's time in Europe had been taken up with outright political activity. He was a Cuban delegate to the Second International Congress of Writers for the Defense of Culture, celebrated in Madrid in 1937, against

the backdrop of the Spanish Civil War. He attended the confer-
ence with André Malraux, Octavio Paz, and Elena Garro. Langston
Hughes and Guillén were also there. Later, in 1967, he was a member
of the Cuban delegation to the Bertrand Russell War Crimes Tribunal in Stockholm decrying U.S. conduct in Vietnam. The "world
of publicity," however, would not leave him alone, even if his involvements with the Cuban Revolution kept his sales appeal down
at precisely the time of life one would have expected him to cash
in. In 1956, Tyrone Power bought the film rights to *The Lost Steps*.
His production company had made all the preparations to begin
shooting, when Power suddenly died.

ZONES

In his Preface to *Music in Cuba*, Carpentier sketches a methodology that only an "American" such as himself could have developed in the 1940s. He intends to proceed, he says, by focusing on
"geographic zones" subject to the "same migrations of rhythms
and oral traditions" rather than on regions or countries. Recent theories of culture have summoned terms such as the "Black Atlantic"
or "contact zones" to suggest the limitations of seeing cultural flows
of influence in strictly bordered or conventional ways. They im-
portantly echo Carpentier's approach in *Music in Cuba*, but they
do so belatedly.

In spite of its eye for Cuban achievements, *Music in Cuba* documents the *mutuality* of the Latin sound. The text, in that sense at
least, is not Cubano-centric. This important aspect of Carpentier's
outlook features most prominently in the opening of chapter 6 on
the career of the *"contradanza,"* where San Domingo (present-day
Haiti) plays a prominent role for the first time. Scholars and musicans from the Dominican Republic and Puerto Rico have understandably taken umbrage at histories of Latino musical genius told
in the form of Cuban origins. Although the focus of Carpentier's
study ends before the 1960s when the *son*, along with styles and
beats from throughout Latin America, evolved into New York salsa,
he repeatedly argues that the Caribbean shares a stock of similar
rhythms under a plurality of names. His elaborate treatment of

the Haitian immigration of the late eighteenth century, of the birth of tango, of the musical contributions of Spain—all suggest his sensitivity to those spurious attempts by some critics from Latin America's largest island to monopolize Afro-Latin music.

After all, the motley forms that are salsa today—although arguably based on the *son*—were primarily the creation of New York Puerto Rican ("Nuyorican") musicians. Carpentier, at any rate, repeatedly makes this sort of point, both in the text and in his interviews and essays during the 1970s. In one of these, for example, he compares Venezuelan and Cuban music, saying that although Cubans have a "richness of execution, of performance," the number of their genres is "highly limited" (21). In Venezuela, by contrast, there is an inexhaustible variety of musical types:

> The similarity among many folkloric American genres is due to the mixing of people from the same origins. The Hispanic ballad, for example, was spread evenly in all of the Spanish-speaking countries after the Conquest. It requires no special explanation. Wherever there were blacks, one could observe dances like the round tambourine dances of Barlovento, the *"resbalosa"* of Chile and Argentina, the *"bamba"* of Veracruz, and some primitive Cuban dances that kept a very strict relationship to one another. (23)

He claimed to study the musical heritage of the entire Antilles "with equal interest"—along with Mexico, Brazil, Argentina, Chile, and Venezuela—in part to investigate "a certain process of inter-migration of rhythms and oral traditions." The years researching *Music in Cuba* had made Carpentier unsentimental.

Music in Cuba, then, had at least two very different kinds of importance. It brought a long-standing problem in the mass culture debates to theoretical clarity by demonstrating that the popular and the classical were complicit and interdependent. In the 1940s, this view was either denied or expressed only in market terms. Then, as now, music that sold well was considered "popular" even if it was strategically developed in corporate boardrooms and produced in slick studios with no public access. Carpentier, by contrast, was able to take popular music seriously as such. His interest was in spotlighting the cultural leadership of those who produced music anonymously, and from below. The classical—and not only in Cuba—had been reinvented by the efforts of a segregated, culturally divergent racial fraction of a class. In this context, the ambiguity of Carpentier's efforts in commercial radio came to a productive head.

By considering a national-popular music, Carpentier mapped out the implications in theory of an already familiar practice. On the one hand, there were symphonic borrowings from black music by Milhaud, Gershwin, Stravinsky, and others. This was the relatively well-known side of the question. But Carpentier also documented the adaptation of harmonic motifs and arrangements "barbarized" in dance-hall music by black instrumentalists trained in the classical repertoire: the sort of process that created the *danzón* of Miguel Faílde in Cuba, and mambo among the Cuban émigrés of Mexico and New York. *Music in Cuba*'s importance, then, was also this: it threw down a challenge that was hard to mistake and difficult to contradict, while arguing that a small island nation had played a key role in world culture. A dependent country with few resources or media outlets had developed a *mass culture* for global export.

Carpentier's investigation into the international migrations that made this happen also signaled the end of an unusually long fallow spell in his own writerly productivity. Apart from his duties at Poste Parisien, Carpentier had been working at the Foniric Recording Studios for the previous four years: "If I wrote very little between the publication of my first novel and 1939, it's due, quite simply, to the fact that I had to spend ten or eleven hours a day in a studio recording in order to make a living."[51] For a while, it was only *Music in Cuba* that occupied him. After the trip to Haiti, however, he quickly published the novella *Viaje a la semilla* (Journey to the source), and began work immediately on *The Kingdom of This World*. At least part of that novel and *Music in Cuba* were composed at the same time, and Haiti was the inspiration for both. It is significant, then, that Carpentier invokes Haiti in the opening pages of the text as the musical cornerstone of the Antilles.

In Haiti, the "people" of the modern era began. Haiti is an island in the heart of the Caribbean, which is the heart of the New

World, which, in turn, might be called the heart of the origins of modernity. For it was in Haiti that Columbus first settled, where France had its wealthiest colony, where the first successful slave-led revolution took place, and where the idea of the "popular"—in dialogue with the French Revolution—was pushed beyond its French limitations. In the New World imagination, Haiti has long played the role of standard-bearer, war monument, and cultural battleground. Carpentier came to appreciate its significance earlier than most of his contemporaries. If Cuba had *negrismo*, Haiti had just responded to a U.S. military occupation (1915–34) with cultural resistance of its own. The part played by Ortiz in Cuba was played in Haiti by the anthropologist Jean Price-Mars, whose books included *La Vocation de l'élite* (The elite's vocation) and *Ainsi parla l'oncle* (That's how uncle speaks, 1928). Price-Mars was the first to recognize the genuine religion in the voodoo cult, based on intuitive reason, communal warmth, and "a cosmic rhythm that, instead of dividing and diminishing, nourishes by unifying."[52] In place of the *Revista de Avance* was Haiti's *La Revue indigène*, founded by Jacques Roumain and five others in 1927, the future cell of the Haitian Communist Party.

Haiti educated Carpentier, just as it had a number of African American and Caribbean authors. Zora Neale Hurston did fieldwork and began *Their Eyes Were Watching God* there; Ishmael Reed's novel *Mumbo Jumbo* rewrites the history of Western civilization by way of New World African dance, and is spiritually devoted to the island. Langston Hughes also remembered being brought up "on stories of Haiti. Its great leaders—Toussaint-Louverture, Dessalines, Christophe—were childhood heroes."[53] Haitian novelists themselves could claim leadership in at least one branch of colonial fiction. Following the example of René Maran's *Batouala* (1921)—a Martinican novel, written in France, which Carpentier reviewed for *La Discusión* in 1923—Jacques Roumain and others launched the genre of the "peasant novel": a twentieth-century blending of colloquial speech and socialist realism that went beyond the coloristic autochthony of "folklore" in a bid for an avant-garde originality that would shun the avant-garde's subservience to form. It was a genre later taken up in poetry by René Depestre and, in his own way, by Carpentier himself.

Carpentier's trip to Haiti drove him in new directions. The style of *The Kingdom of This World* became a model for all of the later Latin "boom," itself adopted in the 1980s and 1990s by writers from India, Nigeria, and other parts of Latin America. It was the first installment in his American cycle; the novel's justly famous preface makes the most concise case for American uniqueness and European lack ever written. There, Carpentier mapped out a theory of American primacy that occupied him for the rest of his career. What needs to be remembered is that it did not do so immediately. *Music in Cuba* appeared first, and it alone brought his earlier pursuits to fruition. The well-known history of *"lo real maravilloso"* articulated in *The Kingdom of This World*'s Preface, and its long, still remarkable influence in practice if not in criticism—all of that came from his work on *Music in Cuba*.

The zones of contact explored in the book are not limited to the Caribbean, however, for North America plays a conspicuous role as well. In spite of the work of people like Langston Hughes and James Weldon Johnson, early attention in the United States to black music has been strangely parochial. It tends to set up arbitrary borders along the Gulf shore in a conventional national bordering that Carpentier's zonal focus supersedes. From the Harlem Renaissance to the Works Projects Administration's collecting and recording of oral histories of former slaves still living in the American South, U.S. and European (especially German) scholarship on black music has been rich and widely available. However, it is almost always dedicated to Afro-North American spiritual, slave song, ragtime, New Orleans Dixieland, Beale Street, Motown, and the rural blues traditions.

Such scholarship has little to say about the chants to the *orishas*, *danza* or *septeto*, *"filin"* or *guaguancó*. These are the forms, among others, that found their way to other parts of Latin America via ballrooms, concert halls, and bars, creeping, under cover, into North American awareness from an early date. Inspired writing on jazz in the United States still often acts as though New Orleans were not a Caribbean city, or as if Miami had not been home to Cuban exiles long before José Martí was writing his encomiums to Walt Whitman during his New York exile of the 1880s. Fruitful, purposive cooperation between the two Americas was of long standing, even if a wall of language separated them. The ways in which Cuban music retained its *cubanidad* abroad (in New York or Mexico City) or acted as a national-cultural emissary in the arenas of entertainment have still not been adequately explored.

It would be saying too much to argue that Cuba went it alone in matters of music. Apart from being pan-Caribbean in the sense that Carpentier describes at length, clearly some of what we know of as "Cuban" music in the twentieth century was filtered through the U.S. jazz combos that visited Cuba in the teens and twenties. Probably the most important Cuban composer of the nineteenth century—Ignacio Cervantes—got his first boost from Louis Moreau Gottschalk, and became the latter's protégé between 1859 and 1861. The *danza* and *danzón* did insinuate themselves into European and North American salon music, as Carpentier notes, but they did so under the auspices of composers such as Rossini and Gounod, who acted as agents for Cuban expatriate pianists who had won important Parisian competitions (as was the case with Cervantes). Even the first Cuban "jazz" tours of Europe in the 1920s performed a hybrid, commercialized product influenced by European protocols of ballroom dress and instrumentation that had been devised by white Cuban arrangers such as Don Azpiazu and Eliseo Grenet. The paradox, in fact, is that the rougher, rawer sound of the *son* as it existed in Cuba before the 1920s (a form that had been in existence for only about two decades) was not as widely exported during the Jazz Age as it is now.

The more or less exclusive focus on the United States when it comes to black popular music had its exceptions among African Americans themselves. Langston Hughes, whose father lived in Mexico, and who mastered Spanish at a young age, thought of the bourgeois black literati of Harlem as the *"old* New World."[54] In the summer of 1927, he first traveled to Cuba as a mess boy on a freighter named the *Nardo*, an experience that later moved him to write the story "Powder-White Faces," about racial discrimination in the brothels of Havana.[55] Several of his poems have distinctly Latin settings ("Caribbean Sunset," "Soledad: A Cuban Portrait," and "To the Dark Mercedes of 'El Palacio de Amor' "). By 1928, the Cuban journalist José Antonio Fernández de Castro published a translation of Hughes's "I Too Sing America," and in 1930, wrote an introductory essay on Hughes for *Revista de Habana,* which stressed his racial pride. Hughes later became very close friends with Guillén, the great poet of *negrismo.*

As the librettist of a pop opera for Broadway, Hughes tried to establish contact with Cuban composers. Already established as a writer there in 1930, he traveled to Cuba "looking for a Negro composer to write an opera with me, using genuinely racial motifs":

> The lady on Park Avenue thought that Amadeo Roldán might do, or Arturo Cartulo *[sic].* I could not find Cartulo, and Roldán said he wasn't a Negro. But Miguel Covarrubias had given me a letter to José Antonio Fernández de Castro, person extraordinary of this or any other world. And José Antonio saw to it that I had a rumba of a good time and met everybody, Negro, white, and mulatto, of any interest in Havana — from the drummers at Marinao to the society artist and editor of *Social,* Masaguer. But I came back to New York with no Negro composer who could write an opera.[56]

In 1931, Hughes arrived in Cuba for a third time, rekindling old friendships. This time he moved on to Haiti, traveling from Cuba directly. Following that trip, he wrote a novella with Arna Bontemps called *Pop and Fifina* and a play, *Emperor of Haiti: An Historical Drama,* performed by the New York City Opera Company in 1949 under the title *Troubled Island.*

It was not always the case that music and literature were so neatly divided in Hughes's world. His experimental fusions had some of the flavor of the early Carpentier. In *Ask Your Mama: 12 Moods for Jazz,* for example (1961), he set his poems to music. The directions for musical accompaniment run down the right-hand margin of the page in a long, thin column, quoting German lieder and calypso while marking the moments when African drums, long silences, jazz solos, or maracas are heard. The poems themselves are often brashly political—about the State Department, Mack the Knife, Leopold of Belgium, and welfare. In one of the poems, "Gospel Cha-Cha," the directions read: "Maracas...in cha-cha tempo, then bongo drums joined by the piano, guitar and *claves*, eerie and strange like bones rattling in a sort of off-beat mambo up strong between verse then down under voice to gradually die away in the lonely swish-swish of the maracas."[57] An impressionistic mix of Cuba and Haiti, the text in part reads: "Erzulie plays a tune / on the bongo of the moon. / the papa drum of sun / and the mother drum of earth / know tourists only for / the money that they're worth / in the quarter of the negroes / mama mamacita papa papiamento."

These U.S.–Cuban interfaces virtually dominate the musical story narrated by *Music in Cuba* in a panoply of similar anecdotes and vignettes. There are few moments when Carpentier compares the technical features of Afro-Latin and African American music. He does do so fleetingly in his discussion of the "offbeat" of ragtime and the "continuous motion" of boogie-woogie. One hardly expects more given the blanket coverage of the North American scene—a coverage that usually impedes writers from making a case for their music outside the North American mass-market loop. But one is still surprised not to see more sustained comparisons. In his *Caribbean Discourse,* Edouard Glissant describes this zonal reality involving the musical styles that emerged from communities at war: "the slums of Kingston where reggae slowly takes shape, the ghettos of New York where salsa bursts into life."[58] In *Autobiography of an Ex-Colored Man,* James Weldon Johnson—himself a Tin Pan Alley composer—pointed to what Cuban composers such as Ignacio Cervantes may well have prompted him to write (and that the Cuban pianist, Ernesto Lecuona, acheived beautifully, although after Johnson's novel appeared): "I had been turning classic music into rag-time, a comparatively easy task; and this man had taken rag-time and made it classic."[59] Brilliant contemporary Cuban musicians such as Leo Brouwer have gone much further. If Stan Kenton, he writes, copped the mambo in the 1950s and if the rumba was bastardized on U.S. soil in the same years, that process never died: "the basic elements of 'beat,' 'go-go,' and 'pop' have Latin roots."[60]

THREE PROBLEMS OF THEORY

Folklore and "Nature"

Carpentier has often been baited as being a Francophile aesthete slumming in the New World. Ángel Rama pegs him as having distant and confused attachments to the Americas reminiscent of a familiar European langor for the foreign and the out-of-reach. The Cuban novelist Guillermo Cabrera Infante paints him as a pretender with a French lisp, as though Carpentier were merely a windbag with no real roots in Cuba at all. But the Frenchness of Cuba—at least the Cuban creole classes from which most of the musicians of the nineteenth century were drawn—places Carpentier's own Frenchness in perspective. It becomes evident by the final chapters of *Music in Cuba* that it was only anomalous for Cuban composers *not* to have studied in France, lived there for a time, or been born there.

Ignoring a very large and difficult oeuvre, or looking for ways to ridicule his political sympathies, many write of Carpentier as a European man calling on the accidents of birth to exploit virgin terrain in the name of a basically Old World project—which was nothing more nor less than a suspiciously exoticized "journey to the source." In these accounts, Carpentier comes off as an avatar of a tired European fetishism of man in nature mocked already in Voltaire's portrait of "El Dorado" in *Candide*, parodied by the decadents, and erased from respectability by contemporary critics of ethnography eager to show the romantic idiocy of claims that any culture is autochthonous.

There is no hiding that Carpentier wrote widely and excitedly about *"la naturaleza"* (nature), most of all in his famous account of his trip to the upper Orinoco in the Venezuelan backlands, *Visión de América* (where he does invoke the words *Genesis* and *El Dorado* in his subheadings). But his point in this travel narrative is further clarified in *The Lost Steps*—the novel he wrote about the same journey, where much of the irony and much of the theoretical distance from the missionary/ethnographer/aesthete is driven home with merciless humor and not a small dose of anger.

Carpentier's apparent emphasis on "authenticity" prompts the kind of suspicion we have all become accustomed to lately in theoretical circles. Viewing his terms precisely, though, and in their historical contexts, alleviates many of these initial doubts. The word *folklórico* or *folklore*, for example, appears constantly in his writing, and yet it has a different resonance in Spanish than *folklore* does in English, where it suggests a staid, purely ceremonial and, above all, dead popular culture staged for middle-class audiences under paternalistic conditions.[61] A more appropriate translation for his use of the term would probably be "popular" or "indigenous" or, best of all, "national-popular." He draws a sharp distinction between the two kinds of meaning, rejecting the spirit of folklore as stilted or (worse) a petrified fraud: "A classical composer doesn't reinvent the chant of a black priest... [W]hen someone persists in trying to do so, he only succeeds at creating a false ingenuousness that fools no one." He goes on to speak of two classes of popular music:

> One is artificial, reconstructed on the basis of documents and without any contemporary existence or influence—the sorts of Latin American dances, for example, that one performs only at conferences or exhibitions or festivals sponsored by official institutes. Then there are the living, contemporary ones in a continual process of evolution that spring from the people in the cities, mainly. The two greatest examples of these in the twentieth century are jazz and Cuban music.[62]

As a theoretical problem, popular authenticity confronted Cuban music in the guise of a fierce ideological war between factions of the national intelligentsia. On the one side—in a very common maneuver found in many Caribbean countries ashamed of slavery's legacies—critics such as Eduardo Sánchez de Fuentes asserted that African influence was completely lacking in Cuban music, and that all important "indigenous" influences came from the Taino Indians.[63] On the other side were the heralds of *negrismo* itself—Guillén, Ortiz above all, and later, Carpentier—who contended that the Indian impact was negligible. To talk about "folklore," then, always meant in the end to talk about race:

> And not only about race, but about the processes of *mestizaje*. Wherever ethnic groups mix throughout the Americas, we discover forms of folklore that maintain an internal kinship among elements traceable to each. Hence, before undertaking a study of American folkore, it is always of interest to learn in what proportion the ethnic groups have blended with one another.[64]

In 1963, on French television, Carpentier was even more direct: "I have to say that the Indians, in general, were not very musically inclined. They excelled in the plastic arts, but the musical expressions of the Indians, with the exception of the Andes, is generally pretty poor" (86). Accused of being hamstrung by idealism, Carpentier was also dispassionate. By arguing that as a result of African influences blacks were culturally more advanced than the safely mythologized Taino, he defied the habits of the educated middle classes of Cuba.

As we saw, invocations of "nature" were central to the estrangement felt by Latin American intellectuals toward surrealism. But Carpentier was not, for all that, a cheerleader for the deep dark essences of the authentic, where the overly urbane supposedly meet their maker—the view, say, of André Gide or Roger Caillois (the European exoticists, in other words, rather than the Latin American intellectuals who mostly knew better). *The Lost Steps* may be the most brilliant attempt in fiction to clear up the confusion surrounding urban humanity in the face of nature. Carpentier's journeys to the Gran Sabana and, later, to the jungles of the upper Orinico made a much simpler, and less suspicious, point than could be found in interwar primitivism. In Carpentier's view, whatever one's ideological stance, the Americas were objectively different. He refused to concede that *nature* was, inherently, an idealistic ruse of the overcivilized or the discontented. As a result, Latin American intellectuals could see what the Europeans could not:

> That primal nature, chaotic, grand — that really exists. And
> it would be absolutely vain to attempt an interpretation of
> America, in whatever region, without taking into account the
> fact of an intact nature, the sort of nature that the Europeans
> have left behind and been unable to see for at least three
> centuries. . . . What is hard to find in the jungle is a mediocre
> person. In every case, they have a humanity that I have simply
> never found among the pallid existentialists so in fashion today
> among those who persist in following the example of what is
> already well on the way to dying in Europe. (28, 29)

Carpentier protested that he had no truck with the noble savages
mythologized by the Encyclopedists of the Enlightenment. "I've
taken my stand precisely against the exotic . . . What I want is that
the elements of Latin America be integrated into a universal culture" (111).

Cubanidad

The Cuba most American readers know begins after the Spanish
governors were replaced by Teddy Roosevelt's Rough Riders at
the turn of the last century. But *Music in Cuba* reminds us of Cuba
during the Spanish dominion, encumbered with clerical protocols
and a vain, derivative and empty-headed creole bourgeoisie, soak-
ing up French fashions. The insipid life of late-eighteenth-century
Havana seen in the ads of the *Papel Periódico* is brought out with
bitterness in chapter 5, for example. Whereas recent literary studies
of colonialism give the Orient and Africa more attention than the
Americas because of their size, economic importance, and history,
the factors that made the New World Conquest unique are overlooked. These were, among other things, an economy based on a
global slave system, exterminations of continental dimension, and
very early successful struggles for national independence. Within
the Americas as a whole, it was the Antilles that had pride of place —
historically first, a strategic crossroads, and a site where the mixing of race and language of New World *créolité* was most advanced.
It is hard to overestimate the degree to which Carpentier under-

stood this priority, developing its consequences in the widest variety of genres with, arguably, the greatest popular appeal.

To understand that the Americas *created* Europe is to understand *Music in Cuba*, just as had been the point of Ortiz's masterpiece, *Contrapunteo cubano* (Cuban counterpoint, 1940). Ortiz's study sought to overturn Melville Herskovitz's theory of "acculturation" published only a few years earlier. As one of the most influential books to come out of Cuba, Ortiz's ethnographic and economic monograph on two commodities — tobacco and sugar — coined the term *transculturation* heralded by Bronislaw Malinowski in his introduction to the book's first edition. Ortiz does not at first seem to argue for any American primacy. He appears to claim only that contact between foreign cultures never leads to a merely one-sided assimilation, but to a subtle, undisciplined exchange of values in which an entirely new culture is produced.

In spite of the messy mutual give-and-take implied by the term (Malinowski applauded this aspect of it), Ortiz's book actually presented a very different scenario than this widely accepted one. The story Ortiz tells is one not so much of mutuality as of reversal, for it gives the formerly assimilated a conspicuous, almost dominant, power. Painting indelible pictures of the beauty of curling cigar smoke and the delicacy of tobacco leaves, Ortiz's poetic economy is equally a sketch of the slow revolution in European customs following their contact with the Americas. Life in Europe was reconfigured, redrawn from top to bottom when it began to import the two commodities the Americas were primarily in business to produce: tobacco and sugar. With Cuba leading the way, the Americas effectively trained Europe in a form of cultural luxury and excess. Supposedly insignificant things like bad habits had become necessities, just as an object of ritual consumption among American natives (tobacco) had became an object of guilty pleasure in Europe.

In *Music in Cuba,* Carpentier adopts an identical strategy, substituting the *son* and *clave* for the insidious pleasures of smoking and sweetened tea. Afro-"American" (i.e., Afro-Caribbean and African American) music had forced its way into every aspect of European culture, becoming a source of pleasure that was also a lesson. And in this process, Cuba had a special role to play. The Americas excelled not only in key commodities of luxuriance, but also in ideological commodities of enjoyment. If certain cultures are primordially mystical or visual, argued Carpentier, others are primordially musical. The mixture of Africa and Spain — in isolation and under extremity — had somehow produced this outcome. Referring to Esteban Salas, he wrote: "Cuba, a country where popular music has always occupied a greater place than the plastic arts, produced admirable classical composers long before it could even boast of its first newspaper, a single painter, or one novelist" (21).

Jazz, Adorno, and "New Music"

In comparative literature, musical theory, and cultural studies, Latin American intellectuals are still for the most part curiously ignored. In theories of globalization, one may hear the names Ulf Hannerz or Thomas Friedman, but rarely Enrique Dussel. Students of film theory will come upon Siegfried Kracauer as a matter of course, but not Fernando Solanas or Jorge Sanjinés. If the issue is nationalism, one reads Ernest Renan or Benedict Anderson, but not José Martí or Eugenio María de Hostos. In spite of recent curricular realignments, older, often high-German or poststructuralist French, intellectual traditions remain center stage.

This is one of many reasons to compare the German theorist and musicologist Theodor Adorno and Alejo Carpentier. Near contemporaries, Adorno and Carpentier both theorized radio, classical music, and a mass culture that (according to Adorno himself) took its leads from New World African sources. Although both identified with Marxism, Adorno's dismissals of jazz are much more famous than Carpentier's arguments on behalf of popular, New World African music. The impression left the public — and it is one that current theory has tirelessly repeated — is that there is a fundamental antagonism in Marxism to the cultural forms of the African diaspora, and that Marxism suffers from a Eurocentric distaste for anything that is not about "class."

The present translation is, among other things, an attempt to show how inaccurate this view is. Not everyone foundered on the twin reefs of a pallid, primarily white populism or a disgust for the messiness of a culture that refused to adhere to a sort of laboratory dialectics. Adorno's views on jazz were neither populist nor patrician; they were neither authoritarianly rigid nor simplistic. However, to see them as summing up an entire era of European Marxist critique *is* simplistic, leave alone what happens to that critique in the presence of intellectuals from the colonies. *Music in Cuba* demonstrates from an unusual angle the novelty of the historical period that Adorno lived — one that, for colonial reasons, is known much better through Adorno's writing than Carpentier's. It was a period in which people from the colonies, attentive to European philosophy, did not feel a necessary antagonism between mass culture and a theoretical break from capitalist disenchantments. However, their views should not be confused with a later cultural studies populism that typically derides the Frankfurt School for its elitism toward commercial culture and mass forms of entertainment. It is true that Carpentier's historical experience would have made him recoil from Adorno's ideal of "critique" (had he read Adorno), for Adorno's style of inquiry found solace in a permanent negativity, shielded from the poor and the unlettered. Carpentier's thought was serious and subtle, and not at all populist in that sense, but neither was it the Frankfurt School's. It represented what, in contemporary terms, might be thought of as a Brechtian position, although explicitly involved in a rejection of an imperial system as well as a protest against the foreclosure of knowledge uniquely available in colonial settings.

Comparing Adorno to Carpentier may, at the outset, seem unfair. Adorno the theoretician has always commanded wider intellectual attention, and Adorno's contribution to a critique of capitalist ideational form relies on a mastery of the traditions of continental philosophy from Spinoza through Heidegger. Holding fast to Marx, and commited to a materialist historiography, Adorno wrote about the necessity of philosophy as such, considering theory a riposte to a consumerism that turned subjects into anti-intellectual automata.[65] Although not a "theorist," certainly, Carpentier succeeded in creating a world of art that was also, it should be remembered, a critique of late capitalism, and that found a way to articulate itself in the modes and practices of intellectuals who were double occupants of Europe and the Americas.

Whether or not Adorno aspired to be an artist, he certainly composed music, although it was never widely performed. Carpentier, by contrast, collaborated with some of the era's best composers; his musical and literary work enjoyed both commercial and critical success. If their involvements gave both some claim to be called performers—and both, apart from being pianists, knew composition thoroughly—only Carpentier had any real success as a composer or producer of musical texts. More decisively, given their goals, only Carpentier had any experience as an actual politician: of being jailed for protests, of running government agencies.

Thus, given their very different intellectual equipment, it is important to remind ourselves of Carpentier's authority. When he writes, for example, of the "new personality" that jazz gave the orchestra, he is not just indulging in some impressionistic gesture of a journalistic amateur. *Personality* is not simply a cognate for *feeling* or *tonal color*, but a judgment on the effect of an imaginative misuse of the static repertoire of orchestral instrumentation. It is a comment informed by a career arranging for studio orchestras and a middle age spent as a reviewer who attended concert halls with the frequency of a conductor: "For me, the piano was a means of knowing the greatest possible number of scores (recall that, in those days [the 1920s], records only offered an extremely reduced repertory of serious music. No production company had dared to record an entire symphony. . .)."[66] Very much like Adorno, Carpentier always has the apt analogy at hand when attempting to illustrate a point, citing the exact movement of the composer in question. This is nowhere more evident than in his claim in chapter 10 that in the fifty-plus *contradanzas* of Saumell "no two pages are alike."

Like Carpentier, Adorno's youth was spent as an apprentice in music. An early student of Alban Berg, Adorno published a hundred articles on music criticism between 1921 and 1932 before he ever published a page of philosophy (a dissertation on Kierkegaard).[67] Both were drawn to writing about the same composers, addressing themselves to precisely the same series of sociological problems—among them, the impact of technical advancements in recording, the vexed relationship of the classical tradition to the rise of jazz, and the role of music itself in being, on the one hand, complicit with, on the other, resistant to, the crushing conformities of capitalist modernity. Although neither talks about (perhaps even knew about) the other, each at times writes as though they had. It is clear from the closing comments of the following passage, that Carpentier could not have had Adorno in mind, and yet Carpentier would have recoiled from Adorno for many of the reasons Brecht did, as the first half of the passage suggests:

> One of the most surprising paradoxes of our epoch is seen in the fact that, especially in the Americas, many people who pretend to have politically advanced ideas feel obligated for that reason to make a profession of faith in the most moth-eaten academicism in the name of who-knows-what sort of wandering concept of "the necessity to express the human" and the "return to the real."[68]

In other moments, he meets Adorno's position head-on, making fun of the "levelheaded professors" who say about jazz that "this noisy, off-balance music, kept in perpetual climax, is alien to our cultural idiosyncrasies."[69]

But it would be too easy to overlook the fact that both Carpentier and Adorno, for very different reasons, attacked jazz. Adorno despised jazz as the aesthetic expression of mass dominance through culture—the destruction of subjectivity. The very form that pretended to rely on improvisation—a performer-centered inventiveness—was actually a formulaic rehashing of the insipid tunes from the popular song industry, shopworn classical phraseology, and narcissistic sexual regression. If, on the one hand, it was guilty of coloristic excess, on the other it was marked by a rigid application of clichéd "techniques" such as syncopation, semivocal and semi-instrumental sounds, sliding impressionistic harmonies, and opulent instrumentation.

Precisely because it presented itself as liberating, it was all the more oppressive. Billed as the authentic expression of black culture, jazz, in Adorno's opinion, had nothing to do with genuine African culture. Musically, its origins could be found in the European salon music and marches of the nineteenth century. To Adorno, Beethoven had already exhausted all of jazz's vaunted rhythmic innovations before any record companies had recorded a single measure of Dixieland. Its currency in African American communities was pathetic rather than exultant, representing a sadomasochistic identification with the oppressor.

Although delivered with brilliance in the name of precise and accurate ends, Adorno's argument sounds hopelessly wrongheaded to anyone who has studied African New World music. In the end, it is impossible to believe otherwise than that Carpentier was just much better positioned to make sense of jazz's social meanings and its technical achievements. The scope of his research made him at once attentive to Adorno's overall theoretical outlook and to all of the resources that Adorno lacked: the archival history of New World African sound. If Adorno called jazz "perennial fashion," Carpentier asserted "it's no vogue ... no fashion" but the "folklore of the modern city":

> It's the first example of a dance music that has created its own means of expression ... [Unlike jazz, neither the minuet nor the waltz] had any unique requirements as far as the "voice" was concerned. Jazz, by contrast, from its earliest days in New Orleans, gave birth to peculiar forms what were amplified, perfected, or diminished — in terms of equilibrium and technical possibilities ... The vocal character of jazz is something new, inseparable from the general climate of the century. Practically without known antecedents, it would have been utterly unforeseeable in the nineteenth century.[70]

The problem with jazz, for him, was very different from Adorno's. It was a geocultural problem of great power dominance — one no less damaging simply because it appeared in black dress. It was a form, in other words, of U.S. values exerting international control. Here he echoes many of Adorno's themes but in the service of different gods. In an essay comparing Josephine Baker (a friend of his from the radio days) and Cuban bandleader Moisés Simons, he speaks unflatteringly of the "monotony" of jazz. He talks about its welcome invasion of Europe, but finds that its charms are all found already in the archaic "St. Louis Blues." Everything after that just plays itself out endlessly.[71] None of this is noticed, he laments, because of the United States' power in the world. He applauds Gilbert Chase for pointing out that "everyone treasures jazz as a popular expression, but it is simply and purely North American."[72]

His critique of jazz, then, is modeled on an appeal to closer and more intelligent gradations within African diasporic culture. This is evident, for example, when he reflects on the musical elements that "make us like Duke Ellington's orchestra more than Paul Whiteman's" in chapter 6. For Carpentier, talking about jazz's African roots raises more questions than it answers, although not in Adorno's sense. Carpentier is acutely aware, as a specialist, that African rhythms adopted by the urban folklores of Brazil or Cuba, for example, "have very little to do with the rhythmic foundations of North American jazz." Writing in the 1950s, he argues that jazz profited from "the rhythms and distinct melodic spirit" of the Martinican *biguine,* and from the runaway success of Simons's "The Peanut Vendor" ("The whole world has a record of our *Manisero* . . . They're listening to it even at the wailing wall in Palestine"). In a wonderful tableau, he describes Simons blowing away Josephine Baker with his piano riffs in Baker's eighteenth-century waiting room decorated with paintings by Watteau. Elsewhere, in a memorable portrait of the Parisian club scene, he gives the nod to the Cuban sound over jazz by looking at Don Azpiazu's big band.[73]

There may be special pleading in *Music in Cuba,* but not all of Carpentier's boasts can be dismissed as cultural nationalism (and we should not forget his attempts to guard against an "excessively eulogistic or irresponsible" criticism in just this sense). He was close enough to events, and knowledgeable enough of the island's two pasts, to be granted some leeway on matters of taste: "[Mambo] is the first time that a musical dance genre made use of harmonic advancements that were, just a little time before, the monopoly of composers qualifying as 'modern' — and, for that reason, it shocked a large sector of the public."[74] In 1951, he claimed that "all of the audacities of the North American performers of jazz have been left in the dust by mambo, 'the most extraordinary genre of dance music of this time.' "[75]

Still, Carpentier does not deny the role of European salon music in the development of New World African music. But he goes beyond Adorno in pointing out that salon music had been Africanized from abroad by the nineteenth century through the labors of such musicians as Gottschalk, Cervantes, and Saumell. If Adorno considers it a clinching rebuke to point out that jazz is not "authentically popular" since its origins in rural African America are tenuous (which is, incidentally, quite false); or if he scorns the publicizers of fashion for being ignorant because they argue that jazz is, in the end, a quintessentially urban and modern form, Carpentier agrees. But he does something very different with the information:

> When talking about mambo, it's a matter of not mixing up or confusing dance music, the fruit of urban life, with folklore. The two are never the same. Dance music of the cities is not a pure outburst of popular inspiration, like the *son*, for example, rural song, regional dance, and so on. It is the product of what in all times is called "modern life" — as the waltz of Romanticism was, ragtime at the beginning of the century — and as such merits one's fullest attention.[76]

The argument over jazz, after all — in Adorno as in Carpentier — recapitulates a similar argument over divergent strains of the classical tradition. Adorno famously despised Stravinsky. Carpentier, like much of his generation, idolized him (even knew him personally).

This remarkable difference echoed an early twentieth-century classical debate that pitted composers who employed folk motifs (Shostakovich, Milhaud, Dvořák, and, above all, Stravinsky) against those who avoided melody and the folk's "representational" sound (Schoenberg, Berg, Hindemith, Varèse). This division is obviously a rough one, because Stravinsky — depending on what part of his career is considered — was both a melodic and a nonmelodic composer. Similarly, inasmuch as experiments in *rhythm* can be used to group composers, Stravinsky and Varèse clearly belong in the same camp. To complicate things still further, Adorno at times attacked Hindemith and Berg, even while Carpentier was not so much *for* musical folklorism per se; he only understood the ideological problem it represented for the meeting of classical and popular music. Carpentier, for example, adored Varèse and Schoenberg *as well as* Stravinsky.

All of that being said, the issue of the "folkoric" is clearly defining in Adorno's loathing of both jazz and Stravinsky. Many of the concluding pages of *Music in Cuba* take up the issue in a sustained way, in passages where Carpentier savors the paradox of Latin American intellectuals who consider work grounded in the music of blacks and other "primitives" to be "no sign of progress," and who urge instead an inspiration based on "the great disciplines of Western culture." For, when they turn to European classicism for comfort, they find nothing but folklore: Grieg, Albéniz, Bartók. These European composers of musical nationalism, he adds, were busy turning for comfort to the New World itself. Even Schoenberg "offers eulogies to Gershwin and shuns the North American atonalists." But Carpentier was never more forceful than in his arguments of the 1970s: "If in that world of the 1920s everyone was a folklorist—Falla, Kacella, everyone—everbody was more or less a sort of nationalist."[77]

The comment is intriguing given how little it fits Adorno, whose rejection of Stravinsky sounds identically motivated in some respects to his rejection of jazz. For him, Stravinsky capitulated to the "power of the collective."[78] Like jazz, the victim of new music was the individual subject, whose critical resources and ability to fight were destroyed by Stravinsky's use of primitive dance, with its spatialization of time, and its substitution of sensation for real feeling. He represented a modern pathology akin to the empty repetitions of schizophrenics. And whereas Carpentier and the anticolonialist intelligentsia saw Stravinsky as opening up possibilities for liberation, Adorno saw him as an ally of right-wing phenomenologists such as Heidegger, whose invocation of the primitive had oppressive effects. Collective expression was, for Adorno, a form of barbarism—antisubject to the core. And so it was as seen against the backdrop of fascism. But then, how could African diasporic art be confused with fascism?

The answer lay in Adorno's comparatively narrow frame of reference, which many favorable critics have tried to explain away.[79] What is striking about the legacy of taste that both Carpentier and

Adorno contributed to making is its continued relevance. The rock and punk music of the youth revolts from the 1960s to the 1980s consciously took off from the very Varèse and Webern that Carpentier and Adorno, respectively, had extolled decades earlier.[80] The same lineage could be found in the neo-bop successes of Anthony Braxton, whose immersion in the vanguardism of Varèse, Webern, and Schoenberg occupied him after he took Paris by storm in the 1970s.[81] Adorno would probably have been horrified that the regressions of listening had diluted and destroyed even Schoenberg. On the other hand, perhaps he underestimated the quality of the best commercial popular music in an era when high and low came together, and was simply wrong about the latter's resources, versatility, and intentions. Carpentier comes off looking prescient in this arc. The anticapitalist popular had, in the figures of Frank Zappa and Anthony Braxton, found a bridge between experimental classicism and the rhythmic innovations and sonic shock of an angry music ill at ease with the world.

CONCLUSION: THE TEXT

This translation is based on the third edition of *Music in Cuba*, published posthumously as part of Carpentier's *Obras completas* in 1988. It differs from the first Mexican edition of 1946 in relatively minor ways. For the most part, it repeats the version of 1979 that had been (in the words of its preface) "lightly corrected" by the author. A few paragraphs were added, and the order of others changed in the second edition; and in the 1988 version, most of the original photos (but not reprinted scores) are dropped. The biggest difference between the Mexican version and the others is its final chapter, "The Present State of Cuban Music," which looks at the "youth" — the composers who picked up the baton following the deaths of García Caturla and Roldán: José Ardévol, Julián Orbón, Hilario González, Harold Gramatges, Gisela Hernández, the "Grupo Renovación" (Argeliers León, Edgardo Martín, Serafín Pró, Antonio Cámara, Virginia Fleites), Carlo Barbolla, Gilberto Valdés, Pablo Ruiz Castellanos. Since these composers had achieved maturity before Carpentier died — and were themselves musicians and critics of stature —

the author felt that the chapter was no longer relevant. I have respected his revision. I have not augmented Carpentier's original footnotes, and I have decided against clotting the text with editor's notes, opting instead to clarify terms with bracketed explanations following their first mention in the text. Adding more biographical information than Carpentier himself provides on figures such as Curt Sachs, Buenaventura Ferrer, Cirilio Villaverde, Bachiller y Morales, Emile Vuillermoz, and many many others mentioned in passing seemed unwieldy. Their uses are contextually clear.

Part of the interest in *Music in Cuba* has to do with its history *as* a text. Political ill will and prejudice have prevented the Cuban Revolution from getting its due for promoting the serious study of New World African music. This is the place to insist that that role is incontestable as a matter of plain scholarly fact. The Cuban revolution was about race, in spite of its largely white leadership. Those who opposed the revolution certainly understood this. The revolution extended the earlier national movement against Spain, and, as it developed into socialism, brought to completion the *negrismo* movement of the 1920s as well as the anti-U.S. struggles of the 1940s. Music—and, for historical reasons that *Music in Cuba* best explains, *black* music—was central to the development of Cuban nationalism, whose modern expression is precisely the Cuban Revolution. The post-1959 era certainly did not launch Cuba's emotional investment in black music, but it was the revolution's intellectuals who did more to dignify African cultures in the Caribbean and to theorize them than any other movement in Latin America before or since. By contrast, the Miami exiles descend from traditions whose banner literally read "Neither black nor red" in the early days of Castro's government. One typical anecdote will illustrate the difference politically and musically betweeen the two. In March 1998, anti-Castro exiles, in one of many such raids, forced a Miami radio station to stop playing music from Cuba— an ironic reminder of David Byrne's liner notes to his "Cuba Classics" CD series titled *Dancing with the Enemy,* where he asks: "Can music be our enemy? Can communists have a good time? Is a music communist? The music . . . has had people in Cuba dancing for the last three decades. Now it's your turn." As a revolution about race, post-1959 Cuba plays to a musical theme. To date, almost all of the high-profile Cuban musicians remained in Cuba and continue to produce innovations that are freely "borrowed" by artists in New York, Miami, Los Angeles, Paris, and Berlin.

As for scholarship, the serious study of Caribbean musical forms exploded in Cuba after the early 1960s, and that explosion, if not inspired by Carpentier alone, received crucial direction from him. As the showcase of a black popular culture industry, Cuba has produced a continuous stream of work on the history and social meaning of the Caribbean sound. It may or may not be true, as Carpentier wrote, that "others have surpassed my work." What is beyond dispute is that the best Cuban musical theorists have been, like him, neither strict historians nor mere chroniclers, neither musical populists nor classical watchdogs. They were a politically sensitive group of musical sophisticates who understood the *simultaneity* of tradition, the peculiar mixture of the classical and the popular, the European and the African, that Carpentier had first fully identified. Among these important writers are Leonardo Acosta, Argeliers León, Leo Brouwer, and María Teresa Linares. They drew on *Music in Cuba* as they headed off in entirely new directions. Others writing from abroad have simply taken from his work without acknowledgment.[82]

Taking stock of *Music in Cuba* is a way of reminding ourselves of the extraordinary intellectuals of the interwar period. By the standards of the United States, Carpentier's views on the African New World, for example, are still radical. His portraits of black musicians as "political" men and women, or his view that the term *"Afro-Cuban"* was superfluous since Cuba's Africanness went without saying — these views surpassed most post-1960s racial consciousness-raising and give no reason to apologize for any purported datedness. The book casts black protagonists in a drama of creation and transformation — and does so, for the most part, without paternalism. Some of Carpentier's enemies have gloated over passages in which he falls into a kind of racial cheerleading. But it is always necessary to recall the contexts of *negrismo*'s creativity. As late as the 1920s, black dance was outlawed. Carpentier, then, was starting from scratch, and his views (and language) evolved over time.

There are some questionable details in the text, certainly. Did Las Casas really see the *areíto* performed, for example? Was the *son* really the creation of the sixteenth-century heroine Teodora Ginés ("Má Teodora"), or is the story just nationalist legend, as Odilio Urfé and Alberto Muguercia y Muguercia have argued? Carpentier was undoubtedly wrong about such facts, and yet the book gets at the truth of the daily life of the Caribbean in ways that few histories have, and Carpentier knew it:[83] "The investigative work done on our music has helped me to deepen my understanding of what can be called the little history of Cuba, or rather, the day-to-day life of the past."[84]

Other questions remain as well. How much is Carpentier the historian and musicologist a novelist *avant la lettre*? In other words, what is the historical status of the tale he tells in *Music in Cuba*? The text is unusual among West Indian chronicles. A region of geopolitical importance and undeniable cultural pull, the Caribbean is also a place where histories are plagued by a frustrating lack of detail. Ill-bred exploiters merged with oral cultures, harried and overwhelmed; they were later joined by the unfortunate, the incarcerated, and the owned. All labored for centuries in the heat and decay of a large, ruthless business enterprise that lived for the day, and noted the march of time by counting slaves as they died in droves. It is a mark of the paucity of documents that their numbers are so small and the names of their authors so well known: Bartolomé de Las Casas, Moreau de Saint-Méry, Jean-Baptiste Labat, (and more recently) Lafcadio Hearn. These figures come up again and again in accounts of the Caribbean—including *Music in Cuba*—to augment histories that stick to broad brush strokes and shimmering generalities.

But what Carpentier manages to do in his narrative is to fill out a *Caribbean* story, not only a Cuban one. Surrounded by rare papers, inspired by the fragment of a sixteenth-century quote or a tattered lead, he bridges the gaps of a spotty narrative of migration and ambition. Thus, in chapter 5, Carpentier tips his hand by referring to Juan Nepomuceno Goetz as "good material for a character in a novel." Like many famous travel writers before him, Carpentier's account is immediate and riveting—although, unlike them, his story is about work, about everyday, normal people under conditions of extremity and demand. Instead of being a diary, memoir, or dispatch to a distant king or queen, however, *Music in Cuba* is a continuous text, mostly without gaps. Carpentier sketches in all the absent transitions as though he were a contemporaneous witness, presenting us with a narrative that is deliberately like a novel. For that we thank him, and go on our way.

ACKNOWLEDGMENTS

When I first began researching this project in 1995, a number of American publishers resisted my arguments for bringing *Music in Cuba* to an English-speaking audience. I therefore want to thank the University of Minnesota Press—and in particular the editors of the Cultural Studies of the Americas series—for supporting the idea. The final product was the work of many farflung editors and translators as well as friends and colleagues trying to keep up with Carpentier's period prose. I hope they will forgive me as I thank them here collectively for their participation in a project that was a long time coming.

MUSIC IN CUBA

Preface

Orphaned by conquest of its indigenous artistic traditions, impoverished in its popular art forms, slighted by its colonial architects, especially when compared to other Latin American nations, the island of Cuba, on the other hand, has powerfully created a distinctive music that has long enjoyed extraordinary success abroad. The worldwide popularity achieved by Cuban dances since 1928 was nothing new for the island. Earlier, Cuban *contradanzas* had garnered similar accolades by European and American audiences under such diverse names as *habaneras, danzas habaneras, tangos habaneras, americanas,* and so on, creating genres that were widely cultivated in France, Spain, Mexico, and Venezuela. Our research has encountered creole *guarachas* from the eighteenth century with rhythms that remain popular today. Many of the percussion instruments that have recently enriched the percussion sections of all dance orchestras, such as the *claves,* were commonly used in seventeenth-century Havana. By the end of the sixteenth century, there were *conjuntos típicos* [folk ensembles] in Santiago, and their *sones* were sung in Cuba for more than two hundred years.

What this reveals is that at every moment of its history, Cuba elaborated a sonorous and lively folklore of surprising vitality, receiving, meshing, and transforming diverse contributions, all of which led to the creation of new and clearly defined genres. We should not forget that, at the same time, other types of musical activity arose, considerably in advance of other intellectual manifestations. Even before Cuba had its first theater or its first newspaper, there was a notable and learned composer such as Esteban Salas in the cathedral of Santiago. We discovered extremely important work after prolonged searching and after many assurances that the work had been lost forever; until now, most music scholars and writers on Latin America are unaware of Salas's work. At the end of the eighteenth century, the names of Haydn, Pergolesi, Paisiello, Grétry, Monsigny, were honored in Havana. As a maritime crossroads, Havana had hosted French companies en route to New Orleans that performed an extraordinarily advanced repertoire for the Americas of that time. Before the mid-nineteenth century, Cuba could boast of a symphonist and composer such as Saumell, who clearly had conceptually defined what later would be called musical nationalism. Espadero and Villate were famous in Europe. Ignacio Cervantes, with his *Danzas,* exercised a definite influence over many musicians of the New Continent.

We make no claim, of course, to exaggerate the universal significance of Cuban music, or the place it should be assigned in the panorama of the world's music. But the study of its development within a specific context, that is, the presence of different ethnicities and their percentage of the population, bring forth a series of exceedingly interesting problems. If we take these factors into account, we observe that they are closely analogous to those similar aspects that a researcher might encounter in other countries of the continent. They contribute to explaining the mechanisms by which certain cultures of the New World are formed. Given these concerns, we have tried to situate the musical events in their historical milieu without losing sight of social, economic, and demographic factors. The study of the census, for example, with its proportion of whites, mulattoes, and blacks, of freed slaves and slaves, has always been necessary to comprehend certain characteristics in the evolution of musical culture and folklore in a country that has endured so many and diverse immigrations.

For the same reason we have tried to create, along with our central theme, a schematic study of the music of other Antillean islands—in particular Haiti—whose slave-led revolution unexpectedly brought to Cuba a number of rhythms and genres, altering certain aspects of its folklore. This method has convinced us that there is much that American musicology stands to gain in studying the music of the continent by *geographic zones* subject to the same

ethnic influences, to the same migrations of rhythms and oral traditions, *rather than by region or country.*

This work has been written almost entirely with primary documents. Given the shallowness or lack of seriousness in the few
books on Cuba's musical history,[1] I felt obligated to return to primary sources of information. There were early warning signs that
a number of generally accepted claims made in the work of even
solid foreign scholars, misled by their credulity, had been the result
of the most ingenuous fantasy. Moreover, almost all the published
work focused on certain particular or anecdotal aspects, influenced
by the private sympathies or personal aesthetics of the writer, and
in no way attempted to offer an overall vision of the development
of the island's music from the onset of colonization.

Given this we embarked upon the patient scrutiny of cathedral
archives — principally of Santiago and Havana — of capitulary records of churches and city halls, of parish closets (with brilliant results in Santiago, but none in Santa María del Rosario), of manuscript documents, private libraries, individual collections, and the
shelves of secondhand bookstores, thoroughly inspecting the newspapers, gazettes, and magazines of the colonial period. In many
cases we had to do research helter-skelter, looking for facts in texts
that dealt with anything but music (histories of tobacco and coffee, judicial decrees and military ordinances, or political essays).
Needless to say, in the course of our labors we have had to wade
through many more texts than appear in our bibliography, and we
have more than once stumbled upon the all-too-familiar obstacles
that so often dishearten the Latin American researcher: libraries in
disarray, the lack of card catalogs, incomplete collections, mutilated
books, and so on. We do not even mention the collectors that behaved like dogs in the manger. Luckily, we have been providentially
favored by the discovery of several scores whose absence would
have reduced this book to being a mere chronicle.

On the other hand, we have counted on a cooperation to which
we can never be sufficiently grateful: that of Monsignor Arteaga,
archbishop of Havana, who furnished us with credentials to go
through the archives of the diocese; of Father Fidel Ruiz, parish
priest of the cathedral of Santiago, who allowed us to copy the scores

of Esteban Salas and Juan París—which we discovered in an old forgotten piece of furniture; of Doctor José Antonio Ramos, assistant director of the National Library, and of Mr. Villanueva, bookseller at the same institution, as well as the librarians of the Sociedad Económica de Amigos del País, so highly conscious of their professional mission. Finally, we should give thanks to Natalio Galán, who worked several months with us transcribing some of Salas's scores, especially those so damaged by time.

This history of Cuban music, the first to be written, does not pretend to have exhausted the subject. Much will be added when scientists undertake the study of the continent's music and its African roots. The examination of certain colonial newspapers buried in unused private libraries could enrich the documentation of Havana musical life during the first years of the nineteenth century. We still have not chanced upon Antonio Raffelin's first or second symphony, which should be retrievable in some North American library. The letters between Gottschalk and Espadero contain much that still needs to be revealed...

But a first book on this subject must conserve a sense of proportion, lest it result in the lack of global vision that has characterized the majority of texts written in Cuba about its music up to now. Accordingly, we have refrained from using certain documents that might have been offered as good research finds, especially when their secondary nature might have obscured the main themes of our narrative. We also left aside the noble area of revolutionary music—more of historical than artistic interest—since we decided that figures such as Perucho Figueredo, for example, author of the Cuban national anthem, ought to be the subject of a different type of research, more closely linked to the patriotic reproduction of iconographic documents or manuscripts. On the other hand, we abstained from lengthy personal comments at the margin of events, believing that basic information should be the main goal of this work, undertaken on almost virgin soil, and whose principal documentary sources are nothing more than the manuscripts or the references lost in ledgers and colonial newspaper collections. We believe that the general thrust of the study traces the continuous development of Cuban music and its culture from the beginning.

Thus, with an opening panoramic vision obtained in this first general overview, we then proceed to study individual cases and fill the lacunae that are still found in the life of Saumell, for example, or to detail the activities of a Raffelin in France, Spain, and the United States. Nevertheless, with this book, we think we have set in place — for other researchers and for ourselves — the necessary point of departure.

Alejo Carpentier
Caracas, November 1945

1. The Sixteenth Century

The degree of vigor, power of resistance, or richness of certain New World civilizations at the time of the Conquest provoked the European invader to greater or lesser activity—but fraught with ambivalence—in matters of architecture and musical indoctrination. When the peoples to be subjugated had shown sufficient strength, wisdom, or industry to have built a Tenochtitlán [Mexico], or to conceive a fortress like Ollanta [Peru], the mason and the Christian cantor diligently entered the action just as soon as the warriors fulfilled their mission. Once the battle of bodies ended, the struggle over signs ensued. The cross had to be raised higher than the *teocali* [Aztec temple]. Over every demolished temple a church had to be erected. The splendor of finely wrought idols had to be eclipsed by liturgies of great pomp. Against songs and traditions that could still arouse a dangerous spirit of rebellion, the spiritual forces of the golden legends and Christian antiphons were marshaled. In brave and prosperous lands, the Conquest hoisted bell towers high against the horizon and set its choruses to singing. In pliable lands, whose inhabitants readily accepted the authority of a king unknown only the day before, the newcomers did not have to work so hard. As a result, the artistic and musical manifestations of sixteenth-century Latin America were of very poor quality, especially in countries whose mythopoetic heritage did not pose a threat to Europeans.

Whereas in Mexico Fray Juan de Haro and Fray Pedro de Gante hastily initiated—three years after the Conquest—the teaching of plainsong to the Indians, replacing the organ with flute ensembles, this strategy of spiritual penetration was of no great concern to the first wave of colonizers of Cuba. True, they massively baptized and indoctrinated whenever possible, but there is no evidence that Christian chants were taught to Cuban Indians before their rapid and complete extermination, expedited in such a reasoned and systematic fashion, comparable to what Father Motolinía chronicled from Mexico. The islands "newly discovered in the Oceanic sea" were rich in neither material nor spiritual resources. More copper than gold lay in Cuban soil. The *Taino* idols, despite their terribly unpleasant faces, offered a coarse and stony nakedness compared to the resplendent robe of the Virgin. They lived in palm-leaf huts, organized in autonomous clans, without a centralizing impulse, and brandished weapons no more threatening than their myths. In such conditions, the choirmasters had more to do among the prospectors for gold — soon exhausted — than in their forgotten world of rules and commandments. Where architecture had not gone beyond the age of branch and fiber, the mason's trowel was an inconceivable luxury. Thus, in an island of thatched huts, the first church was a hut.

In 1509, shorty after Sebastián de Ocampo first surveyed the still-uncolonized island, various castaways were hurled onto the Cuban coast by a tempest. One of them, too sick, could not continue the journey to Santo Domingo, and sought shelter in the hospitality of the Indians of the town of Macaca. Soon he learned some of their native tongue, and because he was so pious, he convinced the *cacique* [chief] to be baptized. The cacique took this, so it seems, as some kind of honorary title bestowed by the foreigner, and believing that the governor of Hispaniola was called the *Comendador*, he chose this title as his baptized name. Excited by the gentleness of the people, the castaway then exhibited a card-sized print of the Virgin he carried with him, and managed to have a hut erected in her honor. "He announced to them (the Indians) that the image represented a very beautiful Lady, benign and rich, called María, the mother of God," and shortly thereafter the good savages were singing an Angelical Salutation to the sunrise and the sunset. Later they "began to compose songs and dances with the refrain of Holy Mary." And within a year, the cacique and the dwellers of the nearby town of Caciba followed the example of Macaca, erecting a hermitage made of palm leaves, in which they sang and paid reverence to the Immaculate Virgin.

The castaway had an unerring vision of how to intelligently colonize. Fray Bartolomé de Las Casas would later recommend acceptance of the *areíto* [indigenous ceremonial song and dance] with Christian wording as a good aid to evangelizing. Unfortunately, by the time some priests were able to apply this system, the indigenous population of Cuba had the word *hunger* too ingrained in their consciousness to be able to think about "composing songs and dances with the refrain of Holy Mary."

In 1511, the city of Baracoa is founded. It is followed later by Bayamo, Sancti Spíritus, and Trinidad. At the end of 1514, Santiago de Cuba is born. Diego Velázquez is already a "distributor of Indian labor." In regard to the immoralities, abuses, favoritisms, and envy engendered by the elastic *encomienda* system [a method of forced labor in land grants bestowed by the Spanish crown], the nascent colony led a turbulent way of life. These grand deceptions embittered the souls of many. The pasturelands of Extremadura were just right for fattening up cattle. No one expected such bounty from these spiceless Indies. Despite the appearance of gold in the washeries, clearly centuries-old alluvial deposits, they were destined to die out under the fingernails of just a few. Those not favored by grants of good Indian labor manifested their discontent more openly. And those with serfs granted by the *encomienda* system were fighting against the clock. "After we came on the scene, the Indians never had a day of respite," confesses Oviedo. "Their entire occupation consisted of work that killed them, and at the end of the workday, they had no other care save to lament and cry out their misfortune and calamity." This regime already encompassed, potentially, the principal reason for the impoverishment of the nascent colony. The truly ambitious considered their stay in Cuba a waiting station, a pause between movements of conquest. The Hernán Corteses, Pedro de Alavarados, Diego de Ordaces, Bernal Díaz del Castillos, already dreamed about the great future myths of America, even though they had yet to guess the names: El Dorado, Potosí, the treasures of the Incas, the fountain of eternal youth. They were preparing their entry into a new mythology, created by their own daring.

Among the extraordinary adventurers who had passed through Cuba there were a few musicians. To our shores arrived the likes of Porras, a cantor, and Alonso Morón, a *vihuela* player, probably a resident of Bayamo and relative of another Morón who marched off to New Spain with his "golden horse." Ortiz the musician, as Bernal Díaz del Castillo insistently called him, is the more clearly defined in this group. A resident of Trinidad, Ortiz was considered a notable player of the *vihuela* and the viola. It is said that he also taught dance. The fact is that his instruments were the first to resonate through the thickets and jungles of the island, the traditional rhythms of the Peninsula sheathed in the guitar necks he brought with him. However, Ortiz's ambition sought greater adventures, and he was far from content to enliven the Sundays and religious holidays of his neighbors in such shameful circumstances. When Hernán Cortés, who as a novelty sported a tuft of feathers, a medal, a chain, and velvet clothing, went in search of men in Trinidad, Ortiz responded instantly to his call. With *vihuela* and viola encased, he took on the great adventure, willing to share with a Bartolomé García the possession of "a good dark horse they called El Arriero." Ortiz was considered by Cortés to be one of his best horsemen. When the conquistador needed an unruly horse to frighten the Indians, he always resorted to the neighing and stamping of El Arriero. Ortiz the musician was part of the entire process of the Conquest. The enterprise concluded, he received at the hands of Cortés, as a prize for his valor, one of the lots of land in Mexico City: it was situated on de las Gayas Street, and there he installed his school of dance and music, the same he had opened in Trinidad. They used to call him *"el nahuahuatlo,"* because of his unique ability in learning *náhuatl* [the indigenous language of Mexico spoken by the Aztecs]. His companion during his Cuban escapades, Alonso Morón, also took up residence in Colima, setting up a school of song and dance. Judging by the date of their arrival in New Spain, it is certain that other musicians, such as the flautist Benito Bejel, the trumpet players Cristóbal Rodríguez and Cristóbal Barrera, the harpist Maestro Pedro, and Cristóbal de Tapia, the drummer of Pánfilo de Narváez, had previously been in Cuba. But their stay there left no mark on the island.

Cuba had received Spain's musical legacy early in its colonial existence from Ortiz, Porras, and Morón, as well as various military musicians of the Conquest.

At the petition of Diego Velázquez, the first bishopric was built in Baracoa in 1518, as a result of Leo X's papal bull. Four years later, this bishopric was transferred to Santiago, its church converted to a cathedral. Its first bishop, Juan de Wite (or Ubite), shouldn't have come to Cuba. For the same reason, his lack of knowledge of the milieu and the true resources available to the colony led him to create offices, positions, and prebends that were disproportionate, dictating acts and ordinances that were practically impossible to carry out. Flemish, so taken with pomp, Juan de Wite saw everything on a grand scale: "And because in the island of Fernandina, otherwise known as Cuba, there has neither been found nor erected any kind of church, nor has any bishopric been instituted ... Leo X, desiring to provide some remedy owed to said island, built, raised, and insituted a church with the invocation of the Assumption of the Blessed Virgin Mary." Music certainly occupied a central place in the sumptuous concerns of the Flemish bishop. They created a choir, a position of choirmaster

> to which no one can present himself unless he happens to be learned and expert in music, at least in plainsong; and whose job will be to sing at the choir desk and to teach those servants of the church to sing; and to order and correct and amend matters pertaining to the choir's singing, and wherever else necessary, and this be on his own and not through third parties.

Also created was a position for organist, "who will play the organ in festivities." And so the ceremonies would lack nothing in magnificence, Juan de Wite endowed the temple with a verger and a dog chaser "to throw dogs out of the church, every Saturday, and during the Vigils or of whatever feast where they wandered about." Finally, with respect to canon law: "We order that the divine and nocturnal offices, during Mass as well as during the hours, observe the rules of the Sevillian church, and when singing, the custom of that church should also be observed."

This founding document, issued in Valladolid March 8, 1523, was, in terms of its details, far from acquiring real shape. The building of the cathedral was not begun until 1528. The organ would not be heard until many years later. However, the choir was instituted with modest resources. In 1524, Diego Velázquez wrote this revealing paragraph of its presence: "I hereby order that on the day I pass away, my body be taken to the cathedral chapter of this city's church...and all the remaining clergymen...intone their litany and vigil with nine readings from Scripture and a sung requiem Mass, with deacon and subdeacon."

Miguel Ramírez, successor to Juan de Wite and first residing bishop of Cuba, did all that was possible to maintain the cathedral of Santiago at such a high level, especially with regard to offices and prebends. Favored by the *repartimientos*, owning good Indian laborers—in defiance of the royal decree that prohibited him from doing so—Ramírez indulged certain luxuries in the temple in exchange for the excessive titles of land in his niece's name. But when Fray Diego de Sarmiento, a hard, energetic, and austere man, became bishop in 1538, he deemed it sufficient to officiate in the cathedral of Santiago with two priests, a sacristan, and two choirboys.

The truth is that the sumptuous organization decreed by Juan de Wite did not correspond, in any way, to the puny importance of a nascent colony. When Sarmiento disembarked in Cuba, "Santiago was, despite its decorative and imposing title worthy of a city, a village of twenty residents, of which twelve were dwellers, four were councilmen, and the other four took turns acting as mayor; to this neighborhood we add the meager garrison, a few priests whose prebends were real in name only, royal officials, and two or three Franciscans slight of learning and abundantly lean."[1] The mines were being exhausted; the Indians were dying out or fleeing to the woods; foodstuffs and goods to the island were irregularly supplied; French pirates had begun their plunder. While a certain Vasco Porcayo de Figueroa hoarded land and serfs, the others grew thinner and indignant for not having passed through New Spain at the opportune time. In terms of the moral climate, one should remember that Governor Guzmán had been accused of "consenting to public sins, blasphemies, gambling, and concubinage." As the great Spanish empire grew on the continent, life in Cuba took on an insecure and difficult existence, corroded in full infancy by an unsatisfied greed, quarrels, frustrated ambitions of men who ultimately were the failures of the great adventure of the Conquest.

Suddenly, a noble figure arose in this milieu, someone who could be considered, chronologically speaking, the first of the Cuban musicians: Miguel Velázquez. As to his Cubanness, he was the son of an Indian woman and belonged to the first generation born on the island. His father was Castilian, a member of the family of Governor Velázquez. And because of his privileged background he was sent to study in Seville and Alcalá de Henares. When he returned to Cuba, the mestizo became councilman for the municipal government. In 1544 he was canon of the cathedral of Santiago. In Spain he had learned to "play the organs" and had thorough knowledge of the rules of plainsong. A true learned soul in that poor colony, he taught grammar, and was diligent in the correct observance of canon law in vocal performances. He was said to be "young at heart but aged and wise in doctrine and deed." And, notable trait, his contact with milieux of superior refinement and culture hadn't extinguished in this son of an Indian woman a profound love for his native land, as was the case with the Inca Garcilaso. Faced with the island's squalor, which he was able to understand better than anyone as councilman, teacher, and canon, he once exclaimed painfully: "Sad land, tyrannized and under lordly rule!"

So we are left with the most interesting fact that the first choirmaster in the recorded history of the cathedral of Santiago, exactly half a century after the Discovery, was Cuban, son of an Indian woman and a Castilian father.

Driven by a provincial desire to downplay the importance of black legacies that have so greatly contributed to the character of Cuban music, some local authorities expended great energies in trying to demonstrate that this music, among its several sources, was of aboriginal origin. The fact is that we are totally unaware of what the music of the primitive inhabitants of Cuba was like. To bring us out of this impasse it would be necessary to have a discovery as providential and improbable as the *areítos* annotated by a Miguel Velázquez, for example, during the first years of colonization. In Cuba's case we could apply the general rule established by Carlos Vega:

When the Spanish arrived, the less developed indigenous peoples and those in a middle range of growth were found on the Atlantic coasts and in the center and south of the Americas. If some of the elements of their material life passed over into swelling the wealth of the victors (in Cuba, the preparation of certain foods, ways of fishing, uses of fibers and leaves, of building *bohíos*), not a sole melody, on the other hand, not a single note, nor a dance ... were adopted by the inhabitants of European origin.

The concept of Taino music held by the colonizers was brutally expressed in letters like the one sent by Bishop Sarmiento to the king of Spain: "As the Indians have nothing else to do, they occupy themselves only in *areítos* and in other vices and dissolute behavior.... Since they are free, they only idle and take part in *areítos;* and by such means they will lose lives and souls, and the residents their haciendas, and Your Majesty the island."

The Siboneyes, few in number, were already at the point of disappearing during the days of the Discovery. "Their culture had not lived through the Neolithic period" (Ramiro Guerra). We know nothing of their music. With regard to the Tainos, true masters of the island, who belonged to "the great family of the Arawaks of South America," we have more reports, although of a descriptive and superficial nature, in the accounts of the chroniclers. Gonzalo Fernández de Oviedo offers us a very detailed depiction of how the *areítos* in Hispaniola were danced:

> These people had the good and gentle manner of remembering past and ancient things; and this was in their songs and dances, which they call *areyto* which is what we call dancing as we sing.... And to greater propagate their joy and mirth, they would take each other by the hand sometimes, and at others would go arm in arm, strung together or grasping in a line (or in a circle), and one of them would take on the task of guiding (be it man or woman), and that person would take certain steps forward or backwards, in an ordered figure like country dancing; and the same thing (and at the same moment) is done by all, singing in a high or low tone depending on the intoning by the guide, and as he does and says, very measured and ordered, the count of steps matching the verses or words being sung. And thusly, the multitude responds with the same words

and steps and order; and as they respond to the guide, he is silent, although he does not cease executing the steps. Once finished the response, which consists in repeating what the guide has said, they proceed unrestrained without pause to another verse or words that the circle of dancers again repeat; and like that, without ceasing, this lasts three or four hours until the maestro or leader who dances finishes his story, and at times this goes on until the next day.

Testimonies of Las Casas and López de Gómara corroborate the exactness of this account.

As for instruments, Oviedo mentions an idiophonic drum, which responds to the same principles of the classic hollowed-out and resonant tree trunks, known to many of the peoples of Africa, South America, and Oceania:

> At times with the singing they mix in a drum, made out of a round wood, hollow, concave, wide as a man, more or less, however they choose to make it; and they sound like the dull drums that blacks make; but they don't cover it with leather or skin, but some holes and stripes that go over the hollow part, from which it reverberates ungracefully. The drum has to be placed on the ground, because in the air it would make no sound.

Las Casas also mentions the "hoarse wooden drums, made without anything stuck to them," adding that the Indians had "small bells, very subtle, made of wood, skillfully crafted, with little stones inside." In some archaeological digs decorative baby rattles were found, as a rhythmic marker for the body movements while dancing. Similarly, the Tainos used the *guano* or *fotuto*, the horn of the conch shell known by many maritime peoples. But we have not seen an instrument with the ability to produce a scale, by which we would be able to establish a revealing kinship. The only *areíto* bequeathed to us is the famous and much-discussed "Areíto de Anacaona," of dubious transcription, reproduced by Bachiller y Morales in his work *Cuba primitiva*. Neither the scale, nor the rhythm, nor the melodic character of the *areíto*, written in our notational system, with its eight measures per stanza and four for the refrain, have the slightest aboriginal air to them. (That is, it does not bear any relationship to or show signs of contact with other primitive musics of the Americas.) Those defenders of its authenticity cling to a phrase by Las Casas, according to which "the songs and dances of the Indians of Cuba were softer, better sounding, and more agreeable than those from Haiti," in order to explain the unexpected melodic appropriateness of that *areíto*, which is precisely what they went looking for in Haiti in order to forge an idea of the music that the Tainos could have produced in Cuba. However, they admit that in the measures reproduced there might have already been a Spanish influence. The truth is that the *areíto* of long ago is surprisingly similar to certain songs and street serenades for infants of the eighteenth century, of the type "Y'avait un petit homme, nommé Titi Carabi, mon ami," and others sung by the sons of French colonizers established in Santo Domingo before the massive slave uprising. As for the words, we find that in one of the verses sung in the court of Henri Christophe, the refrain was initiated with the vigorous and resounding insult:

Aia bombaia, bombé,
lamma lamanaqueana.

These clauses correspond phonetically to those that open the so-called Taino *areíto:*

Aya bomba ya bombay,
la massana Anacaona.

Seabrook reproduces the same lyrics as belonging to a voodoo chant collected by Price Mars, and that Droain de Bercy and Moreau de Saint-Méry had previously cited, with some variations. In order to agree that these words, mixed with voices derived from the *quimbundo* in its subsequent phrases, "could proceed from the language of the aboriginals of the island," we would have to believe that blacks had the gift to assimilate and rapidly transform a newly acquired musical material, and only then could we construe this as a case of a remembered aboriginal melody, with so much of the original model preserved in the famous and only surviving document. We should heed the authoritative statement of Fernando Ortiz: "the indigenous character of this Afro-Francophone couplet is illusory." As for the rest, the only indigenous instruments that have lasted are the maracas and the *güiro*, idiophones that are similar to existing ones found in Africa, and which blacks brought to Cuba, and for that reason, were easily adopted.

The fact of the matter is, that when, at the end of the eighteenth century, Cuban songs appeared that can be studied and compared because of existing manuscripts, or later editions after the date of their diffusion (such as "La Guabina," mentioned in an article from *El Regañón de La Habana* in 1801), there is nothing in them that cannot be conclusively attributable to Andalusian, Extremenian, French, or African influences. If there is something in Cuban music that lies beyond all mystery, it is its direct link with some of its original roots, even in the cases where those roots are intertwined to the point where they constitute a new organism. Luckily for the researcher, the Cubanness of creole music is still a relative phenomenon in the first half of the nineteenth century. The Cubanness is more due to inflections, to modalities of interpretation, to malicious superficialities, than to issues of how clearly they were transcribed. There is no case of a *creation* of new rhythms until after 1850. Thanks to this, certain current genres, quite easy to characterize and very much alive, can be related to an original cell, first effaced, later modified, and finally substituted for, all in the course of an evolution that can be followed step by step for more than a century and a half.

In the first half of the Cuban sixteenth century, Spain comes to us by way of the voice and instruments of the first musicians who pass through the New World. Ortiz, Morón, Porras, and their imitators in playing music and waging war drag along with them a culture that will be inherited by the generations born immediately after the Conquest—just as Miguel Velázquez receives the rules of plainsong and the knowledge of the manuals on playing organ as his patrimony. But another element of capital importance contributes in engaging a folklore in the minds of the population: the ballad. The ballad's legacy was sung over cradles and passed on mouth to mouth. Many conquistadors were illiterate. Others, on the other hand, knew how to sing and versify, and there were some like Diego de Nicuesa, governor of Veragua, "a great man in composing Christmas carols, for the night of Our Lord." The truth is, learned or not, they brought a poetic and musical tradition aboard their caravels, as is demonstrated by the almost incredible propagation of the "Delgadina," whose presence has been revealed in the remotest corners of the American continent (and even in Iceland!) with more or less accented variations—in the wording, in the melody, or both—but with a persisting central idea. Well known is the dialogue between Portocarrero and Hernán Cortés, in which this quote from the former:

Cata Francia Montesinos,	(Montesinos searches for France,
Cata París la ciudad,	Paris searches for the city,
Cata las aguas del Duero,	The Duero's waters search,
Do van a dar la mar...	For where it meets the sea.

elicits the following response from the Conquistador: "Give me, oh God, good fortune in battle, like the knight Roland." The memories of those ballads abound in the conversations of those prodigious men. And the truth is that we find the same ballads in all those subjugated lands, Cuba being no exception. On the contrary, Cuba is one of the countries of America that has best conserved the balladic tradition. In different eras, whether collected in the city or the countryside, we find some of the most famous and universally known ballads because of their mythical-affective content: "Delgadina" (or "Angarina"), "La esposa infiel" [The unfaithful wife], "Las señas del esposo" [The husband's signs], "Isabel," "Las hijas del Rey Moro" [The daughters of the Moorish king]. A short while ago, right in the city of Havana, I heard some young girls who were dancing in a circle singing:

En Galicia hay una niña,	(In Galicia there is a girl,
en Galicia hay una niña,	In Galicia there is a girl,
que Catalina se llama,	Whose name is Catalina,
sí, sí,	yes, yes,
que Catalina se llama.	whose name is Catalina.

Todos los días de fiesta *(bis)*	On every holiday *[repeat]*
su madre la castigaba,	Her mother would punish her,
sí, sí,	yes, yes,
su madre la castigaba.	her mother would punish her.
Porque no quería hacer *(bis)*	Because she wouldn't do *[repeat]*
lo que su padre mandaba, etc.	What her father ordered, and so on
Y mandó hacer una rueda *(bis)*	And he ordered a wheel *[repeat]*
de cuchillos y navajas, etc.	Made of knives and blades, etc.
Y en medio de la rueda *(bis)*	And in the middle of the wheel *[repeat]*
a Catalina arrodillaba, etc.	he made Catalina kneel, and so on.
Y bajó un ángel del cielo *(bis)*	And an angel came down from heaven *[repeat]*
a salvar a Catalina, etc.	to save Catalina, etc.
Sube, sube, Catalina *(bis)*	Go, go up, Catalina *[repeat]*
que el Rey de los Cielos te llama, etc.	the King of heaven is calling for you, and so on.)

This annotation, which I made in a municipal park, is nothing if not a Cuban throwback to an old Andalusian ballad that goes like this:

Por la baranda del cielo,	(On the railing of the sky,
se pasea una zagala,	sauntered a young lass,
vestida de azul y blanco,	dressed in blue and white,
que Catalina se llama.	whose name was Catalina.
Su padre era un perro moro,	Her father was a Moorish dog,
su madre una renegada.	her mother, a renegade.
Todos los días del mundo	Every day of her life
el padre la castigaba.	her father punished her.
Mandó hacer una rueda	He had a wheel made
de cuchillos y navajas	of knives and blades,

para pasarse por ella	to pass her through them
y morir crucificada.	and die, crucified.
Y bajó un ángel del cielo	And an angel came down from heaven
con su corona y su palma,	with its crown and its palm,
y le dice: "Catalina,	and said to her: "Catalina,
toma esta corona y palma	take this crown and palm
y vente conmigo al cielo	and come to heaven with me,
que Jesucristo te llama."	because Jesus Christ is calling for you."

This typical example is not an isolated case. In *guarachas* that speak about cats, there are reminiscences, in the lyrics, of the classic "Don Gato," so popular throughout all Latin America. There isn't a Cuban woman who doesn't know the more recent ballad "La muerte de Alfonso XII." And children still sing the "Mambrú." In a *guaracha* from the mid-nineteenth century published in 1882 in the Plaza del Vapor, in Havana, you can read this quatrain, whose first two verses could have been written by Nicolás Guillén:

Tú eres un negro bembón	(You are a juicy-lipped black
y yo soy mejor que tú;	and I am better than you;
si te doy un bofetón	if I give you a whack
te hago bailar el Mambrú.	you'll dance the Mambrú.)

One can still hear on the island a roguish version of the "Delgadina," which ends in this very creole manner:

Angarina se murió	(Angarina died
en un cuarto muy oscuro,	in a very dark room,
y por velas le pusieron	and as candles they had
cuatro plátanos maduros.	four plaintains of gloom.)

From early on the ballad was sung in Cuba. Its imprint is very alive and profound, in the songs of white peasants, and principally in its Extremenian versions. Any Cuban *guajiro* [peasant] can "intone" some of its traditional popular songs:

Ese caballo fue mío,	(That horse belonged to me,
valiente caminador;	so valiant afoot;

| fue de un gobernador, | under the governor's boot, |
| de la Provincia del Río, etc. | from a province by the sea, and so on.) |

sung to the music of "Moralinda," cited by Bonifacio Gil García, without the slightest desire of modifying it, since it corresponds totally, in regard to melody, rhythm, and mode, to its habitual forms of expression. At most, he will lengthen a note, with a point of augmentation, shortening the next note. But here is an even more eloquent example: a short time ago, a Havana radio station achieved great success with the popularity of a completely peasant song titled "La guantanamera," which had been brought to the capital by authentic balladeers. Over the melody, as if they were hallelujahs, was a narration of current events. Well, fine: but the music that corresponded to the first two phrases of "La guantanamera" was nothing other than the Extremenian version of a very old ballad, "Gerineldo."

Add to this first influence the knowledge of how to play the European instruments brought by the first musicians of the Conquest. By 1550 hadn't those flageolots, harps, *vihuelas,* sackbuts (trombones), and small flutes that were played in Mexico during the banquets offered to Hernán Cortés to celebrate the peace treaty signed by Charles V and Francis I perhaps first passed through Cuba and Santo Domingo? From the beginning of colonial times, public "merriments" were held in Santiago to celebrate auspicious events. These "merriments" were now observed and heard by a new type of human being that came to swell the ranks of the Cuban population against their will, bringing with them their own innate musical genius: blacks.

Although it is not possible to state precisely when the first blacks came to Cuba, we know they were on the island as of 1513. Hernán Cortés took some blacks to Mexico. In 1526, Fernando Ortiz tells us, two Genoans brought a shipment of 145 black slaves from Cape Verde. In 1534, the colony had some one thousand Africans.

In that emerging society, blacks were considered as less worthy than Indians (many first-wave colonizers had joined up with Indian women and had mestizo children), constituting the most inferior and ill-treated class of the population. Frequently they were the victims of abusive decrees, such as the one that prohibited black and mulatto women from adorning themselves with costly materials, or even to dress, for that matter, like white women. And nonetheless, in those years, the condition of blacks wasn't as exhausting and humiliating as it would be later when the slave trade became firmly organized as a great profitable business, with the creation of an authentic creole bourgeoisie, proud of its stature, prestige, riches, and surnames, buttressed by the work of slaves that guaranteed the welfare and foundation for an entire economic system. For now, in such a sparsely populated land, the equality or similarity of conditions in the face of certain public calamities, epidemics, hurricanes, incursions by pirates, lack of goods, and poverty gave to the black population, at certain critical moments, a greater human stature. There were certain days of shared anguish in which the whiteman had to make common cause with his slave. There were even cases where the heroism of a black man would cause shouts of admiration from whites. The poet Silvestre de Balboa, in his *Espejo de Paciencia* [Mirror of patience] devotes several eight-line stanzas to narrating a unique battle in which the black man Salvador Golomón kills the pirate Gilberto Girón with a pruning machete (1604), thus liberating the captive bishop Fray Juan de las Cabezas Altamirano:

Andaba entre los nuestros diligente	(Among us, a man so diligent,
Un etíope digno de alabanza,	An Ethiopian, praiseworthy, willing,
Llamado Salvador, negro valiente,	Called Salvador, black and valliant,
De los que tiene Yara en su labranza,	in Yara's soil he goes tilling,
Hijo de Golomón, viejo prudente:	Son of Golomón, old and prudent:
El cual, armado de machete y lanza,	Who, armed with machete and lance,
Cuando vido a Gilberto andar brioso,	When he saw Gilberto impetuous,
Arremete contra él cual león furioso.	like a lion attacks him, furious.
. . . .	. . . .
¡Oh, Salvador criollo, negro honrado!	Oh, creole Salvador! noble black!
¡Vuele tu fama, y nunca se consuma:	Your fame soars, never to end:
Que en alabanza de tan buen soldado	Nor should praise of your attack
Es bien que no se cansen lengua y pluma!	Ever grow weary from tongue and pen!

In 1539 there was a black sheriff in Havana, "distinguished for his learned ways." The black man Estevancio, taken to Florida by the conquistador Pánfilo de Narváez, was known for his "miraculous cures," to which his comrades in fortune showed no disdain. An auto-da-fé held in Cartagena de Indias [Colombia], in 1628, reveals the existence of an Antón Carabalí, from Havana, who would recommend amorous herbal remedies so that "men could lust for and love women dishonestly." In an old Havana record from the sixteenth century we see a witch doctor promising to cure a sick person in the presence of a notary public. These diverse facts or events show that the social cohabitation of black and white was then, for different reasons, much closer than in the eighteenth century, for example, in that the discriminatory line or boundary was established in a more pronounced fashion in daily life, creating a border between races that, although it never took on the almost impermeable barrier erected in the southern United States, still maintained, for a long time, a white monopoly over the most honorable and lucrative occupations. Furthermore, at the end of the sixteenth century, the law offered greater facilities for manumission. The number of free blacks grew. Among the first property deeds in the city hall of Santiago, it is not strange to find blacks applying for lots of land. In 1768, there were 22,740 free blacks in Cuba.

From the outset, the Christian church exercised a powerful attraction for the blacks brought to the Americas. The altars, the accessories surrounding the cult of worship, the images, the religious garments, were crafted to seduce souls strongly attracted by a sumptuous world of rites and mysteries. Deep down, of course, it did not mean that the ancient gods of Africa were renounced. Ogún, Changó, Elegguá, Obatalá, and many others continued thriving in the hearts of many — such a living presence that there was a growing number of faithful in Cuba, Haiti, and Brazil. But the African transplanted to the New World never believed that these two worlds, Catholic and African, could not be shared in admirable harmony. After all, in the end, they were all Powers. Better still: by way of a process of sycretism, widely studied by such specialists as Ramos, Fernando Ortiz, Nina Rodríguez, Price Mars, Maximiliano the Elder, and others, many Christian divinities or saints enriched the African pantheon (principally, Yoruba), substituting ancient anthropomorphic or zoomorphic representations with idols or higher gods that were more abstract, whose names they adopted. In this fashion, Saint Lazarus became Babalú-Ayé; the Virgin of Regla is Yemayá; Saint Barbara is associated with Changó; Ochosi with Saint Norbert; Elegguá with Saint Anthony (and the Soul in Purgatory), and so forth.

Another factor that drew blacks to Christian temples was music. In a period where churches were, in a certain way, the only concert halls, what happened in them concerned blacks. Of course, between the culture represented by the chants intoned "according to the customs of the Sevillian church" — as Juan de Wite would have it — and the rhythms that blacks carried in their veins, there was a huge abyss. But black people, it should be noted, had no difficulty in rapidly assimilating the music of countries they were taken to, making it their very own. In the United States, they learned the Protestant hymn. In Santo Domingo, they made French songs and dances their own. There were, in Cuba, as we will see later, blacks who specialized in *tiranas* [old Spanish folk songs] and *seguidillas* [flamenco songs and dances], theater ditties, *contradanzas*, and minuets.

"The first news we have of music on the island is quite deplorable," affirms, irately, the chronicler José María de la Torre. "It is enough to know that black women sing in the churches and that among the instruments played is the *güiro*." The truth is that, in Santiago de Cuba, the dearth of instruments, and very often of organ players, justified the use of profane musicians for the solemnities of worship. In the end, it was confirmation of an analogous process from the Middle Ages, where the doors of minor parishes were opened to minstrels. Musicians were still scarce in Cuba. In a "Report on the Residents of Havana and Guanabacoa," written in 1582, there is no mention of any resident being a musician. On the other hand, in Santiago de Cuba there was a small orchestra composed of two flautists, a bass viol player named Pascual de Ochoa from Seville, and two free black Dominican women from Santiago de los Caballeros, two sisters, Micaela and Teodora Ginés.

This orchestra, put together for parties and celebrations, also played in the churches.

From 1553 on, Havana was the official residence of the colonial governors of the island. The security offered by its port, the creation of shipping routes to Veracruz, Trujillo, and Cartagena, increased the importance of the city, transforming it into "the key of the New World." The news of these events arriving in the easternmost province caused the disintegration of that first Santiago orchestra. One good day, Pascual de Ochoa and Micaela Ginés decided to try their fortune in Havana, leaving Teodora behind. At the turn of the century we find these musicians teamed up in a quartet with a Spaniard and a Portuguese: Pedro Almanza from Málaga, violonist, and Jacome Viceira from Lisbon, "clarinet."[2] This group would swell and enrich its sounds with accompanists "strumming, scratching gourd instruments, and playing the castanets." Of their activities, we have this from a chronicle of the time:

> They attend acts called dances and diversions, which have previously been agreed to be held. These musicians are always committed and to get them to play your preferred tunes you have to pay them an exorbitant sum, bring them horses, serve them rations of wine, and make for them and for their family members (aside from what they drink and eat during the performance) a plate filled with everything that's been served so they can take it home with them. These same musicians appear at the solemn celebrations of the parish, held in honor of Saint Christopher, Saint Martial, Corpus Christi, and so on.

Nonetheless, the economic situation of the illustrious quartet doesn't seem to have been as brilliant as the chronicler would have us believe. We have exact proof of an agreement from the town hall of Havana, dated January 10, 1597, in which

> a petition was seen and read submitted by the minstrels who currently reside in the city, seeking some manner of salary for sustenance, and acknowledged and discussed by the town council, it was agreed that the city... should provide one hundred ducats per year to all four, which corresponds to twenty-five coins apiece per year and that said year be counted from the

first day of this month onwards, paid quarterly, and with the obligation that they [the minstrels] attend the public celebrations of the city and the other events as ordered by the town hall.

Suddenly, an established event had taken place that would have considerable influence on Cuba's musical formation: already in the sixteenth century (this will be more decisive throughout the nineteenth), the musical professions excluded tacitly, because of a scarcity of skilled performers, the possibility of racial discrimination. As José Antonio Saco observed in 1832, with words that would have been equally as poignant in 1580: "Music enjoys ... the prerogative [of mixing blacks and whites] because in the orchestras ... we confusedly see all mixed together, blacks, browns, and blacks."

Teodora Ginés, a freed slave, remained in Santiago. Má' Teodora, as she was called — an allusion perhaps to her age that might have made the fatiguing trip to Havana too difficult — was famous for her songs. One of them has made it down to us. It happens to be the only composition that can give us an idea of what popular music in sixteenth-century Cuba was like: the famous "*Son* de la Má' Teodora."

Sánchez de Fuentes, faithful to a merely personal conviction, which took him to the worst of dead ends, sought to find in this cheerful and lovely song an "aboriginal influence." Others have considered it as a sudden and decisive affirmation of an idiosyncratic Cuban sound — born by spontaneous generation — which is said to have endured until the present. The truth is that even a quick look at this Antillean "primitive" piece allows one to bare its roots quite easily. It simply deals with the copy of an Extremenian ballad, whose melody has been slightly modified by the habits of popular intonation (the word *la* in the eighth measure, for example), with the clauses being separated by a rhythmic refrain, strumming over the strings of the *bandola* (or *bandora*, or *mandola*), the mandolin. The lyrics match the classic octasyllable of the ballad, so well studied by Vicente Mendoza, with its stress on syllables 1, 3, 5, and 7.

DON-de es-TA la MA teo-DO-ra

In regard to the phrases that function as a strophe ("¿Dónde está la Má' Teodora?" . . . "¿Con su palo y su bandola?" etc.), the rhythm is a perfect match to one of the Hispanic patterns as established by the very same Vicente Mendoza used in determining the origins of the Mexican *corrido*. In passing, let us say that we do not trust the exactness of the generally admitted notation of this song. It is not probable that the trochees of the initial verse would transform themselves into iambic meters, as the voice proceeds over the same type of phrasing and accent of the previous verse after the first refrain. This inversion of values does not respond to any need whatsoever, constituting a useless complication, at odds with sound popular logic. But this is a detail that does not affect the real nature of the problem. Concerning the melody, the "*Son* de la Má' Teodora" maintains a close kinship with a whole series of Extremenian ballads. Take the ballad of "Delgadina." It seems almost like a textual quote of a good-sized fragment of its melody, in the case of the Santiago-based song, with a slight type of modal modification — very much less so, in this case, than other ballads that made their way to the Americas. We do not seek to demonstrate, of course, that good old Má' Teodora would have consciously appropriated the melody of a ballad sung in Cuba in that period, nor that the "Delgadina" was necessarily a victim of theft. But the sound world of both is the same. The balladeer or songwriter of Santiago had assimilated what had been heard on the island, and she brought it back in her own fashion, adding to it a refrain with a flourish that, and this is no coincidence, has the same rhythm that used to be the introduction to, in the 19th century, the *coplas* of *La Resbalosa*, a black dance performed in Argentina and Chile. An interesting detail: the *bandola* [mandolin] seemed to have lost two of its strings, transforming itself into something like a *tres*, which is still prolifically used in Cuban popular music. If the *coplas* are of Spanish descent, the strumming or flourishes are of African inspiration. The two elements, brought into mutual presence, are the origins of a Cuban accent.

The literary form of this *son* presents a certain number of characteristics that have endured until today. The expression of "rajar la leña" [chop the wood] is taken here to mean "to be at a dance," that is, working. It's interesting to note that this kind of idiomatic substitution—the idea of a noisy party, by means of an ironic allusion to work—is something that created a true tradition in the popular music of Cuba. Just as "rajar la leña" was said for playing music, "cazar el verraco" [hunt the boar], "sacar la manteca" [remove the lard], were equivalents of "to dance." On May 1, 1945, you could still find a popular dance event advertised under the rubric of "sacar el boniato" [pull out the *boniato,* a tuber]. Let's not forget that "rajar la leña," "cazar el verraco," "sacar la manteca," and "sacar el boniato" were typical occupations of the rural population of Cuba at the dawn of colonial times.

The type of refrain, with its ending repetition, ad libitum, to the point of exhausting the dancers, can still be observed with the *sones* called *montunos*—the most rudimentary ones—of the type "Mujeres, no se duerman" [Women, watch out], and others. But let's go back to "Má' Teodora":

"¿Dónde está la Má' Teodora?"	(Where is Má' Teodora?
"Rajando la leña está."	Chopping wood she is.
¿Con su palo y su bandola?"	With her mandolin and her cane?
"Rajando la leña está."	Chopping wood, she is.
"¿Dónde está que no la veo?"	Where is she? I can't see her.)
"Rajando la leña está,	
Rajando la leña está,	
Rajando la leña está,	
Rajando la leña está," etc., etc . . .	

The form of "call and response" between the soloist and the chorus comes from sung games played in Africa. Although the *areítos* mentioned by Oviedo seemed to have had that same structure, one must reject the hypothesis of an indigenous influence. The antiphonal or response-type character is found in almost all the collective chanting of all primitive civilizations. Fernando Ortiz points out its presence in almost all the religious chants of the Yoruba. If the blacks who came to the Antilles found the Indians singing in the same manner, they could not see this as an advance over their own cultures. Lydia Cabrera has collected in Cuba an old chant, of a more primitive essence, which responds to the mechanism of the "*Son* de la Má' Teodora":

SOLOIST:

¡Aquí no hay visita, Kende Ayere!   (Here there's no visitor, Kende Ayere!

CHORUS:

¡Walo-Wila, Walo-Kende, Ayere Kende!

SOLOIST:

¿Quién es la visita, Kende Ayere?   Who is the visitor, Kende Ayere?

CHORUS:

¡Walo-Wila, Walo-Kende, Ayere Kende!

SOLOIST:

¡Compadre caballo, Kende Ayere!   My buddy the horse, Kende Ayere!)

CHORUS:

¡Walo-Wila, Walo-Kende, Ayere Kende!

This expeditious structure of verse and refrain from line to line had already caught the attention of certain Golden Age authors from Spain as characteristic of African music. When Simón Aguado, in 1602, had blacks singing in one of his *entremeses* [a one-act farce], he had a tenor sing the following:

Dominga ma beya,	(Dominga da prettiest
tu, pu tu tú,	
que una cara estreya,	A face like uh stahr
tu, pu tu tú,	
casamo en eya,	Let us git married
tu, pu tu tú,	
y como e donceya,	And since she so fair
tu, pu tu tú,	
hijo haremo en eya,	We giv'er lotsa chillun)
tu, pu tu tú.	

Just as "Má' Teodora" ends its *son* with an obstinate repetition of the refrain, one could still hear thirty years ago, marking the rhythm of the Havana *comparsas,* this sole phrase sung to the point of exhaustion:

Sube la loma' é San Martín, (Go up the hill of Saint Martin)
sube la loma' é San Martín . . .

If examining the *"Son* de la Má' Teodora" is extremely interesting, it is because it reveals, as a starting point for Cuban music, a process of transculturation destined to amalgamate meters, melodies, Hispanic instruments, with clear traces of old African oral traditions. Blacks, situated at the lowest level of Spanish colonial society, aspired to ascend to the social level of whites, adapting themselves, as far as possible, to the type of art, habits, customs being offered as a model. Despite this, they never forgot their instinct for percussion, transforming the mandolin into a creator of rhythms. Thus, in the *son cubano,* as in the Brazilian samba, the guitars have a more percussive than melodic role. The bass players in street groups did not use the bow. Only the *tres,* derived from the ancient four-string guitar, tends to follow the song, adorning it with cadences and trills.

The *"Son* de la Má' Teodora" was still being sung in eastern Cuba at the beginning of the nineteenth century, in the masquerades of San Juan and Santiago.

2. The Seventeenth Century

At the beginning of the seventeenth century, the island of Cuba had roughly twenty thousand inhabitants,
whites, blacks, Indians, and mestizos. The sugar industry was beginning to develop, with an increased demand for black slaves. The first sugar mill on the island—La Prensa—had been founded in El Cerro in 1576. After acquiring a taste for spices, Europeans took to tobacco, as later they would become enthralled with coffee and chocolate. Quickly, the great oil painters depicted the gestures and expressions of smokers. With all of this, Cuba was laying the foundations of its economy.

The existence of huge sugar cane plantations in the vicinity of Havana detracted from Santiago's importance. In 1612, the bishop Alonso de Almendáriz made an arbitrary transfer of the cathderal of Cuba from Santiago to Havana. Despite annulment of the order by a royal decree, Havana continued to powerfully attract ecclesiastical personnel as a city of greater opportunity and resources. The metropolitan government had to intervene on certain occasions and call back the prebendaries who were overstaying their welcome in what was de facto becoming the capital of the island. The absurdity was such that its maximum executive authorities were living at the other end of the country, even when the cathedral was still in Santiago.

The truth is that the cathedral of Santiago was in plain decadence, musically speaking. In 1622, Juan de Mesa Borges was appointed as organist because, "as explained, many years had gone by in which the divine offices lacked the solemnity of a good organist... because there was no intelligent person to play it" (Morell de

Santa Cruz). The chorus had been reduced to two cantors who, without a doubt, in certain festivities, were assisted by black women singers and by some local instrumentalist. In 1632, Juan de Mesa abandoned his post, with Juan de Zabaleta taking his place, "with the accustomed salary of one hundred pesos and a pension for playing the bassoon." In 1644, Fernando de Espinosa was appointed, "with an income of one thousand five hundred coins," a raise made "so that desertions would cease, since their frequency was too great for those who obtained such work." In 1655, musical matters were going from bad to worse, since "the first steps made this year were to try and remedy a truly grave defect in the cathedral since the chorus was without plainsong books for its function." The field master don Álvaro de la Raspuria, who was about to be transferred to Mexico, was put in charge of buying there the necessary books.

In that period, the city of Bayamo seems to have been more greatly favored in terms of religious music. It was the second largest settlement on the island, "as much for the number of its residents as for its wealth in livestock and its commerce in cattle, hides, leather, and other products, all of contraband nature" (Ramiro Guerra). The worship ceremonies there must have been uniquely magnificent in contrast with those of Santiago, especially if judged in the light of this eight-line stanza by Silvestre de Balboa, written in 1604:

Estaba apercibido ya en la iglesia
Blas López, sacristán de aquella villa,
A quien todo el Bayamo estima y precia
Como a Guerrero la sin par Sevilla;
Y con la dulce voz de que se precia,
Con los cantores de su gran capilla,
A este motete dio principio y gracia,
Cual el famoso músico de Tracia.

(It was all arranged in the church
Blas López, sacristan of that town,
All Bayamo esteems him, holds him dear,

As does Seville with Guerrero, all year;
And with the sweet voice, a marvel,
with the cantors of his great chapel,
to this motet he gave life and grace,
like the famed musician from Thrace.)

It would not be so daring to deduce that while Santiago made its greatest efforts to retain a loyal organist, Blas López, with the choirmasters of his "great chapel"—a chapel sufficiently skilled to perform motets—would have already made known to the residents of Bayamo the magnificent musical presence of Francisco Guerrero, who died five years before Balboa had written his poem, and whose works were receiving wide distribution in Mexico.

Havana's first church was set on fire by pirates in 1538. Under the aegis of Mayor Juan de Rojas, they began making the rubble-work for the Church of Saint Christopher in Havana in 1550. A certain Antonio Vicente, the Puerto Rican Hernán Rodríguez, Juan de Zerpa, and Juan Trimiño were among the first choirmasters of the brand-new parish. Clearly, Santiago and Havana were totally unaware of the sumptuous liturgy displayed in Mexican sanctuaries. The slight spiritual and physical resistance of the autochthonous population had blunted the constructive energy of the colonizers. Everything was focused on things that yielded an immediate profit. There was a greater need for slaves than for choirboys. In addition, even then it was already being said that there was a kind of slackness with regard to anything religious, to be observed later in the historical and cultural development of Cuban nationhood. Cuba might have had good sacred orators, but it never produced great mystics. Religious literature on the island has had few and mediocre practitioners—and not for lack of faith, but because of a poor disposition for the fervent embracing of causes, the gestures of contriteness, which are among the more significant traits of *el criollo*, the Creole. In the middle of the seventeenth century, the bishop Vara Calderón was obliged to prohibit the holding of public dances in the churches, and to hire black and mulatto women to wail at funerals.

The festivities, however, seemed to have greater brilliance when celebrated as a collaborative effort of all residents. If in 1557 Havana counted no more than one musician, the Flemish Juan de Emberas, who would beat a drum when there was a ship in sight, by 1573, the town council of the municipal government commissioned a Pedro de Castilla to "come up with a dance" for the feast of Corpus Christi, a festivity traditionally observed in Cuban towns and cities. From early on, these festivities featured giants, Moors, midgets, and dragons — and without a doubt the heel-tapping dancers alluded to by Cervantes. Showing an analogous process that saw medieval theater emerge from religious ceremonies, theater in Cuba was born during the feasts of Corpus Christi. A few exact dates will allow us to locate their first manifestations. In 1573, it was agreed that Pedro de Castilla would "create an invention for the procession." Five years later it is stated "that there be a good and joyful work in order to make the feast or holy day a solemn one," pointing out that its author was a Juan de Vargas. In 1590, twenty ducats were paid to the "farce actors" of the plays "performed on the day of Corpus Christi." Francisco Mogica was rewarded for being "the author of said work." News of this type became more frequent: in 1598, Juan Batista Siliceo wrote or staged two comedies; in 1608, the town council spent 4,258 coins for making giants "that will be used for other feasts." In 1621, "the proposition is accepted to build or make the giants, the Father, the Mother, a bull, six small horses, and a dragon for 150 ducats a year." And the following year: "Alonso Méndez asks for one hundred coins as payment for having done the dance of the monkeys the day of Corpus Christi, and let it be stated that the costumes had been provided, except for one, and it was agreed that he be paid, but discounting the costume he didn't hand in, the one of the monkey."

At first, these "dances" were done, no doubt, with the fifes and drums of the garrison. According to Irene Wright, there was also in Havana a guitarist and hornpipe player here and there. But we should not forget that in 1597, four minstrels lived in the city. From that time on, the dances grew in stature with the flow of years. When in August 1605 news of the birth of a prince arrived, this event was celebrated with true pomp:

> After Mass was celebrated in the afternoon, there was a gallant
> masquerade in which no man was left on horseback, nor young
> men, nor students, all who had invented something.... And
> later games with cane sticks were organized and there was a
> triumphant float with much music and characters, and twenty-
> four bulls were paraded about on two different days with new
> lights and volleys.

The tradition of Corpus Christi, independently of other feasts
of circumstance, lasted in Cuba until the beginning of the nineteenth
century. And the outer trappings must have changed only slightly
if we go by the narrative of Emilio Bacardí, which refers to the year
1800:

> In the procession different masks and figures appeared,
> representing angels, devils, gypsy men and women, lions,
> tigers, and above all a gigantic snakelike figure called the
> dragon. All these *comparsas* had their own dances; in both the
> general procession and the festival celebrated over an eight-day
> period, different busts of saints were carried and some of these
> were preceded by African chants, drumming and timbrels
> [tambourines].

This description differs little from what we already know from
the archivist of Havana's ordinances. In a city where black and mulatto women were hired as mourners, and where brown-skinned
people could establish inns for travelers, it is certain that "African
drums and tambourines" would be out in the street during the
first Corpus Christi feasts. Once again, black people had the opportunity to assimilate Iberian melodies, at the same time enriching it
with rhythmic and percussive elements. Two musical cultures —
one inherited from the Christian West and the Moorish tradition;
the other, elementary, constructed on the basis of rhythms and percussive qualities considered as inherently worthy values — would
find themselves meeting in that maritime crossroads that was Cuba.

Before 1603, there was already a grammar professor in Havana
who taught Latin to families of the well-to-do. His salary of one
hundred ducats was paid by the town council of the municipal
government. In 1605, a Gonzalo de Silva offered to give organ and

song lessons, probably the first professor of music known to the population.

While the cathedral of Santiago underwent a moment of need, from which it would emerge with renewed splendor in the second half of the eighteenth century, religious music continued to flourish in Havana. In 1612, an organ was installed in the largest parish. Coupled with the appearance of floats and other refinements introduced thanks to the commercial boom in sugar and tobacco, greater attention was paid to the loftiness of religious offices. Work began on a music chapel — with a pretty irregular functioning, as we shall see further on — which lent a greater aura to the solemnities. The Havana clergy, with the expressed disgust of their Santiago brethren, were actively involved in intrigues to ensure that the cathedral would be transferred to the economic capital. Using the promising argument of music, and leaning on the testimony of an ally from Santiago, the bishop Don Juan de Santa María wrote to the king in 1666:

> For the classic feasts [holy days] that are held in this temple [of Havana] also pertaining to others with similar functions, there is a Chapel of Music with teachers, instruments, and corresponding choirmasters, who officiate with a serious and measured harmony during vespers, matins, and Masses, all such festivities being executed with majesty and pomp, because the clergy in this city are numerous and respectable and commonly authorize said celebrations . . . and thus give a particular splendor to the solemn and grave functions of this parish, of whose knowledge and experience Dr. D. Alonso Menéndez, canon of the Holy Church of Santiago of Cuba expressed no doubt, to expose and secure for Your Majesty; therefore, by transferring said cathedral to this church, we would execute the capitulary functions and divine offices with a pomp and circumstance almost equal to that of Puebla and Mexico.

But this was not all. To maintain a certain level of solemnity, one had to have available, at all moments, learned cantors. For this purpose, the following was created:

the school of Señor San Ambrosio, selected by the most
distinguished Evelino in 1689 or the year before, for the
education and teaching of twelve-year olds who, by serving at
the altar and in the chorus of the main parish, would learn from
a tender age the rites and ceremonies of the divine offices, and
who, upon assuming clerical duties, would be more prepared
and suitable for executing the ministries of the church, to which
end a preceptor of grammar and a professor of song were
provided, also giving them a parish priest who would guide
them and provide discipline in all other matters, which pertain
to the honesty of customs and for the correction of puerile
pecadilloes. (Arrate)

But in last resorts, the learning imparted at the Colegio San
Ambrosio was pretty deficient, if we judge by a severe censuring
measure by Bishop Hechavarría y Elguezua, in which the prelate
complained that proper attention was paid only to Latin and plainsong. Once again — so characteristic of the evolution of Cuban culture — the teaching, practice, and cultivation of music was far ahead
of other artistic disciplines. On the island, music always rushed
ahead of literature and the visual arts, acquiring a maturity when
other spiritual manifestations — except for poetry — were only in
an incipient phase. Cuba already had admirable religious composers and serious performers of scored music long before the island had produced a single novel or published a newspaper.

Fernando Ortiz, in his valuable essay *La clave xilofónica de la
música cubana*, traces a vivid picture of popular Havana life in the
period of the eighteenth century:

> Havana, maritime capital of the Americas, and Seville, its Iberian
> counterpart, changed year after year, for three centuries, their
> ships, their people, their riches, their customs, and with them
> their rogues and spirit of mischief, the pleasures of their joyful
> souls, given to the enjoyment of all earthly and human beauty
> that they were fortunate to find. . . . But another race spilled
> forth their passion, pleasure, and art, from the heat of the
> equatorial jungles, into the seething brews of Seville and
> Havana. For centuries, abundant torrents of muscular strength
> and spiritual spontaneity were extracted from the entrails of

Africa and taken to white-controlled shores on either side of the Atlantic, conferring greater ardor to the soul and commotion to the flesh. Havana was famous for its diversions and libertine behavior, as is every bustling port. It enticed long stays from sea travelers or newcomers from the fleets along with noisy and festive slaves and loose women in the sleazy taverns with black women selling pig innards, in gambling houses set up by admirals and generals, and in the dives, even less holy, sheltered in the *bohíos* [huts] and houses with mud-plastered walls, within or outside the city perimeters, located by el Manglar, los Sitios, and Carraguao.... Songs, dances, and music came and went from Andalusia, America, and Africa: Havana was the center where they all came together with the greatest heat and warmth and with the most polychromatic iridescence.

Doubtless, America began early on to create a music with very diverse expressions—according to the ethnic factors that were present—capable of creating fads that made their way back to Spain. Cotarelo and other authors have widely informed us of this in their selection of texts alluding to dance and music. In a classic *entremés* (one-act farce), the dancer who performs the "dance of Gayumba" exclaims:

Lo que cantan en Indias,	(What they sing in the Indies
cantarles quiero.	I want to sing to you.)

Lope de Vega alludes to a chaconne, which was danced by "taking the apron with both hands." The chaconne goes like this:

De las Indias a Sevilla	(From the Indies to Seville
ha venido por la posta.	it has come in the mail.)

The gesture accompanying it reappears in a poetic description of a *batuque* [rumpus], in the eighteenth century:

Fingiendo la muchacha que levanta la falda	(Pretending to lift her skirt, the girl
baila ante el mocetón que más le gusta ...	dances before the strapping lad she likes...)

In the *entremés* of *Los sones*, by Villaviciosa (1661), they speak of a *zarambeque* [a gay noisy dance with blacks or Moors]:

...que es baile tan rico	(...a dance so sweet
que es de las Indias.	that is from the Indies.)

In another *entremés*, a black woman dances

...con vueltas de zarambeque,	(circling with the steps of the zarambeque,
teque, reteque, teque, reteque.	teque, reteque, teque, reteque.)

The saraband, like the chaconne, was "something from the Indies." The *zambapalo* (from *zamba, samba* [an ancient West Indies dance]), danced in Spain in the sixteenth and seventeenth centuries, is thought to have been created in the Americas. Similar is the case of the *retambo* or *retambico*, dances with vigorous movements, always sexual, in which the dancers "look like they're in the throes of passion," wearing a kerchief on their neck, on the shoulders, in their hands, and "kicking the apron," exactly as would currently be done by a Cuban rumba dancer with the tail end of her dress. There is also a constant phonetic analogy between the names *gayumbas, Paracumbés, retambos, cachubas, yeyés, zambapalos, zarambeques,* and *gurrumbés,* all referred to by the Spanish Golden Age poets and those such as *rumbas, bembés, sambas, batuques, macumbas, guaguancós, candombes, tumbas, chuchumbés, carrumbas,* and *yambús,* which proliferated in Cuba, Argentina, Chile, Mexico, Brazil, Colombia, and wherever black slaves existed in the Americas. Referring to the fandango, the *Diccionario de Autoridades* defines it as a "dance introduced by those who have lived in the kingdom of the Indies, which is performed to the sound of a festive and joyful playing." Moreau de Saint-Méry in 1789, described a dance of African origin from Haiti—given the probably erroneous name of *la chica*—which is the same dance "that is called *calenda* in the Windward Islands, *congó* in Cayenne, and *fandango* in Spain." In my childhood years I saw the *kalinga* or *karinga* (*calenda*) danced in the Cuban countryside. Fray Iñigo Abbad, depicting the customs of Puerto Rico in

1782, designated black dances with the name of fandango. In 1943, the *houngan* [voodoo priest] Abraham, informant to the Ethnographic Museum of Port-au-Prince on matters related to voodoo rites, danced a *fandán* in our presence, offered as a "Spanish dance." Curt Sachs, a specialist in choreographic matters, concludes: "The fandango, with its variations, the *malagueña*, the *rondeña*, the *granadina*, and the *murciana*, which were newly arrived in Europe in the seventeenth century, had their origins in the West Indies. But even if this statement is justified, these dances come from a two-thousand-year heritage, from Spanish soil, going back to the Phoenicians, who contributed to their formation."

One thing is certain: the primitive dances brought from the Iberian Peninsula acquired a new form in the Americas as they came into contact with blacks and mestizos. Their tempos and movements modified, enriched by gestures and figures of African origin, they tended to make the reverse journey, returning to their [European] source, but with novel aspects added. In the heat of ports, dances that were reminiscent of African dances were also born, though stripped of their ritual connotations. But the Americas, in their formative nation-building period, gave much more than it received.

Much has been written concerning the origin of the identical rhythms of the tango and the habanera, despite their different names. According to Friedenthal, it was taken to Spain by the Moors. According to other authors, it forms part of the popular Hispanic tradition, although this last thesis is frequently supported by dubious quotes. Curt Sachs, so taken with examining a problem in depth, eludes this issue of origins, expeditiously affirming that "the tango is not a pure black dance." (In the middle of the nineteenth century, Bachiller y Morales gave the name tango to all dancing done in the streets by slaves.) The fact is that we find its rhythm accompanying the first *contradanzas* published in Havana in 1803, and also in *guarachas* long before that. Their wide diffusion in Cuba at the end of the eighteenth century — as much found in the *danza* of the salons as in popular dances — implies the presence of a long-acquired habit that was shared by both blueboods and freewheeling mulattoes.

It is difficult to imagine that the famous *tanguillo* from Cádiz had imposed its rhythm in a few years on such an immense geographic sweep of the New Continent, manifesting its influence with equal vigor on the Mexican *bamba*, the Haitian *merengue*, the music of Brazil, the Argentinian tango, and so on. Its rhythmic presence in the Americas is much earlier than the first references to it in Spain. Why were the melodies of the French *contradanzas* performed in Santo Domingo [Haiti] at the end of the eighteenth century based on a tango rhythm? Why did Cuba, after receiving these *contradanzas*, adjust so well to these arbitrary conventions? If the Spanish influence was strong in Cuba, its sway was much weaker on the neighboring isle under French colonial rule for two centuries. This rhythm existed long ago, on both sides of that divide. In "La Guabina," sung in Havana long before 1800, we already find, perfectly etched, the characteristics of the so-called Andalusian tango. Furthermore, if Argentina, for example, having lost its black population, needed the tango rhythm to come from (or go back to) Spain by way of the zarzuela [light comic opera] and the habanera published in Europe, thereby creating what is now their national dance, Cuba never showed much interest in this rhythm, which formed part of its dances as an old routine incapable of engendering anything new. When songs appeared on the island under the rubric of habaneras, their catchiness was due to their enchanting ballad-like melodies and the charm and wit of their lyrics. In no way where they perceived, musically speaking, as something new or particularly interesting. This without saying that at the beginning of the nineteenth century, the rhythm that nowadays is so suffused with voluptuosness and languidness, was played at an incredibly swift tempo, serving more as a bass line to the Cuban *contradanza.*

So many reasons lead us to believe that the tango rhythm was known in the Americas before appearing in Spain, and that blacks were the ones responsible for its diffusion. Besides, it should not be forgotten that the dances born in the New World in the first period of colonization were not that different from each other, despite their diversity of names. They belonged to two large groupings, endowed with identical characteristics, wherever these types of racial contributions happened to coincide. And they were produced in the same countries whose folklores appear marked by the presence of the tango rhythm.

In 1776, a fleet from Europe that had made a long stopover in Havana took some immigrants of "broken color" to Veracruz [Mexico].[1] These foreigners brought a Cuban dance called *El Chuchumbé*, which immediately became an extraordinary success. The riffraff of this maritime city began dancing this sweet Antillean novelty with the greatest of joy. The verses, brimming with licentious intent, already had the tone, the twist, the kind of guile that we will find in Cuban *guarachas* of the nineteenth century:

¿Qué te puede dar un fraile	(What can a friar give you
por mucho amor que te tenga?	no matter how much he loves you?
Un polvito de tabaco	A mission without position
y un responso cuando mueras.	and a prayer when you die.

Por aquí pasó la muerte	Death came 'round my door
poniéndome mala cara,	Making a long face,
y yo le dije cantando:	And I told him, singing:
¡No te apures, alcaparra!	There's more to the show, so take it slow!

Mi marido se murió,	My husband died,
Dios en el cielo lo tiene	God in heaven has him;
y que lo tenga tan tenido	may he keep him so well-kept
que acá jamás nunca vuelva.	that he never returns.)

El Chuchumbé is danced with "swaying motions … contrary to the honesty and bad example of those who only watched the dancers fondle themselves from step to step." Such was the popularity of this dance, so strong in its intentions and gestures, danced "in ordinary houses lived in by mulattoes and by folks of broken color; not serious people, nor among circumspect men," that it was denounced before the Holy Inquisition of Mexico to have it banished. The answer did not take long. After ordering a "detailed and thorough" investigation, the Holy Office railed against *El Chuchumbé* with its irrevocable condemnation, deeming that the Cuban dance was causing grave damage to Veracruz, "particularly among the maidens" directly alluded to in the refrain, and because it offended "proper education and good manners."

El Chuchumbé was not invented on the boat traveling from Havana to Veracruz, as is sometimes imagined. It was not spontaneously generated. It formed part of a vast and motley family of *paracumbés, cachumbas, gayumbas,* and *zarambeques,* close of kin to the saraband and the chaconne mentioned by the poets of the Spanish Golden Age, always accompanied by the "kicking of the apron," the gesture of "the lifted skirt," the choreographed pursuit of the female by the male. The latter is an eternal theme and basis of the fandango, as danced in seventeenth-century Spain, and of which Casanova said the following: "the man and the woman of each couple adopt a thousand attitudes, make a thousand gestures that are of such lasciviousness that nothing can be compared to it." It is quite interesting to compare references that reveal the existence of a similar type of dance in precisely the geographic zone that for a long time would be welcoming identical intermigratory rhythms. Referring to the *Chuchumbé,* the informant to the Holy Inquisition in Mexico writes the following: "The verses are sung while others dance, a man with a woman or four women dancing with four men; the dance is performed with gestures, shaking, and swaying, contrary to all honest intentions . . . because in them they embrace and belly joins with belly."

Father Labat describes a very similar dance he saw in Santo Domingo in 1698:

> The most gifted voice among them sings a song . . . whose refrain is repeated in chorus by all the spectators. The dancers are placed in two long lines, the men on one side, the women on the other. They jump, turn, and spin, they draw close to each other, two or three feet from one another; they retreat following the rhythm, until the sound of the drums brings them together again. . . . It seems as if they were striking each other in the stomach; in reality, it is only their thighs that touch. But they draw back in the act, turning in a circle, with absolutely lascivious gestures. From time to time they embrace.

When Carlos Vega affirms that the majority of travelers who describe similar dances copied the prose of Father Labat, he may be thinking of the text written by the informant of the Mexican Holy Inquisition. The same gestures, the same placing of the dancers are pointed out; the embracing, the same "belly joining with belly," something that appears more attenuated in the account of the French friar. Roquete, in his *Dictionary of the Portuguese Language*, defines the *embigada*, a step in the *batuque* dance, as "the impetuous collision of belly button with belly button."

In 1789, Moreau de Saint-Méry describes a dance derived from the previous ones:

> The talent, for the female dancer, stems from the perfection shown in moving her hips and the lower part of her kidneys [*sic*], conserving the rest of her body in a kind of immobility without losing the soft movements of the arms that hold either end of a handkerchief or the edges of their skirts. A dancer approaches her; he pounces forward and falls into the rhythm, just as he is about to touch her. He goes back and then forward again, inviting her to be part of a most seductive struggle. The dance becomes more animated and soon it becomes a picture whose features go from voluptuous to lascivious.

This description, more detailed and better written than the previous ones, contains all the choreographic elements of the *Chuchumbé*, adding what is the cornerstone of the rumba: that certain way of moving the hips, keeping the rest of the body immobile, while the hands hold the two corners of a handkerchief or of the skirt (here we're bordering on the Brazilian *batuque*!). The rumba was not danced any other way twenty years ago in the Alhambra Theater. And it probably was not danced any other way by the "caricatos habaneros" [Havana caricaturists] in the Villanueva Theater, that fateful night of January 1869, when the Spanish "volunteers" [pro-colonial militia with a taste for brutality] opened fire on the audience.

Max Radiguet, when describing the *resbalosa*, a dance done by black men and zamba women in Argentina, establishes the same analogy:

> The woman held in her right hand a handkerchief unfolded, to which a circular motion imprinted a slow rotation that seemed to beckon the gentleman. The man, with the elbows outward and hands close to the hips, would draw closer, balancing himself with confidence. Then the female dancer, with many coquettish gestures, began a series of slides and pirouettes, apparently trying to avoid the gaze of her companion, who, in turn, exhausted himself in vain efforts to see her face.

Here, the woman dancer behaves similarly to the way described by Saint-Méry. The male dancer, described in turn, makes the classic gesture of the rumba dancer seen today.

Lafcadio Hearn, when speaking of the *congo* dance performed in New Orleans, paints a similar picture. Miguel Cané, referring to Martinique, alludes to the same dance: "the women place themselves facing the men . . . wavelike movements in which the head remains stationary . . . they approach their partner, draw close, and rub up against him," and so on. This identity of figures and gestures is accompanied by references to instruments that today constitute the basis of Afro-Cuban percussion. The drums, of course. In Louisiana, the jawbone, known in Cuba under the name of *quijada* [jaw]. In Santo Domingo (Saint-Méry), a resonating box equipped with small keys of different length, which is played with the fingers: the Cuban *marímbula*. In Puerto Rico (Fray Iñigo Abbad), "timbrels [tambourines], gourds, maracas, and some small guitar." In Cuba, in the first years of colonization, the black women that sang in the churches were accompanied by gourds and *güiros*. This without forgetting common idiophonic instruments: the box struck with a stick; the *catá*, still played by "black Frenchmen" of Santiago; *econes* or cowbells, the *bran-bram sonette* of Haiti, an arsenal of percussive instruments to which the Cubans added the *claves*, an instrument that originated in Havana, whose "sonorous sticks" were, primitively, the *claves* or pegs made of hard wood used in the making of ships, as shown by Fernando Ortiz. It is interesting to point out in passing that the *clave* rhythm, as Emilio Grenet has intelligently observed, is the only one that can always adjust itself, without variation, to all the types of Cuban melodies, thereby constituting a kind of constant rhythmic element.

When the town council of Havana gave instructions in 1573 that the procession of Corpus Christi should be attended by all free blacks "who could lend themselves to supporting this feast in like fashion to that of Seville," they must have danced dances similar to those that would soon arrive from Spain "brought by the mail." What is known today as the rumba would be known under twenty different names in the American continent, dances with very slight variations. They were sexual dances, with a couple dancing apart, with identical gestures and intentions, their roots extending all the way back to certain African ritual dances—dances that in Spain and Italy were generally known as sarabands, causing the fury of austere spirits, before losing their primitivism and passing on to the salons, and inscribing themselves into the choreographic culture of Europe in the eighteenth century.

Lacking other references, we are left with a certain number of obvious facts. In the seventeenth century, Cuba already possessed instruments and dances identical to those we can still see today in its popular dances. The island formed part of the vast sector of the continent subjected to African influences, exporting dances that had more power and force of diffusion than those that were imported. Its influence was not specific, forming part of an activity generally verifiable in countries that had received large numbers of black slaves. It is almost certain that the rhythm designated much later as tango rhythm or habanera rhythm was already known. With regard to the rumba, it was already in the air with all of its characteristics.

Along with these African-type dances there was the *zapateo* [heel-tapping dance from Spain], of clearly Andalusian origins, at least with regard to Cuba, even though some type of heel tapping is observed in other provinces of Spain. The *zapateo*'s presence was widespread. In 1782, Fray Iñigo Abbad saw a similar dance in Puerto Rico: "Each one invites the woman, who, if she doesn't have slippers, asks for them. And they start making turns in the room. The man does nothing else but raise and lower his feet with great clarity and force. The major ability consists in making as much noise as possible." We see this in Moreau de Saint-Méry: "This dance consists . . . in a step in which each foot is put forward and withdrawn successively, percussively done in precipitated manner, sometimes with the toe, other times with the heel. The dancer turns in place and around his couple, who also turns and changes location shaking the corners of a handkerchief." It would be wearisome to enumerate all the popular dances from Mexico, Agentina, Chile, and Venezuela that are derived from the *zapateo*. Its inter-American migrations were as considerable as the African-based ones.

The *zapateo* persists in Cuba as the almost exclusive patrimony of the white Cuban peasant, forming a specific block of genres with its *puntos, décimas,* and songs, derived directly from the Andalusian and Extremenian ballad. There are specific references to *zapateo* dances in Cuba in the first years of the eighteenth century.

3. Esteban Salas

As we have seen, the rapid growth of Havana helped submerge Santiago's cathedral into a shameful mire of mediocrity. Whereas in the economic capital "the instruments officiated with serious and measured harmony," in the city still linked by ancestry with the name of Cuba, there was a scarcity of plainsong books and organists remained in their positions for less time than dogcatchers and vergers. The bishop Juan García de Palacios reacted against this sorry state of affairs in 1677, creating a "music chapel" overseen by a chaplain named Maese Olivares. But despite its pompous title, it had only two singers. In 1680, given the scarcity of singers, Santiago took a notable step in artistic quality in hiring Lucas Pérez de Alaiz, a good choirmaster from Burgos. In addition, he was an excellent guitarist. But, in any event, a chronicle of the time says this: "in matters of sacred music, good taste was absolutely hopeless."

In the first half of the eighteenth century, profane music fared much better in Santiago than its religious and solemn counterpart. The city housed a true family of musicians: the mother, Doña Bernarda de Rodríguez de Rojas, a creole woman born in 1686, was a harpist; her husband, Leonardo González was a composer of *seguidillas;* their daughter, Juana González, singer and violonist, had married Lucas Pérez Rodríguez, son of the cantor of the cathedral, who would be his father's successor. There were already small groups of guitarists and mandolinists, like the one organized in Santa Clara in 1722 to the great joy of the population. Popular songs spread from mouth to mouth, like "Allá voy con el tamborilo," "Vamos a la cueva," "¿Dónde está cayuco?" (presumably *sones*), but they have not made it down to our times. We know for certain that when Bishop Francisco Gerónimo Valdés founded the Seminary College of San Basilio el Magno in 1722, a professorship was established for the teaching of plainsong. But this was not enough to lift the cathedral of Santiago out of its musical torpor. The cantors and prebendaries dreamed of Havana. And when they needed a Christmas carol to liven up Yuletide festivities, they would rely on the goodwill of resident Leonardo González, more efficient in addressing the needs of a raucous party than in the art of fashioning shepherd's songs.

In December 1755, faced with the growing threat of the cathedral's transfer to Havana — "the [Rodríguez] brothers felt troubled about this exaltation of the vassal becoming a Queen" — the town council approached King Ferdinand VI requesting permission and funds to establish a chapel of music that would go beyond mere words in an official declaration. Charles III responded to the petition, after ten years of waiting. On April 26, 1765, a royal decree was issued that fulfilled these long-held yearnings.

Esteban Salas y Castro, the first Cuban composer whose work has come down to us, was in Santiago a year before.

There is no way to explain how the work and the personality of Esteban Salas have remained until now in the most absolute obscurity. He is not even mentioned in authoritative or officially sanctioned books or studied in conservatories. His name does not appear in any Cuban biographical dictionaries. Laureano Fuentes, who quotes him in passing in his book *Las artes en Santiago de Cuba*, does not seem to have made the slightest effort to locate his scores. Salcedo, an austere maestro from Santiago, categorically stated that the composer's entire work had been lost. Nonetheless, given his important role in the history of Cuban music, Salas was, without a doubt, the person who has most merited careful research.

The prolonged searches that led us to discover a good number of Salas scores sheds light on a figure of revelance not only for Cuba, but for the musical history of the entire continent. Preceding the Mexican Aldana, a contemporary of some of the Venezuelan maestros of the eighteenth century, Salas helps us round out our vision of the religious music of the Americas at a moment when, due to inadequate study, it could appear to be creatively impoverished, when in reality it constituted one of the most interesting and rich stages of artistic production in the New World. Salas was much more than an honest Latin American priest (they were many and most barely left a trace) who considered his position as choirmaster a kind of bureaucratic post and composed sacred music according to established rules because he did not have the oeuvre of others at his disposal. Salas was the starting point for the practice of serious music in Cuba; that is, he initiates a distinction between popular music and cultured music, with an evolving coexistence between the two. Of course, this parallel feature has always existed in all civilizations between the temple and the people. But in Cuba until then, religious music consisted of a commonplace textual reproduction, a timid rendering drawn from readings of books received from Spain, Italy, or Mexico. If Blas López had composed something of note in Bayamo, this effort had not created a sense of continuity. Under the leadership of Salas, on the other hand, the cathedral of Santiago was to become a true conservatory, to which many musicians remained linked during the nineteenth century. He acquired disciples and trained performers. The example of his continuous work originated a demand. After him, no worthy composer in Santiago could be considered as such if he had not composed for the church. Salas's work created an order of discipline unknown in Cuba before then. Thanks to him, the chorus of the cathedral was also a concert hall. Haydn entered the island through its doors.

Esteban Salas was born in Havana on December 25, 1725. There he undertook his general and musical studies, first in the greater parish, where he learned the organ, plainsong, and composition. Later, he studied philosophy, theology, and canon law at the University of Havana.

Salas was a figure of angelic purity. The few tribulations and sorrows of his life reveal an ingenuous soul, trusting, incapable of tolerating any deception. From an early age he observed absolute chastity, living like a priest, although he thought himself not worthy of tonsure. A true mystic, he had taken vows of poverty and always dressed in black. He was short, thin, and lean. His wide forehead drew attention. It is possible that some black blood coursed through his veins, since, and despite his aquiline nose, his skin was quite dark and his lips were thick and fleshy.

Notified of the royal decree to establish a music chapel in the cathedral (this founding becomes a reality long before the issuing of the royal decree became known), the town council, eager to have a maestro who measured up to the task, focused its attention on Esteban Salas, whose fame as a good musician had already made it to the easternmost province. More recently, a certain Bernardo Guzmán had directed the musical affairs of the sanctuary; but his incompetence in fulfilling positions of greater responsibility was unquestioned. The first priority for the canons once their petition was made and heeded was to find Guzmán's successor.

Salas arrived in Santiago on February 8, 1764. He was already past middle-aged, and his extreme modesty at first created a bad impression. Untrusting, the canons immediately subjected him to tests, demanding that he compose a hymn to the Virgin. Salas emerged triumphant from that test with his motet *Ave Maris Stella*. Somewhat appeased, the town council requested the writing of a *Psalm*, which was deemed satisfying for even the most demanding member, and thus he was awarded the position of maestro. He began to work right away, asking for an annual stipend of one thousand four hundred pesos for the maintenance of the chapel, and a salary of three hundred and seventy pesos for himself, "taking into consideration his continuous labors and the costly expenses of life, since he had to pay for a house comfortable and spacious enough for the duties of teaching." In a pertinent warning to the public treasurer, never punctual in the payment of wages, he expounded on the poverty of the musicians who would be performing under his direction and the necessity for said musicians to live in a dignified manner, and not have to sell their services for sinful diversions. Right away he created the positions: three trebles, two altos, two tenors; two violins, a bass viol, two bassoons, a harp, plus the organ. A total of fourteen performers. Not many, but it constituted a good start for a church that until then had only employed temporary organists and a chapel with two choirmasters. Thanks to the efforts of its excellent director, over the years, the group would become enriched with flutes, oboes, violas, and horns, swelling until it had become by the turn of the century a small classical orchestra capable of performing symphonies by Haydn, Pleyel, and Gossec, as well as religious music by Paisiello, Porpora, and Righini.

Salas endured a deep anguish in 1766, when a terrible earthquake demolished eastern Cuba, causing cracks in the cathedral and destroying the chapel of Our Lady of Carmen. Truly devoted to the Virgin, he cried over the ruins of her temple, envisioning the noble goal of reconstructing the chapel through his own effort. He then wrote, in collaboration with the poet Pérez y Ramírez, several *autos sacramentales* [religious-allegorical plays], staged to raise funds for reconstructing the chapel. Ultimately, enough money was collected to raise the scaffolding, and the musician lived the happiest day of his life when he saw the stone from the quarry arrive, acquired through the efforts of his artistry. We have documentation that one of the plays was a *Don Juan*, but have not been able to find either the text or the music.[1] This *Don Juan* would have been composed some thirty years after *El príncipe jardinero y fingido Cloridano* by Santiago Pita, the first significant drama written in Cuba, and one of the most important documents of our dramatic literature of the eighteenth century.

Endowed with extraordinary organizing skills, Salas made his musicians and singers work diligently, familiarizing them with difficult techniques. With the goal of training performers in the art of the fugue, he wrote a series of *Pasionarios* [Passion songbooks], which confronted the performers with all the problems of the genre, imposing new methods on the basso continuo player, too accustomed to improvising on a mere tonal indication in the style of the time. He trained two disciples: Manuel Mitares and Francisco José Hierrezuelo. Tirelessly, and with a surprisingly fresh inspiration, he composed Masses, motets, Christmas carols, psalms, and hymns, written in a handwriting that is clear, precise, recognizable, thereby easing the work of deciphering those of his manuscripts most damaged by time.

In 1785, the chapel suffered a grave setback because of a budget reduction. In protest, the musicians abandoned the temple. Salas energetically stood up to the town council, obtaining not only what the performers wanted, but a salary increase and the creation of four new positions, to be paid for out of the church's reserve funds. (Salas was unaware that this victory, eight years later, would occasion some of the bitterest days of his life.) His fame grew. The canons urged him to join the religious order. But since he deemed himself unworthy of wearing a habit or saying Mass, he continued on the margins of his own world, wearing an abbot's garments. In 1789, the bishop Antonio Feliú y Centeno arrived in Santiago. While the town council paid him the usual reverential gestures, the bishop observed that Salas, his head now full of white hair, remained among the altar boys. The prelate went toward him, took him in his arms, and asked him with a gentle air of authority to become ordained. This time, Salas broke with one of his precepts of humility. He took his initial vows in November of the same year. In March 1790, he became a priest. On Good Friday he officiated at his first Mass, composing for this solemn occasion a truly monumental *Stabat Mater.*

Soon after, the town council granted him the rectorship of the seminary and the professorships of philosophy, theology, and morality, which Salas accepted on condition that he receive no stipend for these duties. He wrote several philosophical texts. Each year, with absolute regularity, he composed delightful pastoral poems—*Coronas humildes para adornar la cuna del Salvador* [Humble crowns to adorn the Savior's cradle]—which he would transform into *villancicos* [carols] at Christmastime. He seemed to have reached the peak of his career in 1793, when the Superior Council of the Indies demanded the restitution of the supplementary funds allocated over the preceding eight years toward the improvement of the music chapel. Taken by surprise, without knowing how they would raise the money, the canons blamed everything on Salas. Pained and disconcerted, Salas wrote a long letter to the king, explaining what had happened. The response took seven years. During that time, the anxiety and uncertainty undermined his health to the point where he was near death. When a royal decree, filled with indulgence, put an end to his affliction, on November 27, 1801, Salas was the ghost of his former self. He died in 1803, after having carried out his functions for thirty-nine years, "with the approval of all."

On the July 15, Esteban Salas, priest, born in Havana. In Communion with our Holy Mother Church, died having received all the Holy Sacraments; and his body was buried in the Holy Church of Carmen by the Illustrious Dean and Town Council; signed by the priest and rector for Your Majesty of the Sanctuary of the Holy Cathedral of this city, so be it recorded. (Signed) Dr. Juan Francisco Sánchez.[2]

The bishop ordered that his funeral rites be executed with the greatest solemnity and pomp. All of Santiago joined in mourning. The day of his funeral, a printed sheet, with a list of mourners, made the rounds, from hand to hand. On that sheet was the following sonnet:

No es muerto Estevan, no, que vida ha sido
De perdurable paz su monumento:
Por él con subterráneo apartamiento
A la mansión de Dios se nos ha ido.

Ya desnudo del hombre malnacido
Dejó la patria y valle turbulento,
Viajando en derechura al firmamento
Por la lóbrega senda del olvido.

Puerta dichosa fue, no sepultura,
la que le abrió el destino en su partida,
Dándole franco el paso a su ventura;

Porque la muerte al fin aunque temida
Es del justo varón llave segura
Con la que entra en los Reinos de la vida.

(Esteban has not died, no, his life
Has been a monument of enduring peace:
Through it, in a subterranean release,
He has gone to God's abode, beyond strife.

Stripped of the ill-born man
He left valley and homeland, turbulent,

Traveling straight to the firmament
By the dark path of oblivion.

It was a blessed door, not a tomb,
That destiny opened as he disappeared,
His venture, given spirit, illumed.

Because death, in the end, though feared,
Is, for the just, a trusty key to assume
Entry into God's reign revered.)

When Esteban Salas y Castro died, the town council ordered an inventory of his works. Said inventory does not appear among the documents that make reference to the music chapel. But in a catalog of the archive, established in 1880, we have the following: two Masses in G Minor, "for voices, organ and orchestra"; a Mass in B minor, for three voices and orchestra; a Requiem Mass, for four voices and orchestra; another Mass for three voices; two *Lecciones* [Lesson extracts from Scripture]; a *Salve e tota pulchra;* and various Litanies. There is word of other compositions as well: "Hymn to the Virgin," *Pasionarios, Psalmodies, Litanies for the Heart of Jesus, Litanies for the Holy Trinity;* sixteen *Salves* and motets, written for the *Octave of the Assumption;* a Mass in C Major; a hymn titled "Hail the Divine Daybreak." And to this must be added the *autos sacramentales* and songs composed with Pérez y Ramírez.

Through our efforts we have found the following scores: a splendid *Requiem Mass* for four voices and orchestra, with a new copy dated from 1849; a Mass in F, of considerable proportions, of which we have the original and a subsequent copy; various *Lecciones,* for one voice and orchestra, written in Salas's hand. Finally, the manuscripts of some thirty *villancicos* [Christmas carols] written for one, two, three, four, and six voices (only one) in different states of preservation. And we say some thirty, because certain *particellas* have been so mistreated by time and humidity that it is impossible to know if they pertain to one or several works. Fortunately, sixteen of the original manuscripts offer three completed parts and are well conserved. The Masses and larger-scale works are not dated. The *villancicos,* on the other hand, always have the date of the year of the Christmas or the Saint's day it was written for. They were composed between 1783 and 1802.

All Salas's scores are written with a surprising mastery of the craft. In the *villancicos* he uses two violins and *basso continuos*, to which he adds two flutes and a horn in exceptional fashion. In the major works he uses two flutes or two oboes, two violins (doubled to four in the ensemble), violas, and a *basso continuo*. In his Mass in F Major, he employs two horns and excludes woodwinds. Except in the passages conceived as accompanied recitative, the instrumentation plays a great role in his oeuvre, giving some of the movements of his *villancicos* the flair of a *sonata da chiesa*.

Salas's style comes directly out of the Neapolitan school and it is likely that he was unduly influenced by Francesco Durante, showing a decided affinity for the techniques the maestro's disciples used indiscriminately in religious music and comic opera. At times he abuses the succession of thirds and the "pigtail" style; but, in his very personal style, a passage of greatness from a score always arrives in time to remind us of the presence of a master, expressed in a unique voice. There is also something of Pergolesi in certain passages of his *villancicos* that recall the writing found in *La Serva Padrona* — a logical influence in the Cuba of the time since Pergolesi was one of the first European composers known to the cultured society of the period. At the beginning of the nineteenth century, it was still a tradition to sing Pergolesi's *Stabat Mater* during Holy Week in gatherings of good aficionados. Salas also knew the work of Paisello, and owned several of his scores.

Salas's *Villancicos* — totally removed from the polyphonic Spanish *villancico* tradition — are accomplished works in exquisite style. Breaking with the traditional pattern of refrain-verse-refrain, he imbues them with three well-defined parts: a recitative, a pastoral, and an allegro. Frequently, he begins by way of a small instrumental prelude, along the lines of an Italian overture. The pastoral carries all of the composition's melodic interest through the instruments *supported by the voices,* instead of the opposite. Salas was used to moving with a unique freedom within the genre. In his *Villancico de Navidad,* of 1783, he completely abandons the tradition of pastoral poetry, putting into the concoction verses of his own full of elevated mysticism:

> *Lo inmenso se circunscribe de un Portal a breve estancia, por tal que ocupen los hombres de el celeste Palacio las mansiones varias.*
>
> *En el seno de María los senos suyos dilata, dilata, la suma bondad de Dios para que todos tengan en su Templo casa.*
>
> (The immensity, for a brief sojourn, circumscribes an Entrance, in which men occupy the different abodes of this celestial Palace.
>
> In Mary's bosom, her breasts swell, they swell with the supreme goodness of God so that all may have a dwelling in his Temple.)

The *Kalenda* from 1791 begins with three verses sung in duet, before moving on to an ample three-voiced fugue over a popular motif that jubilantly closes the score. In the *villancico Pues logra ya el hombre miserable...*, the finale, placed after an ample pastorale (in twelve by eight), is an instrumental allegro of enormous mien, whose measures in triplets evoke the writing of Father Soler:

Despite his love for the maestros of the Neapolitan school, Salas does not hide his Iberian roots, which manifest themselves in his more solemn works, often unexpectedly, making one think of the newer turns and phrasings of the most modern Spanish school. We find in the "Introito" of his Requiem this phrasing conceived in the manner of a popular song:

In the *villancico Pues la fábrica de un templo*... (1783), we find these bars (the first measures of the "Vivo," reproduced here from an autographed transcription by José Ardévol) with a markedly Spanish character, which could be likened to certain passages of Scarlatti's sonatas:

Refinement, good taste, fresh ideas, never abandon Salas. Furthermore, his language is concise and direct. There is no wasted space. He uses the canon and fugue frequently, but he does not gratuitously abuse contrapuntal play. Sometimes he initiates a fugato without any other purpose than to impart greater dynamism on a crescendo. In the Masses, however, he tends to take the canon to the limit of its possibilities. Except for certain "recitative" parts, he never "accompanies" the singers, thereby transforming the orchestra into an enormous guitar. Frequently treated with a notable independence of rhythm, the voices and instruments always know where they are headed, and a strenuous effort is required of both. His Requiem is a unique example of technique perfectly wed to expression. Each one of its parts, brief, full, well-rounded, establishes a contrast with the previous and subsequent parts. Then, between a gradual rising of exquisitely crafted harmony dominated by lyrical values and an offertory that begins in a canon, he places a dramatic fugato in three voices, a capella, in an almost despairing tone. In the splendid canon encompassed in the Mass in F, we find this passage traced out with a unique sense of freedom:

In sum, Salas was the classic composer of Cuban music. A classic who was not an isolated phenomenom, since he established solid connections with the European music of his time, imposed certain enduring disciplines, and for the first time brought to the island certain lasting stylistic characteristics, some of which even passed over to specific expressions of popular music. Later we will see how certain musical habits of the eighteenth century marked the *criollo* sound of the island in its formative phase. The first French *contredanses* introduced into Cuba, written for violin *avec dessus de viole*, created modalities of musical writing that carried over, at the beginning of the twentieth century, into the *danzón*. Manuel Saumell, in his *contradanzas* composed at the height of the Romantic epoch, made many references to Mozart. The peculiar and insistent use of thirds in all of Cuban music has its origins in the preoccupation that the first composers of the nineteenth century showed in *writing correctly*, according to respectable models. Salas's oeuvre, heard year after year in Santiago, constituted one of those indisputable models, along with the works of the Neapolitan school. The inscriptions on the covers to the scores demonstrate that they had a long life before they were displaced by a "religious music" that would replace the great ordered counterpoints and harmonies of the eighteenth century for arias and duos with accompaniment. His *villancicos Oigan una nueva*, [Listen to the new tidings], *Cándido corderito, Un musiquito (Mi sol, la sol-fa-mi-a le dice al niño Dios)* [A little musician (My sol, la sol-fa-mi-a says to the infant Jesus)], were sung again in 1810, even when their composer had already died. His Requiem Mass was recopied, for the purposes of a new performance, in 1849.

4. Salon and Theater at the End of the Eighteenth Century

In 1774, the island of Cuba had a population of 96,430 whites and 75,180 blacks, of whom 44,633 were slaves. Eight years earlier, a certain Gelabert had established the first coffee plantation, not far from Havana. Sugar, coffee, tobacco, cattle raising, forestry, bee-keeping, and copper mining already constituted — and would for a long time — the basis of the Cuban economy. The sources of income, always well invested and ever-growing, had given rise to a Creole bourgeoisie ready to transform its coats of arms of leather, grain, and leaf into good heraldry from the Indies. Gone were the times when Havana was a mere rest stop for navigators, a place of solace for foreigners, with an affable population resigned to living like a poor relation of the inhabitants of New Spain or the Viceroyalty of Peru. A fertile soil earned the respect of the natives. There was a greater attachment to the land. The Creole began to gain greater consciousness of his rights. In those years, the umbilical cord that tied the colony to the warehouses of Spain had stretched thin. In the end, there was a higher standard of living in the colony than in many estates of Castile. There might have been a lack of noble emblems, but no scarcity of sugar mills. Mahogany, *ácana* wood, the *jiquí* became genealogical trees. The shipyards worked to swell the king's fleets. Many of them harbored the spirit of the miller of Sans-Souci.

The British capture of Havana in 1762 was a barometer for this incipient expression of Cubanness. Havana society chose not to attend an evening party given by the Count of Albemarle, but it also harshly criticized the inept performance of the Spanish military chiefs. The hero of the day was Pepe Antonio, a creole guerrilla from Guanabacoa. The popular *décimas* sang their praises:

La audacia y valentía	(The audacity and courage
de los pardos y morenos,	of the browns and blacks,
que obraron nada menos	who fought with valor
que blancos sin cobardía.	no less than whites.)

The priest Rafael del Castillo y Sucre, enthused by the bellicose feats of the black fighters, exclaimed:

> And have you forgotten, memory of mine, the many spirited blacks who won their right to immortality with their valor? Live in peace, fortunate comrades of those brave volunteers, may our religion never forget to recommend them to posterity in our sacrifices, prayers, and eulogies, nor allow us to be insensitive to the sight of wounds that should not be over-looked by the most illustrious warriors, nor forget the spilled blood that I would never disdain to mix into my own veins.

One hundred ladies from Havana "signed a written document to the queen, in which they revealed bitter complaints against the authorities who, by their lack of decision and ability, were deemed responsible for surrendering Cuba's capital" (Ramiro Guerra). In the streets *décimas* made the rounds, filled with authentic creole *"choteo"* [an irreverent humor that takes nothing seriously], in which they asked for a governor who would be:

Sabio, cristiano, prudente,	(Wise, Christian, prudent,
de experiencia y muy valiente	experienced and brave
y que no sea traidor,	and who would not be a traitor,
. . . .	. . . .
que el que hubo fue un alcón	since the previous one was a hawk
sin justicia ni razón	without justice and reason
y que me ha dejado en suma	who left me
cacareando y sin pluma	cackling and without feathers
como el gallo de Morón.	like the rooster from Morón.)

Discontent was widespread. That is why when the occupation initiated by Great Britain began, long-standing resentments surfaced in the heat of battle. For the common folk, this was, in the end, a conflict between the king of Spain and the king of England. The mulatto woman from Carraguao did not feel any connection to this dispute. British officials were received in some homes. Two women even married in a Protestant ceremony, embarking with those invaders of a different faith, who were from a country as distant as Spain. A young woman, rescued by her father at the moment when she was going to hide in the holds of a British ship, inspired this streetwise quatrain:

Las muchachas de La Habana	(The girls of Havana
no tienen temor de Dios,	have no fear of God,
y se van con los ingleses	they run off with the British
en los bocoyes de arroz.	in barrels of rice.)

On an island that was beginning to create its own way of life, culture was able to advance at a quicker pace. Three centuries after the Conquest, the actors and musicians of Spain started to turn their eyes toward the Indies, cradle of new cities, rich enough to satiate their greed and allow them to dedicate their leisure to fineries of the spirit. In Cuba, as in Santo Domingo, sugar cane had engendered the use of carriages. These carriages now became useful for going to the theater.

Since the times in which Pedro de Castilla had "created an invention for the procession of Corpus Christi," there had been slight progress in the Havana theater scene. A chronicle—apparently apocryphal—speaks of a comedy presented on the night of San Juan (June 24) in 1598, titled *Los buenos en el cielo y los malos en la tierra* [The good go to heaven, the bad stay on Earth], with the audience "so pleased and satisfied that it insisted that the play be performed all over again." In the middle of the eighteenth century, the mansions of the wealthy used to feature the plays of Calderón, Lope, and de Moreto. But aside from this, Havana audiences only enjoyed functions put on by some mulattoes, "awful amateurs," in a house located at the end of Justiz Lane, which served as a theater and was called Casa de Comedias [House of comedies].

Thanks to the intiative of the Marquis de la Torre, Havana had its first theater in 1776. They tried to build a coliseum "where comedies could be presented that otherwise were provisionally being performed in someone's home with great discomfort for the numerous members of the audience." This work was considered necessary, because "it would be convenient to have public diversions in such a populated city as Havana, as is the case in all populations that are orderly." This was how the Teatro Principal was built, near the bay, a crowning completion to the promenade of the Alameda de Paula. The theater's presence was a powerful stimulus to musical performances.

A curious little theater gazette published in 1815 states that *Didone Abandonata* [1724] by Metastasio, was sung [sic] in Havana in October 1776, the year in which the Teatro Principal was inaugurated. The tragic poem by Metastasio inspired many composers, as is well known. Was *Didone Abandonata* performed with an original score, or was it an embellished version with intermissions, arias, and divertissements by several authors, typical of that era? There is no surviving document that will tell. Anyway, this function, probably organized by aficionados, was not an isolated case. A report on the need to make repairs to the building, written in 1792, enumerates the kind of spectacles that the residents of Havana came to know in those years: "good comedies, tragedies, dancers, small [chamber] operas, zarzuelas [light opera], tightrope walkers, acrobats, shadow plays, automatons, and other types of recreation that are frequently offered in this transcript."

When the first issue of the *Papel Periódico de La Habana* was published in 1790, a Spanish company had already established itself as a permanent act at the Teatro Principal. In the October 24 issue, there is an advertisement for comic actors who will perform Rojas Zorrilla's *Los áspides de Cleopatra* [Cleopatra's asps], an *entremés* [one-act farce] created by the ingenuity of Havana resident Ventura Ferrer, and a *tonadilla* [ditty] for duo called *El catalán y la buñuelera* [The Catalan and the donut maker] by Pablo Esteve. For October 31, there is an ad for something of greater musical interest:

the famous comedy *Cristobal Colón* will be performed, with two
new changes thought up by the author[1] of this large theater;
during the first intermission *seguidillas* with obbligato flutes will
be sung, and later a concerto for obbligato violin will be
performed; during the second intermission, a *tonadilla* for three
voices will be sung and, once finished, a concerto for obbligato
flute by Don Miguel Labusier will follow.

Of course, we should not get too excited about the quality of
these "concertos." They really were not concerti, but more a kind
of piece to be performed by a brilliant soloist, as demonstrated by
that other ad from 1791, so revealing of the kind and caliber of the
event: "during the first intermission the glass harmonica will be
played, and during the second a pianoforte concert, titled *Los enre-
dos de los demonios* [The devil's twisted ways] composed by Mr.
Fallótico."

This José Fallótico was a character of a certain importance in
the burgeoning musical life of Havana. A kind of one-man orchestra, alert to every possibility for making money through music, he
was ubiquitous, like the rabbit in the fable. When he was not presenting himself as a concerto player or composer, he organized
"musical diversions, danceable diversions, and other pleasant spectacles" at people's homes. In November 1791 he premiered a great
zarzuela titled *El Alcalde de Mairena*, "in which Mr. Lucas Saénz will
sing two buffa arias, imitating the sounds of various animals."

On September 6, 1792, he published the following humorous
ad in the *Papel Periódico:*

> A notice for the public. On Saturday the 8th of the current
> month, José Fallótico will give two mathematical pieces on
> Cuba Street, at the house on the corner of San Ignacio Street,
> facing the house of Madame Countess de Casa Bayona.
>
> 1. A little shepherdess, seated on a pyramid placed on a
> table in the middle of the living room, will sing a refined aria
> with the entire orchestra. A solo will be played on the glass
> harmonica.
>
> 2. The little shepherdess will again sing an extremely
> refined *tirana* [old Spanish folksong], and as soon as the song
> concludes, all of those in attendance can approach the singer

and speak to her, and she will respond to whatever matter is brought up.

The function will conclude with the renowned Máquina Périca, representing the triumphs of Europe.

The company of artists who worked with the restless Fallótico imitated actors from Madrid theaters who traveled throughout Spain. It was typically comprised of ladies, swashbucklers, bearded souls, comedians, and ridiculous old men. The principal actors were Lucas Sáez and Juan Acosta; the actresses: Plonia, María del Carmen, and María Domínguez. According to a tradition from the origins of Spanish theater, and which the *entremés* [one-act farce] had helped preserve, all of the artists in the company were capable of singing and dancing as well as speaking in verse. Hence, in 1791, the company decided to publicly present a more substantial spectacle:

> On the 17th of the current month, the great and famous opera *Zémire y Azor o el amor de un padre y deber de una hija* [Zémire and Azor, or the love of a father and the duty of a daughter], in four acts, translated into Spanish, will be performed.
>
> The music is by the celebrated composer Gretri *[sic]*; it will be embellished with various scene changes and flights of fancy, and, particularly in the third act, which features a scene change with a magic mirror, in which three persons will sing a trio. This function will be embellished with a gigantic dance.
>
> At seven sharp.

This presentation of the Grétry opera was so successful that a few days later it was staged again, "the dance component being augmented with various new figures."

It should not surprise us that the company acting in the Teatro Principal had enough orchestral resources to dare to perform the Grétry score. The stage *tonadilla* was at the height of its splendor. Subirá astonishes us when he timidly points out, deducing from "allusions contained in these plays" and of squabbles between theater company directors and editors coming out of the theaters of the Indies, that "the diffusion of the *tonadilla must have been* great overseas." In Cuba, this scenic diffusion was extraordinary, even inspiring a modest local production, already made manifest by those first ads. When the *tonadilla* genre went out of fashion in Spain due to a *décalage*, a kind of chronological time warp always observed in Latin America with regard to types and styles that have been exhausted on the Old Continent, but that rebound in delayed fashion throughout the Americas (impressionism, Romantic opera, the mazurka, or the *valse-hésitation*), all of Santiago was still singing the verses of *El trípili-trápala* [Spanish song and dance popular at the end of the eighteenth century]. More than two hundred stage *tonadillas* were sung time and again from 1790 to 1814, the year in which they started to be displaced from Havana programs, finding a new life in the provinces. The best creations paraded on the stage of the Teatro Principal: *El amante tímido* [The timid lover], *La anatomía* [Anatomy], *Hipólita y Narciso* [Hyppolite and Narcissus], *La lotería* [The lottery], *Los genios encontrados* [Crossed tempers] by Blas de Laserna; *La maja y el oficial* [The belle and the officer], *La paya y los cazadores* [The song and the hunters], *El granadero* [The grenadier] by Pablo Esteve; *El compositor* [The composer] by Misón; *El maestro de música* [The music teacher], *El recitado* [The recitative], *El sacristán y la viuda* [The Sacristan and the widow] by Rosales; *El calesero y la maja* [The coach driver and the belle] by Guerrero; *La recomendación* [The recommendation] by La Riba; *El inglés y la gaditana* [The Englishman and the Woman from Cádiz] by Pablo del Moral; *Las mañas de una casada* [The wiles of a married woman] by Galbán; *La ópera casera* [The domestic opera] by Manuel García. To this we must add an endless repertoire of *"chascos"* or tricks (of the donkey, the abbott, the blind man, etc.), of *"fingidos"* [pretenders] and *"burlados"* or those being made the butt of jokes (lovers, painters, Italians, shepherds), of *"lances"* [quarrels or jams], without forgetting all those titles where the following characters are featured: sacristans, Frenchmen, Moors, beggars, astute ladies, the all-too-familiar gypsy women, *malagueñas* [women from Málaga], country bumpkins, Galician women, Catalans, dandies, and musketeers. As in Spain, certain *tonadillas* that seemed forgotten would surface again unexpectedly, always finding a warm reception. In 1815, even though the genre was disappearing from Havana stages, *Los maestros de la Raboso*, with the inevitable *El trípili-trápala*, continued to grip audiences, before it took Santiago by storm in 1822.

As we will see, stage versions of the *tonadilla* will have a great influence on Cuban *bufo* theater. Already at the end of 1791, we find announcements proclaiming "*seguidillas* composed with an American ingenuity." At times, the *tonadillas* received from Spain were adapted to the local milieu. In 1802, a "*tonadilla* for three" was premiered, under the title *Un gaditano en La Habana* [A man from Cádiz in Havana]. A local author wrote, in 1807, a *tonadilla*-like *sainete* [one-act farce] — according to the purest traditions of the genre — *El chasco del ratón o la educación del día* [The mouse's tricks, or a day's learning].

The *tonadilla* of Laserna, Esteve, and Rosales — with their beautiful melodies, their agile duos and small choruses, with their instrumental introductions of such excellent quality, as in *Los ciegos fingidos* [The fake blindmen] — at times demanded a measure of ability from the orchestra musicians. Of course, it was a routine, and certain stereotypical passages of *seguidillas* and *boleros* were performed according to well-known formulas, as is done by jazz musicians nowadays. But it is interesting to observe that both in the past and now, a certain type of music imposed a kind of technical functionalism on the group. Just as in jazz orchestras where the saxes play the clarinet's role, and the trumpets echo violin parts, the oboists from the *tonadilla* orchestras played the flute, and the horn players bugles, when a production demanded it (Subirá). Added to this was a cello and a bass, aside from the indispensable violins.

The instrumental groupings that offered these *tonadillas* to the Havana public adjusted themselves to these rules. The flautist Labusier also played clarinet "concertos." Proof of the widespread use of horns in the Havana of those days is demonstrated by the fact that the first *contradanza* edited in the nineteenth century (1803), "San Pascual Bailón," especially indicates the use of two horns to play the initial theme. In reality, little was needed for the Teatro Principal's orchestra for it to be a true classical orchestra . . . A regulation from the music chapel of the Havana cathedral, written in 1802, established that, "being a source of great dissonance that musicians destined to the worship of God . . . be occupied and employed in music for theaters, we resolve that musicians of the holy church are not permitted to sing or play in these establishments under any circumstances."

What this reveals is that, in the case of presentations, the usual orchestra was expanded with musicians from the cathedral. In order to offer the proper performance of an opera, the number of violins and cellos was doubled, and the church provided other instruments that were lacking: oboes, violas, bassoons ... In those cases they would count on the size and type of orchestra used by Haydn.

After the fortunate effort made by Spanish comic actors nine years before, in December 1800, the opera *Zémire et Azor* [1771] was sung again for Havana audiences. But this time the performance was of much higher quality, given by a French company, en route to New Orleans, with tenor Faucompré and Madame Villeneuve in the leading roles. On November 30, they had debuted with a program of comedy and opera, consisting of *Love's Disillusions* by Molière and *Ariadne* by Cambert. A few days later, for a change, the usually bitter *Regañón de La Habana* wrote in an admiring tone: "the music, the execution, and the staging [referring to Grétry's score] filled the audience with pleasure, even those who did not know the language. What intelligence and mastery in the singing! What assurance and skill of movement, what stage presence!" *Zémire et Azor* was presented three more times in January 1801, adding up to a total of five performances in Havana.

The artists of that company continued their season with increasing fortune, giving audiences a new taste of what good lyric theater could be like. Successive productions featured *La Serva Padrona* [The maid-mistress — 1781] by Pergolesi; *Le tonnelier* [The barrel maker — 1761] by Audinot; *Anita et Lubin* by La Borde; *Le Déserteur* [The deserter — 1769] by Monsigny; *Le tableau parlant* [The talking picture — 1769], *Silvain* [Silvan — 1770]), and *Les deux avares* [Two avaricious souls] by Grétry; and *El marqués de Tulípano* by Paisiello. For the benefit of Faucompré, a "second presentation" of *La belle Arsène* [1773] by Monsigny was staged. If we take into account that all of these operas had premiered in Paris thirty years before (on average), we can see that Cuba showed the classic lapse of time in its knowledge of European musical productions, a pattern that would continue well into the twentieth century. The prelude to Wagner's *Parsifal* was played in Havana for the first time in 1902; Debussy's *Prélude à l'aprés-midi d'un faune* in 1924; Stravinsky's *Firebird* in 1927. It is important to keep these facts in mind, at a time before records and radio, in order to explain how musical impressionism was so influential in Cuba, especially between 1920 and 1925, and why some orchestral procedures so dear to *The Rite of Spring* [1911–13] began affecting certain composers when Stravinsky had already written his *Sonata for Piano* [1924], and was on the road to his *Symphony of Psalms* [1930].

The atmosphere had changed completely when a company of "Havana comic actors" was formed in mid-1802, made up of Victoria and Loreta Fleury and the actors Francisqui and Laboterry, backed up by some amateurs. The "inventions and diversions" of José Fallótico had been forgotten. The public's musical palate had a taste of the French company, making it a more demanding audience. Hence, the new company made a serious effort to emulate these daunting foreigners, with a Spanish translation of *Radamisto and Zenobia* by Crébillon, with an expected and daring production of *Temístocles en Persia* in the works, probably written by Philidor. But the company enjoyed only a mediocre success, trying to shore up the box office by acquiring new artists: Polanco, Josefa Titi, Leonarda Sánchez among the women, and the male singers Latorre and Cabello. Great difficulties must have beset traveling productions in those days, to judge from an ad from 1804: "Because actresses have not arrived from Spain, no doubt because of the war, we cannot offer complete productions at this time." Nonetheless, the audiences were growing accustomed to these miscellaneous offerings, which featured, along with *sainetes* and *tonadillas*, auditions of musical fragments. On Thursday, February 12, 1801, *Papel Periódico* had published its first concert program — a true concert — which can be found in the Cuban press of old. Because of its historical value we transcribe said program, thanks to the artistic initiative of foreigners who were passing through:

Great Instrumental and Vocal Concert

Don Jorge Eduardo Saliment is honored to announce to the public that on Saturday the 14th of the current month he will

give a concert with a large orchestra, in which the following
pieces will be played:

FIRST ACT

An overture by Pleyer [sic] with the entire orchestra.
An obbligato flute concerto by Hoffmeister, performed by
    Mr. Saliment.
An aria to be sung by Mrs. Cassaignard.
An obbligato horn concerto.

SECOND ACT

A flute solo played by Mr. Saliment.
An aria by Mrs. Cassaignard.
An obbligato flute concerto.
A duet by Saliment and Mrs. Cassaignard.
A finale by Haydn.

    On Inquisidor Street, the block before last, number 101,
house of Don Silvestre Bozalongo, dance teacher, one peso
tickets will be available at the house.

Now, with complete performances an impossibility, fragments of
Zémire et Azor would be sung (obviously, this opera was a great favorite among Havana folk!); imitations of *Le Déserteur* by Monsigny;
a scene from Paisello's *La molinara* [The maid of the mill — 1789]; a
duo from *Antigona* by Paisiello; and arias by Grétry, Cimarosa, and
Pleyel were offered. The "concerts" also grew better in terms of
quality: in 1804, Dalayrac's overture from *Raoul, sire de Créqui* (1789)
was performed (it premiered in Paris fifteen years earlier!), a "Concerto by Mr. Stamitz" (!), "accompanied on the fortepiano by a distinguished recently arrived woman foreigner"; in 1805, "a violin
concert by Mr. Vioti." Nonetheless, the atavistic bad taste of the
Spanish actors always became manifest, here and there. In April
1805, we find this:

Today the famous opera *La Serva Padrona* will be performed, in
which Miss Rodríguez and señores Comoglio and García will
sing and it will conclude with a trio titled "El Pollo, Gallo y
Gato" (The chicken, rooster, and cat), in which the peeping,
squawking, and meowing of these animals will be imitated.

The sensibility of Havana audiences became much more refined in the last years of the eighteenth century. It is not yet a true culture; but music in its diverse aspects had become part of people's customs. In 1792, María Luisa O'Farril received great applause in the aristocratic salons with her clavichord performances. The ads in *Papel Periódico* set the tone for the milieu, with this unadorned document—which at times strips away in an ugly fashion the habits of a bourgeiosie that cultivated its spirit with the sweat of more than sixty-four thousand slaves.

> SALES: A clavichord or fortepiano, very beautiful, British, three unisonous voices, for 400 pesos. (February 1791.)
>
> For sale: a clavichord that functions like an organ and also will accept young bulls as payment. (May 1792.)
>
> Musical papers, to wit: *tiranas*, boleros, *seguidillas*, arias, with other kinds of church music and some concertos. (July 1792.)
>
> A fortepiano of excellent tones, made in London. (September 1792.)
>
> A superbly made violin, with exquisite tones, at a fair price. The butler at the house of the Marquis of Justiz will provide information. (February 1794.)
>
> An organ for orchestra with four pipes, on which are inscribed the overtures of the best operas of Grétry and Paisiello, at a price of 300 pesos. Available at the watch shop of D. Gabriel Bernal, facing the jail. (March 1794.)
>
> Two lovely transverse flutes, at an equitable price. (May 1794.)
>
> Two clavichords, a black woman (!), and a dresser with a bookshelf. Lieutenant Major D. Ramón Bretos will provide more information. (June 1794.)
>
> A used spinet, for 50 pesos. A new dark colt, and an ambler, for 100 pesos. A black creole boy, seven years old and free of smallpox, for 200 pesos. At Obispo Street 38, more information will be provided. (August 1794.)
>
> A cembalo, of exquisite tones and made of a unique wood, made in Seville by the craftsman Mármol. (February 1795.)[2]
>
> Various kinds of music from Spain, composed by the best composers of the North (?), at an affordable price. Don Cayetano Pagueras will provide more information. (July 1795.)

Strings for violins, guitars, and harps, made in Rome.
Supply is in great condition. (November 1795.)

A new psaltery... (November 1795.)

A host of violins... (May 1799.)

Principles of guitar playing by musical example. (March 1804.)

A three-tiered clavichord, with excellent tones, valued at 80 pesos, will offer for 30 pesos. (May 1804.)

A more instructive description is not possible. In the last years of the eighteenth century, keyboard instruments, violins, flutes, harps, guitars, favored by salon society, nourish a little industry. The clavichord is visibly displaced by the piano, sold for ever-decreasing prices. Cayetano Pagueras, cantor of the cathedral, offers serious music. There are *tiranas,* boleros, and *seguidillas* for the frivolous; sonatas, "concertos," and arias for the dedicated amateur. Music makes inroads into the world of the privileged classes. But this refinement, coupled with wealth, does not free a society, which cries out its misfortune like a classical heroine, from the cruelty sanctioned by business as usual. A black woman is sold with a group of musical instruments and furniture. A little seven-year-old black boy, free of smallpox, is a piece of merchandise worth two ambling colts and four spinets in good condition.

5. A Plot in the Cathedral of Havana

When the position of choirmaster became vacant following the death of Esteban Salas, his assistant and disciple, Francisco José Hierrezuelo, who had served for thirty years, believed that he was legitimately authorized to take over. The town council called for competitive examinations, which placed Hierrezuelo up against one adversary: the priest Juan París, a solid and conscientious musician. Hierrezuelo was sure of victory. His long collaboration with Salas, his intimate contact with the canons and musicians of the chapel, made him a favorite over an outside opponent.

However, on the day of the exams he was dealt an unpleasant surprise. In the chorus stood an exceptionally learned German priest named Juan Nepomuceno Goetz, unnoticed. When he saw him, Hierrezuelo was startled. Burning with rage, without paying due measure to his words, Hierrezuelo refused to take the exam, accusing the bishop of acting treacherously. He stated that the prelate had encouraged the candidacy of the foreign maestro "with a declared passion," and that his unexpected appearance in the chorus was an obscure conspiracy schemed up in order to strip him of his rights as Salas's legitimate successor. Faced with such insolent behavior, the Four Arts tribunal was disbanded and exams were suspended until a new decision could be reached by the town council. But Hierrezuelo, blinded by indignation, took up the pen. Enraged, he ratified his clumsiness in writing, fashioning a true allegation: he was the victim of an odious machination of forces; craftily, the presence and candidacy of the German had been kept quiet; Goetz had neither "sufficient nature nor title to qualify him for benefits or offices of an ecclesiastical nature; he, Hierrezuelo, was a Spaniard, baptized by his country, and he had to "look after her honor, and not strip the wages of the faithful vassal of the sovereign by illegal measure"; the Laws of the Indies, he affirmed, were opposed to having foreigners occupy religious positions. He threatened debates, scandals, an uproar...

If it is true that Hierrezuelo's allegation underlined Goetz's calm and docile attitude, "being of special note that the foreigner has until the present behaved with better conduct, veneration, and respect than the Spaniard"; and so insistently had the illegality of this affair been stressed that the bishop, fearful that the case would transcend local boundaries, preferred that the German voluntarily renounce his aspirations. But Hierrezuelo's adventure cost him dearly: despite a letter in which he cried out his own repentance, bowing to the dust and accusing himself of criminal ravings; despite his tears, supplications, and ejaculatory prayers, he was only able to obtain from the town council, and a deeply affronted bishop, a modest position in the chapel, thereby giving up his ambition of ever becoming a maestro.

With the slate cleared, Juan París passed an exam that was a mere formality, and took the place that had been so brilliantly performed by his predecessor.

> Among other exercises, he composed a hymn-like motet to the Holy Trinity, which he himself sang in two parts with bass and violins.... He also sang a role that suddenly occurred to him, and that was the renowned and famous composition *Himno Stabat Mater Dolorosa,* which was one of his favorites, as it had also been for his deceased predecessor Esteban Salas.

Juan Nepomuceno Goetz only stayed a few years in Cuba, yet his sojourn on the island, with the conflicts it caused, sheds such light on the Cuban musician's condition in those times and teaches us so clearly how they were trained and how they lived, what their habits and miseries were, that we should linger briefly on the story of a plot that took place in the Havana cathedral chorus—a plot that reveals the presence of a new climate, born of a growing creole moral force. The Goetz-Gavira-Pagueras-Rensoli dispute offers four depictions of musicians; four typical portraits of maestros and performers that then existed in the Americas, and to which we owe, ultimately, the formation of our musical culture.

Despite the Santiago cathedral's desire to acquire the luster of pomp and solemnity so greatly sought after; despite the fact that it had—finally!—reached the level of prosperity that Juan de Wite had dreamed of at the outset of colonization, Havana continued to insist on being not only the sugar capital, but the faith capital as well. In 1764, looking for a solution to the problem, the illustrious bishop and historian Morell de Santa Cruz petitioned for the creation of an ecclesiastical province, thereby creating the bishoprics of Havana and Puerto Príncipe, but his plea was ignored. In 1787, the episcopate of Havana was created, and on December 8, 1793, a royal decree that satisfied all concerned established a division between the diocese of Santiago de Cuba and Havana.

Before becoming a cathedral, the greater parish of Havana had a music chapel, as we saw in the report written by the bishop don Juan de Santa María. But said chapel, as the capitulary act of 1815 reminds us, "was not constituted nor was it an obligation." It was "available to other congregations of other parishes and convents in celebrating their major festivities" (and to this end a small allowance was apportioned to this major parish). Beginning in May 1779, the priest Francisco María Lazo de la Vega, a Franciscan, took on the position of choirmaster for irregular functions. In 1796, Havana fulfilled its ambitions to have a cathedral, and it was ordered that a music chapel be built as splendid as the most renowned sanctuaries of the New World.

Asked by the town council about the upcoming measures, Francisco María Lazo de la Vega said that: "until now the provisonal chapel only consisted of one maestro, two sopranos, two altos, two tenors, two basses, and a violin . . . whose voices and instruments were not able to preserve all of the serene harmony that the majesty of worship merits, and even less for a cathedral in Havana." With the appropiate chores accomplished, by February 1797 the chapel was established in total splendor, including four *seises* [singing and dancing choirboys], two altos, three tenors, two oboes, two bassoons, a *triplín*, two horns, four violins, and a bass. In 1799, all of the positions were filled, with the exception of the third tenor.

The priest Lazo de la Vega had carried out his functions with honesty and devotion, but without a great display of energy. A composer of *villancicos*, he was cautious about publishing the lyrics of those carols to be sung "in solemn matins of the birth of Our Lord Jesus Christ," as Esteban Salas in Santiago used to do. In the last few years of the century, his health began to decline. Overcome by the ailments of old age, he had to abandon the chapel, and died on July 6 of the following year. When the position was vacated, twenty-eight-year-old first violinist José Francisco Rensoli from Trinidad [Cuba], the singer Luis Lazo, the maestro Cayetano Solís, and the Catalan Cayetano Pagueras, a religious composer and first contralto of the chapel, all sought to take the competitive examinations. With greater age and experience, Pagueras was a strong candidate. At fourteen he had been an organist in Barcelona. Living in Cuba since the mid-eighteenth century, he had married a creole woman and considered the island "as his native land through marriage." Invited on one occasion to move to Puebla de los Ángeles [Mexico], his nostalgia for the tropics did not allow him to finish his trip. As a candidate for examination, he prided himself on being a "maestro in the four arts: plainsong, organ playing, counterpoint, and composition."

The exams were about to take place when an unexpected factor created unrest in the small musical world of Havana: a certain Juan Nepomuceno Goetz, in a letter sent from Santiago on July 29, 1803, offered his services to the cathedral, having learned of Lazo de la Vega's retirement. The candidates' indignation was boundless when they found out that the town council had invited him to move to the capital "in order to learn more about his merits." Who was this Juan Nepomuceno Goetz? A most solid musician, good material for a character in a novel. A letter in his handwriting gives a portrait of his life from the beginning. German by birth, he becomes a resident in the diocese of Constanza right after his ordination. Having become a professor of philosophy and morality at the Imperial and Royal University of Vienna, he moves to the New World, motivated by his desire to travel. He is appointed music chaplain of the cathedral of Santo Domingo; later, as a priest and rector, he moves to the city of San Fernando de Montecristi, before ascending, with the same position, to the wealthy parish of Le Môle Saint-Nicolas. He witnesses the slave uprising and the British occupation of his parish. When Toussaint-Louverture succeeds in driving the British out, Juan Nepomuceno starts ringing the church bells and goes running through the streets, carrying the image of the Lord. But the joy caused by the fleeing heretics is short-lived. In the shadow of the black caudillo's two-cornered hat, war flares again like fire, and the voodoo drums throb too often in the mountains. Having had enough of revolution, deprived of alms, eaten alive by yellow fever, Goetz seeks refuge in Santiago de Cuba, where his knowledge of languages make him known as "the foreigners' priest," that is, primarily of French émigrés. This was the moment when, declaring himself "fit for the teaching of figural music and plainchant," he expressed his desire to become choirmaster at the cathedral, with the already known results.

Wary after his adventure with Hierrezuelo, Goetz arrived in Havana at the beginning of November 1803 with added moral ammunition: he had applied for his naturalization papers as a Spanish subject. On November 22, impressed by his visible mastery, the town council appointed him interim occupant of the desired position, hoping he could soon execute his duties legally. Needless to say, Pagueras and Rensoli, also in the running, immediately formed a common front of passive resistance, their intrigues boosted by the forceful character of the new arrival. In addition, the old age or ill health of Lazo de la Vega had fomented the indolence and lack of discipline that so easily affect the Creole when he loses interest in routinized work. This, too, would be used at an opportune time.

When Goetz appeared before the cathedral chorus, he was surrounded by pale, half-scared smiles. He had not only displaced a Cuban aspirant and a Catalan who was passing as a Cuban, but also showed the utmost seriousness, weighing the value of each performer. Without the slightest compunction, after looking, interrogating, hearing, he writes a first report to the town council, filled with definitive statements about the personnel placed in his hands:

Cayetano Pagueras: Second contralto; terrible voice, no expressiveness. Almost blind. When he sings, everyone starts laughing, and the dogs run from the church. A good composer and very helpful, but he doesn't know how to sing his own works.

Don Luis Lazo: Third contralto. Knows nothing of music and never will. He entered the chapel fraudulently, and when he sings, he does so from memory, and for this reason is totally inept; the same holds true for the position he occupies, superfluous.

Don Juan Alcayado: Third tenor. Terrible voice. He hardly attends, and when he does, he speaks constantly, disturbing the others. He creates disorder in the chorus and looks disdainfully upon the chapel. A totally useless human being. The position of third tenor is hereby abolished for its superfluousness, it is not needed.

He alludes to the musicians' poverty, asking "that they be paid the first day of each month . . . since this is beneficial for so many of the poor, but also to the honor of the cathedral in which they are sheltered." Always inclined to praise a musician with true talent, Goetz asks that he be supported in his preference for the most apt performers, "in order to fill positions with the most capable of individuals." He asks "that those being moved from major to minor roles, titles brazenly held, should be considered finished, and asked to take the exam again, both the theoretical and the practical parts."

Reasoning as a good musician who prefers the quality of sound more than sheer volume, he reduces the number of positions instead of increasing them. According to his *Plan de las voces e instrumentos de que debe componerse el Coro de Música de la Catedral*, the following group was established, approved by the canons on April 17, 1806: choirmaster, four sopranos, two contraltos, two tenors, a baritone; two clarinets, two bassoons, two horns; four violins, bass viol, and bass.

In those times there was a unique character at the cathedral who would play a considerable role in the Cuban musical scene at the beginning of the nineteenth century: Joaquín Gavira y Rondón. A man with a violent disposition, quite disorderly in his personal life, a solid performer but with a bohemian temperament, Gavira — as Goetz said — was a good musician. As a boy soprano he had sung in the cathedral for more than six years. He would often proudly assert "that he had become a composer at a tender age," and he would embellish his signature with a very studied fluorish in the form of a pentagram in the key of G. An infantryman with the Seventh Regiment of the Militias, he wanted to give up the uniform for the bow. Born in 1780, he aspired to be first bass viol player in 1802, invoking, so as to soften the hearts of the canons, his condition as the son of a widow, as well as past services rendered by his family to the cathedral. Like so many musicians of the period, Gavira was extremely poor. He embodied a Cubanness with singular energy, a sign of the times that had become manifest in all social classes since the British occupied Havana (1762). Not only did the Creole start claiming his rights on a par with the Spanish, but in certain kinds of activities, being from the island instead of Spain was seen as a privilege. Referring to a rival presenting his candidacy against him in competitive examination, he stated that "a foreigner should not be preferred to a native."

Having such ideas would draw him to the plotting of Rensoli and Pagueras and other musicians who were trying to make life difficult for Goetz. Removed from the militia corps thanks to the town council's pressure on the military authorities — "since he could not attend rehearsals at the chapel," Gavira was the heart and soul of the creole conspiracy against the ex-professor from Vienna. Even though the position of bass viol was more prestigious musically, the need to earn an additonal two pesos impelled him to apply for the fourth violin spot. Goetz, when he began his dismissals, promoted him to second violin. But by then war had been declared. Used to the docile indulgences of Lazo de la Vega, the performers abhorred their demanding maestro, usurper of the post, who took note of failings, screamed during rehearsals, and never hesitated to point out the technical deficiencies of the worst performers. Gavira was not an easy man to handle. When he became enraged, he lost control of himself, and was capable of truly violent gestures. In

1804 he had been arrested for striking another musician with a piece of iron in the Carmelite church of Santa Teresa. One day, in the large theater, he caused a phenomenal scandal when he insulted a black musician of the orchestra calling his performance deficient. This reputation of irascibility and danger must have seemed useful in the campaign of systematic sabotage against Goetz. In 1805, the first grave incident takes place in the chapel. Having just finished the first night of matins of Maundy Thursday, Goetz severely scolded the Mexican bass player Sebastián Solís for arriving late. Solís excused himself. Goetz became enraged, lashing out with violent words. Solís yelled back, accusing Goetz of trying to humiliate him in front of his companions. "Not even blacks are treated this way!" he exclaims. "To me you're more than a black man!" responds Goetz. "And if you answer back I'll have you removed from the chorus with the back of my hand!"

From that moment on, life in the chapel becomes a living hell. Gavira goes to the rehearsals with a rapier, as a mute reminder to the maestro. He does whatever possible to create disorder, with or without reason. He creates difficulties "introducing at the most serious moments restlessness and uneasiness. He converts the "simplest event into the bloodiest of stories." One day he showed up without an instrument, offering some obscure reason. "Faced with the dilemma of having to play, he borrows the most worthless and least appropriate violin." He is the principal reason for the "chapel's awkwardness and lack of success." The other musicians second the motion, showing irritation and discontent with the dismissals. But Goetz does not yield. He asks the town council for a vote of confidence in 1806, and his interim position is ratified. In December, the situation becomes worse. Goetz, seriously upset, speaks of the squabbles among the positions created and unresolved problems, "fearing that a death might occur in the church."

Goetz endures this life for a few more months, knowing that soon a royal disposition will arrive granting him Spanish citizenry. He is counting on this to end an insufferable situation. At last, in October 1807, the king's letter arrives. Now, supported by his "prerogative of being a naturalized citizen of Spain, with permission to reside and remain in its dominions," Goetz initiates the decisive battle to entrench himself in the position. Wanting to elicit the admiration of his musicians and regain their respect, this maestro, whose proficiency had been amply proven in four years of service, applies to take the competitive exam, thereby obtaining general and irrefutable approval of his capacities. But the musicians, unwilling to concede that triumph, organize a cruel scheme: Joaquín Gavira writes the apppropriate document to the town council, stating his intention to apply for the position. This time, Goetz cannot take it anymore. In a letter begun with plentiful apologies, so that the dean and the canons not be offended by the rude language, he lists the scandals and evil actions undertaken by Gavira, explaining his decision to resign the position "if the expulsion of that offensive musician is not arranged."

Goetz was too good a musician for the Havana of those times. His intentions to have the chapel function in German style, as would have been possible in Mainz or Leipzig, created insoluble problems. In a city with so few performers, a strike led by Gavira would have left the cathedral without a chorus and orchestra. Sensing the reality of the situation, the town council yielded to the musicians in revolt. Goetz abandoned the island at the beginning of 1808, and all traces of him after that were lost. When an inventory of the music he left behind was undertaken, nine Haydn symphonies were among his papers. In February of that same year, the rebellious clique secured a complete triumph with the appointment of José Francisco Rensoli, from Trinidad, to fill the position deserted by the foreigner.

Masters of the territory, Gavira and Rensoli repeatedly insisted on allowing black musicians into the cathedral, as substitutes or supernumeraries. Rensoli, quite cognizant of the precarious economic situation of his men, sometimes allowed them to play in the Bejucal fair or in festivities outside the city, compensating them for the rigors of the severe rules that impeded their performing in the theaters and dances of Havana. But as far as black performers were concerned, the Creoles were unable to overcome the racial prejudices of the town council, which did not want to see "Ethiopians" in the chorus. In 1809, Gavira, "threatened by the diagnosis of the illness of Lazarus or of general paralysis," as a consequence of some slight indiscretions clarified by a medical report, requests permission to be transferred to the baths of San Diego, "and as there is no other white person to occupy his spot in this chapel," he implores "that Juan Peña, a black man, be accepted to fill in the lack." The proposal is denied. The same year, Rensoli faces a similar problem with the defection of two musicians. Having learned from previous experiences, he resentfully writes to the dean: "In spite of the fact that among people of color there are superior performers, and that they could make beautiful music, *as they have done on other occasions*, I have refrained from calling on them . . . because I believed that you were repulsed by their presence." As in the days of the "Má' Teodora," the creole musicians were not adverse to rubbing elbows with blacks in their orchestras.

Outside the church, Gavira kept working actively to generate a taste for good music. In 1811, he founded the first classical trio with black cellist Bartolo Avilés and a certain Mazzuchelli. He had excellent disciples, one of whom achieved prominence, José Domingo Bousquet, a great violinist, son of a doctor who had accompanied Napoleon on his Egyptian campaign. It took until 1852 for him to become choirmaster of the cathedral, and he died in 1870, extremely destitute, sheltered in a convent. As for Rensoli, he carried out his functions honorably until 1845.

When he related his impressions of Havana, the reverend Abiel Abbot — not inclined to admire Catholic ritual — wrote, wonderstruck, in 1829: "The music of the cathedral of Havana is the best I have ever heard." The church's archive had 623 scores in those years, all of which seem to have been lost forever. In them were works by Lazo de Vega, Goetz, Gavira, Pagueras, and Rensoli, as well as Masses written by the great European masters.

6. Introduction to the *Contradanza*

Despite their proximity and identical natural surroundings, Cuba and Santo Domingo already had very different histories. A cultural center, a cradle for poets, boasting of a university and theaters at a time when Cuba was arduously beginning its life as a poor colony without a literary milieu, Hispaniola had gone from being a rich and treasured land to the sad condition of a fiefdom for adventurers. All of the western part of the island — not to say the almost legendary Tortuga — had been populated by buccaneers and French settlers with deplorable habits. (Ogeron stated that there were not enough chains for so many bandits.) As if that were not enough, in 1697, with considerable lack of political acumen, Spain ceded to France, in the Treaty of Ryswick, the part that France had occupied, at its own risk. Spain thus lost total control over an island that previously had been the true operational center of the discovery of the Americas.

During the times of Governor Ogeron — years before the treaty signing — the French zone of the island seemed destined to engender individuals unworthy of human respect. Wanting to increase the birthrate, the French sent to their colony, ostensibly "to give them the only and last sprucing up needed" *(sic)*, any hussy that could be rounded up in the dungeons of the Salpêtrière, "des salopes ramassées dans la boue, des gaupes effrontées."[1] Many settlers, faced with the fear of being eaten alive by the plagues carried by these "ladies," preferred to cohabit illegally with slave women, who at least had firm, healthy flesh. At the beginning of the eighteenth century, the colony of Saint-Domingue was an abominable factory of all the vices, violence, abuse, and wastefulness within reach of an adventurer. On the settlers' table, the local pork, roasted over a pit, had given way to the *pièce montée* delicately adorned with its feathers, and the rough firewater to wine from Beaune. Nonetheless, the situation was the same intellectually and morally.

However, a series of unforeseen circumstances came to almost suddenly modify, in less than thirty years, the colony's social panorama. The revocation of the Edict of Nantes, the growing poverty of the rural nobility, and the existence of official ranks peopled with ruined noblemen pushed their way toward the French colonies of the Americas, a class with bourgeois tastes that aspired to find arable land in order to rejuvenate fortunes that, for centuries, had existed thanks to tilling. All of the officials who went to the New World in those days called themselves *de* Marmée, *de la* Martinière, *de la* Motte, *de* Periguy... There is not among them a simple Mister Jourdain. As soon as they inserted themselves into a society whose incipient wealth was not exempt from brusqueness or vulgarity, these tarnished nobles who owned nothing but the particle "of" imposed French habits and fashions, trying to create, in the shade of palm trees, lifestyles accordant to their education. With this example, the colony was transformed in a short period of time. The grandchildren of pirates, the sons of buccaneers, the settlers, the mixed bloods, acquired new customs. Other true pleasures are recognized, beyond the carnal or the culinary. Tailors, wig makers, hairdressers, seamstresses, printers, and musicians flocked to the colony. In 1764, the first issue of the *Gazette de Saint-Domingue* appeared. The same year—when in Havana there was only the "house of comedies" in Justiz Lane—a theater in the Cape City, on Vandreuil Street, premiered Molière's *Misanthrope.* Many women who impatiently waited for their husbands to strike it rich, always speaking of a return to France postponed year after year, must have shed a tear hearing Célimène's reply:

> Moi, renoncer au monde avant que de vieillir
> Et dans votre désert aller m'ensevelir!...
>
> (I would renounce the world before growing old
> and allowing myself to buried in your desert!)

The example of the Cape was followed by other cities. In Port-au-Prince, in Leogane, in Saint-Marc, in Les Cayes, new theaters were opened in which, alternating comedies with music, *El legatario universal* by Regnard and Beaumarchais's *The Barber of Seville* were staged and *Anette et Lubin* was sung, as well as newly written comic operas. One day, in Paris, Governor Bory met up with Jean-Jacques Rousseau at the Café de la Régence:

"I've seen your *Adivino de aldea* staged in the French Cape..."

"So much the worse for you!" responded, bitterly, the singer of *La Nouvelle Héloïse*, who must have not had great faith in the singing talents of performers in the colony.

This feverish attempt to imitate the refinements of the metropolis invades the people, even modifying the contours of folkloric expression. The creole songs acquire an unexpected accent à la Racan to them, with their dark-skinned beloveds called Lisette and Colin, but not forgetting, despite the names, the delicious island slang:

Didi mon perdi Lisette
Mon pa souchié kalenda
Mon quitté bran-bram sonnette
Mon pas battre bamboula.

Of course, the drumming on the *bamboula* continued (the boulá drum of the *rada* rituals), the *calenda* rumba was not forgotten, and the belt with cowbells (*bran-bram sonette*) was frequently shaken during the *houmfort* of the voodoo cult. But even among blacks a great diversity of gestures and intentions was established. The *Yanvalou*, the *Dahohomé-z'epaules*, the invocations to Erzili, the Assotor Drum, all maintained their tradition, principally in the slave workforce, where the magic rituals, the religion of Papá Legba and Ogun Ferraille were on the way to becoming a political weapon. For the concubine mulatto woman of the French settler who liked to be called Madame; for the musician who made a living playing at white parties; for the quadroon, the bold or simply dark-skinned person admitted to masqued balls as long as he did not abandon his box seat; for all those who could join in with the pleasant life of the city, voodoo was a sinister throwback to rural life, a carryover reminiscent of whips and stocks best left behind in the narrow street, even though a drum call from the bush elicited a more heartfelt response than the pain of Phaedra or the death of Hyppolite. Moreau de Saint-Méry, a keen, unique observer of everything, tells us:

> Blacks, imitating whites, dance minuets and *contradanzas*. Their sense of attunement confers on them the first quality needed by a musician; for this reason many are good violinists, since this is the instrument they prefer. Quickly, they know, for example, that the B note is found over the third string, and the first finger should be placed on that string; by just hearing a tune, or remembering it, they learn it with utmost ease.

Let us recall that the customs of the colony had been modified by a bourgeois caste that had brought with them the generalized habits of the modest castles in Périgord or Gascony and of the provincial salons. From this milieu, the *contradanza*, a bourgeois dance that never made it to Versailles and that was disdained by the Destouches and the Campras, was suddenly the supreme embellishment of French Cape and Port-au-Prince dances. Derived from the English country dance, taken to Holland and France at the end of the seventeenth century, the *contradanza* had acquired a French status through and through, spreading principally among the middle class. It was an honest figure dance, with a certain good-natured gallantry, and did not require an enormous choreographic ability from the dancers. But this dance did have an inherent element that was powerfully seductive to blacks. As Curt Sachs tells us:

> The circle and the single file are the basic forms of all choral dancing, and the majority of the figures go back to the Stone Age.... Even the way the men and women are placed in a double row, facing eaching other and divided in pairs, has already been pointed out in numerous African tribes, among the *bailas* of Rhodesia, the *bergdamas* and *bolokis* of the Congo. The fundamental primitive theme, is once again, the battle of the sexes with the ensuing attack and flight, union and separation.

In essence, the *contradanza* responded—although with more reserve and rules—to a mechanism analogous to the *calenda*, the conga, and other rumbas created by blacks and mestizos in the Americas. This collective dance, so action-filled, took greater license as it grew more popular. Hence the black musicians of Santo Domingo adopted it with enthusiasm, imbuing it with a rhythmic vivacity overlooked by the original model. The *contradanzas* of lesser composers such as Vincent, Séchard, and others (the greater composers did not cultivate this genre) acquired a unique trepidation, filling the bars with dots [points of augmentation] and sixteenth notes. The so-called tango rhythm was featured in the bass. The percussion accentuated the cunning of the black violinists praised by Saint-Méry. Once more there was a process of transubstantiation at work, due to what Carlos Vega so aptly calls "a way of doing things."

On August 14, 1791, Santo Domingo is shaken by an enormous event. The voodoo drums in Bois Caiman drone on. Under a torrential downpour, two hundred delegates from the slave plantations of the Northern Plain, assembled by the illuminated Bouckman, drink the tepid blood of a black pig and take an oath of rebellion. Eight days later the hoarse voice of the great shells soared over the mountains. The slaves disappeared into the jungles, after having poisoned the wells. In February 1793, the French National Convention abolished slavery in the colonies. Despite British occupation at Le Môle Saint-Nicolas and other places that were loci for insurrection, whites were no longer respected by their former slaves. After the first slaughters, many fled the disorder. Those settlers who could find a passing boat went to New Orleans. But, for those who only had a schooner at their disposal, the Cuban coast offered surer and closer refuge.

Many fugitives arrived in Santiago in the utmost misery, and depended on public charity for a while. But, with the passing of the great terror, tired of the soup that a townswoman made for them, they began to refashion themselves. The educated French ladies "established drawing, sewing, and French schools, and with this kind of self-sufficiency money flowed into the households; others taught geography, music, dance, and they had excellent disciples in matters of manners, in how to exhibit their refinement; others in the playing of the piano" (José María Callejas). A musician,

Monsieur Dubois, formed the first black musical group in Santiago. But that was not all. Revolutionizing the tranquil customs of the inhabitants, the French constructed a provisional theater, made of palm trees, for performing dramas, comedies, and comic operas. Actors recited Racine's verses and a Madame Clarais sang Kreutzer's *Joan of Arc*. In a café-concert hall, inaugurated under the name of Tivoli, one could hear good music performed, or rounds of applause for a ballerina called "La Popot." The daughters of the settlers sang *bergerettes*. Concerts were offered that invariably ended with a minuet, with a trio featuring Monsieur Dubois on clarinet. Years later, the musical activities of the French acquired greater importance. A certain Karl Rischer and Madame Clarais, who together had brought a clavichord, founded an orchestra composed of the following: piccolo, flute, oboe, clarinet; trumpet, three horns; three violins, viola, two cellos, and drums. A curious fact: in those first years of immigration, one could witness the unique case of Tivoli audiences singing, with equal enthusiasm, *The Marseillaise* and the *Hymn to Saint Louis*. Far from the guillotine, which seemed insignificant compared to the machete-wielding followers of Toussaint-Louverture, the exiles sang the praises of both the monarchy and the republic.

Before the arrival of the French, the minuet was danced only in the exclusive circle of the Cuban aristocracy. But the fugitives popularized it, bringing, in addition, the gavotte, the *passe-pied,* and, above all, the *contradanza* — a fact of capital importance in the history of Cuban music, since the French *contradanza* was adopted with surprising swiftness, staying on the island and transforming itself into a Cuban *contradanza,* cultivated by all the creole composers of the nineteenth century, even becoming Cuba's first musical genre to be triumphantly exported. Its derivations originated a family of types that are still alive. The genres known today as the *clave,* the *criolla,* and the *guajira* were born from the considerably Cubanized *contradanza* in 6/8. And from the 2/4 *contradanza* came the *danza,* the habanera, and the *danzón,* with its ensuing more or less hybrid offshoots.

Later, we will see how Manuel Saumell gathered in his exquisite oeuvre all of the rhythmic and melodic elements of all these genres.

Even before 1850, Saumell's *contradanzas* already traced the shapes and contours of an ensemble of patterns that will embody and nourish, under diverse names and contested claims to paternity, the Cubanness of a wide source of music being composed on the island.

Many blacks accompanied the whites fleeing the Haitian insurrection, some out of loyalty to their masters, others brought as domestic slaves. These were the grandparents of those blacks still called "French" in Santiago and who retain a certain number of songs and dances created in Haiti. Each Saturday, they gather to dance at one of the two associations that subsist in the city, losing themselves in dances generically known as *tumba francesa*, a faithful reflection of eighteenth-century creole traditions. Their drums are wide and stubby, barrel-shaped, adorned with drawings. They are played with drumsticks — like Haitian voodoo drums — although they use the tension of the rim in order to have a smooth drumhead, and not the "buttoned-down" tension with wedges, more characteristic of the island where they originate. The dances are performed with the couple dancing apart, with gracious figures, copied from the old dances of the Cape and Port-au-Prince, although the accompaniment on percussion — three drums with drumheads and an ideophonic drum made of wood called *catá* — creates a rhythm of monotonous intensity alongside the sung melodies.

The "French blacks" would also play an important role in the formation of Cuban music — made from inherited and transformed elements — with a fundamental rhythmic element to be slowly incorporated into many of the island's folkloric genres: the *cinquillo* [one-two-three-one-two]:

which also tends to be written, in more modern fashion, in this way:

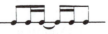

The *cinquillo* is of obvious African origin. It has the rhythmic regularity, the symmetry of certain percussive rituals of voodoo. Its diffusion and persistence can be observed in regions of the Americas where blacks were the majority or a significant part of the population. It accompanied the dance *La resbalosa* in Argentina, when it was still a dance of "blacks and zambos." It is a fundamental rhythm in Santo Domingo and Puerto Rico. It is the basis for the Haitian *méringue*. The peculiar placement of the two eighth notes on either side of the bar of a measure is found in the *rada* percussion of Haiti, and even appears in some of the *batá* rhythms of Cuba. To sum up, its inter-American migration follows that of all African-based dances performed throughout the continent. That it existed in Cuba before the arrival of the "French blacks" is quite likely. But it must have been confined to the slave barracks, since it passed into salon dancing in the days of the Haitian immigration. In the neighboring isle, its presence was so active that it was incorporated into the *contradanza*. It is interesting to note that in a *contradanza* published in late-eighteenth-century Paris—a time when Bernard of Saint-Pierre had made the Antilles fashionable—and which arrived in Cuba by way of Port-au-Prince with the meaningful title of "La insular," we find the use of an insistent rhythm (foreign to the nature of the *contradanza*) inexact and clumsily notated, but with the same placement of short and long sound values of the *cinquillo:*

The melodies of the first songs in creole patois brought by the "French blacks" to Santiago were all constructed on the basis of the *cinquillo*. The *Tabatié mue tombé,* collected by Emilio Bacardí, offers eight bars with *cinquillos* out of fourteen total. The *Cocoyé* (or *Cocuyé*), a series of verses of the same origin, so disseminated in Santiago that they grew to be a kind of national song, turned the *cinquillo* into a kind of obsession. Certain passages return to a merely percussive function, which reflects its more primitive existence:

When it was introduced on the island, it became one with the eastern *contradanza*. Dance orchestras took it on to spice up their performances. All of the Santiago-based repertoire, which included "La Santa Taé," "La francesita" by Boza, and many other hits of the day, presented the same characteristics. But—and this is a curious case—the *cinquillo* took more than fifty years to reach Havana. Manuel Saumell, who knew everything about *contradanzas*, seems not to have suspected its existence. The same holds true in the compositions of his successors of lesser note, such as Tomás Ruiz, Díaz de Comas, Fernández de Coca, without forgetting that modest master Lino Martínez. This shows—and we will return to this point—that the modifications of European genres on the island by African-based rhythms functioned by modalities of interpretation— modalities not written down for a period of time, as happens with certain jazz pianists, but that soon created enduring habits. In the days when a trip from Havana to Santiago was a fifteen-day adventure (or more), it was possible for two types of *contradanza* to coexist: one closer to the classical pattern, marked by the spirit of the minuet, which later would be reflected in the *danzón*, by way of the *danza*; the other, more popular, which followed its evolution begun in Haiti, thanks to the presence of the "French blacks" in eastern Cuba. Because, when speaking of the Cuban *contradanza*, one must not forget that two parallel and different types existed during the first half of the nineteenth century: Santiago's and Havana's. (Almost all *contradanzas* written in Mexico, for example, were of the latter type.) Only in the last decades of that same century would the *cinquillo* reach to the capital, feeding into the *danzón* and the bolero, and becoming one of the integrative elements of Cuban music.

The first person to understand the rhythmic and melodic value of black Antillean music was not Cuban-born, and perhaps this is why his vision was not clouded by local prejudices. One night in 1836, finding himself at the café La Venus, the excellent Catalan musician Casamitjana (author of Cuban songs well loved in Santiago) witnessed the passing by of a noisy carnival procession, led by two mulatto women, María de la Luz, and María de la O., who were singing the *Cocoyé*. On the spot, astounded by the revelation, he wrote down the verses and the rhythms, writing a score for the Regiment of Catalonia band. Days later, the work premiered at an open-air concert, to the scandal of "distinguished members of the audience." But by then the applause of the common folk filled the plaza, disarming the faces of disapproval made by the fops.

The *Cocoyé* would have a long life. This invention by "French blacks," adopted by black Cubans, with its *cinquillos* and deftly placed melodies over percussive basses, would be transcribed again for a band in 1849, by Manuel Úbeda, a composer of religious music. Reinó, author of an imitative fantasy called *El viaje a Güines* [The journey to Güines], very popular throughout the island, made a new arrangement of the *Cocoyé* for a band. Desvernine employed its themes for piano compositions. Finally, Amadeo Roldán would use its melodies in the *Overture on Cuban Themes* (1925), and in the song "Oriental" of his *Tres pequeños poemas para orquesta* (1926).

In 1809, colonial "chauvinism" aimed its sights against the *danzas* brought by the French, warmly received in the salons of the aristocracy as well as in the dance halls. An editorial from *Aviso de La Habana* started the movement with these ideas:

> In all times, we have been a people distinguished by honest simplicity, with no affectation, until French libertinism conquered our compatriots . . . inflicting great harm on our ancient customs. Now that we detest with all our heart the principles of that degraded nation, and since we have sculpted in marble the felony committed against the august person of our adored king Señor Don Ferdinand VII (may God look over him), why are we not going to feel odd with the *balsa* [waltz] and the *contradanza*, always indecent inventions that diabolical France has introduced in our midst? They are, in their essence, diametrically opposed to Christianity: they are made up of gestures, lascivious wiggling, and an impudent ruffianism that provoke, like concupiscence, heat and fatigue in the body.

But no one paid any attention to the condemnatory phrases uttered by the bilious gazetteer. The *"balsa"* and the *contradanza* had taken root too deeply in the tastes of the Creole for him to feel tempted to show his loyalty to Señor Don Fernando VII by denying himself something of utmost delight. In a two-by-four, three-by-four, and six-by-eight rhythm, the Creole's heart started to draw further away from Spain. Fourteen years later, José María Heredia would have to flee Cuba for his involvement in the conspiracy of Los Rayos y Soles of Bolívar.

7. Blacks in Cuba

In the 1827 census (*Censo de la siempre fidelísima ciudad de La Habana* [Census of the ever faithful city of Havana]), one finds the following curious fact: among the 16,520 white males dedicated to different occupations, there are 44 musicians; among the 6,754 males of color, free, and in similar conditions, there are 49 musicians. Proportionately speaking, it is a figure three times as great. In an oft-cited paragraph from his *Memoria sobre la vagancia en la Isla de Cuba* [Memoir on vagrancy in Cuba], José Antonio Saco wrote in 1832:

> The arts are in the hands of people of color. Among the greatest
> evils this unfortunate race has brought to our soil is to have
> distanced the white population from the arts. Destined for only
> the most mechanical of occupations, blacks were exclusively
> entrusted with the labors proper to their condition; and early
> on, the master became accustomed to treat the slave with
> disdain, and quickly began to see in like fashion the work he
> performed, because all occupations are worthy of praise or
> derision according to the good or bad qualities of those who
> undertake them.

But it was not just "the habit of despising the work done by blacks" that determined the distancing by whites — not an absolute distance, moreover — from the work of being a musician. Various factors came into play against music as a profession; first, the prejudices of a colonial society, that recently had attained prominence, consigning its sons to law, medicine, the church, a military career, or, for lack of anything better, public administration, reserving for itself the monopoly of the most "honorable stations." If the aroma of cane molasses still clung too closely to the body, a toga, a sable, or a tonsure was an excellent cover for the lack of *sine nobilitas* [signs of nobility].

On the other hand, the musician's profession was not an enviable position because of its inherent instability and poverty. In Santiago, the priest Juan París, the successor to Salas, had to lend money to one of his muscians so that he could "purchase a decent enough suit to attend a funeral." Ever since a Havana ecclesiastical ruling prohibited their participating in orchestras and opera or *tonadilla* choruses, the choirmasters and musicians of the cathedral filled sheet after sheet pleading to the dean and town council that the treasurer give them back pay, or that the record keeper not discount poorly explained absences from their wages. In spite of all this, the positions were ferociously defended as the only providence possible. Concerts were too risky an adventure to become a way of subsistence. And as for theater, the arrival of companies with a vocal repertoire was too irregular to create a continuous demand for orchestra musicans. Hence, whites, privileged in work opportunities, turned their backs on such a dangerously insecure profession.

For blacks, however, the problem took on a different hue. Barred from the law, medicine, ecclesiastical careers, and the better administrative positions, blacks considered music a very reputable profession, one that allowed them to scale the heights of the social ladder. Moreover, besides playing an instrument, most held another job. Many black musicians back then were tailors or cabinetmakers. Despite a generally recognized ability, certain noble paths of employment were closed off to them. Blacks could not aspire to work at the cathedral in Havana without a document proving a "clean bloodline." The "Ethiopians," as already seen, were excluded from the chorus. What road was left to the black musician when a theater company in transit did not require his services? Dance. Dance, which Creoles at the beginning of the nineteenth century encouraged with incredible constancy, since it was their favorite diversion. Dancing, where Spanish, French, and mestizo dances were thrown in together, originating new directions and rhythms, eventually imparting a unique character to the island's music.

In 1798, the chronicler Buenaventura Ferrer estimated that some fifty public dances were held daily in Havana. The enthusiasm was "almost crazed." Open to all, "young lads of idle occupation were accustomed to spending all night there." These dances were held in houses with various rooms selected for refreshments and gambling. The *zambumbia,* Loja water, and sangria fueled the ardor of those in attendance. The party started with a minuet, while the caller, holding a cane, would survey the dancers. (There was a Don Liborio who was famous for this.) Once the serious dancing concluded, the *contradanzas* began, being the latest fashion since the onset of the French arrival in Santiago. By the third *contradanza,* "the dancers had cast aside all notion of reason and good judgment" (*El Regañón de La Habana*). To make sure the body was kept limber, during intermissions they danced *zapateos, congós,* boleros, and *guarachas.* When those attending the parties were not very distinguished, everyone sang slum songs, derived from or contemporary with the *chuchumbé,* rich in puns and libidinous allusions: the "Cachirulo," "with the verses of Father Pando speaking to a pious woman"; "La matraca," "La cucaracha," the song "¿Cuándo?" —that impatient and yearning "¿cuándo?" [when?] which, played over different rhythms, has been sung with the same lyrics in all of the countries of Latin America:

¿Cuándo, mi vida?	(When, my heart?
¿Cuándo?	When?)

To this more risqué repertoire they added "Que toquen la zarabandina," where a "friar Juan de la Gorda Manzana" [Friar Fat Apple] worked as an official dealing with licenses. And never forgotten or excluded was the irreplaceable "Guabina," with its style typical of Havana *bufos:*

La mulata Celestina
le ha cogido miedo al mar,
porque una vez fue a nadar
y la mordió una guabina.

Dice Doña Severina
que le gusta el mazapán,
pero más el catalán
cuando canta la guabina.

Entra, guabina, entra,
por la puerta de la cocina.

(Celestina the mulatta
is afraid of the sea,
because once she went swimming
and was bitten by a *guabina*.[1]

Doña Severina says
that she likes marzipan,
but even tastier is the Catalan
who sings the *guabina*.[2]

Enter, *guabina*, enter
by the kitchen door.)

The graceful and charming mulatto women were the queens of these dances.[3] They competed with the black women in wearing clear-colored and showy dresses, bangles, bracelets, and earrings with big hoops, while the men would sweat away in their "linen, drill, or cotton underjackets," without removing their cloth hats.

> There was no shortage of young Creoles from decent and well-to-do families, who, without embarassment, mixed in with the people of color and took part in their diversions . . . some out of mere taste, others motivated by less pure intentions. Apparently, some of the males . . . were not bashful with the women of their own social class, if we are to judge by the ease with which they stopped dancing and spoke to their acquaintances or friends, according to the close observation of the women who, as mute spectators, watched from the windows of their own houses. (Cirilo Villaverde, *Cecilia Valdés*)

Deprived of lovers in the narrow circles of bourgeois society of the times, the son of a good family sought to satisfy his desires in the world of the daughters and granddaughters of slaves who had made them wealthy, forgetting the "inferiority" of people of color for a few hours. What was not allowed in the church choirs could well serve for intimate recreation. This detail is interesting because it explains a phase of *mestizaje* [racial mixing] of certain salon dances where customs filtered through from the bottom up, that is, from the dance halls to the lordly mansions. It is significant that, in 1856, during a great formal dance in Santiago in honor of General Concha, the most aristocratic elements of society furiously surrendered themselves, at one point, to the rhythms of a *contradanza* titled "Tu madre es conga."

It seems that the young bourgeois who rode in carriages and wore top hats and watch chains, who gathered at the dance halls, found an élan in the way black orchestras played, an intensity, a rhythmic force that was unpretentious. In numerous chronicles and articles of the colonial period a growing preference for "orchestras of color," when speaking of dances, is mentioned. Certain *contradanzas* "had greater appeal" when played by blacks. Blacks and whites performed the same popular songs. But blacks added an accent, a vitality, something unwritten that "perked things up." In short, what happened was something similar to what makes Duke Ellington's orchestra more appealing than Paul Whiteman's. The black musician was elusive, inventing between the written notes. White musicians stuck to the notation. Thanks to blacks, there was a growing hint in the bass lines, principally in the accompaniment of the French *contradanza*, of a series of displaced accents, of ingenious and graceful intricacies, of "ways of doing" that created a habit, and originated a tradition. A small detail is more instructive than a long explanation. As is known, the ill-named "habanera" rhythm already appears, without the slightest alteration, in the Cuban *contradanzas* at the beginning of the nineteenth century:

Well, then: in the famous *contradanza* titled "Tu madre es conga," danced in honor of General Concha, this rhythm appears modified in this unique fashion:

Even those who cannot read music will be able to observe the identity of both rhythmic figures with regard to their constitutive elements: an eighth note with a point of augmentation, a sixteenth note, two eighth notes. But in the second case, a simple linking of notes has completely transformed the rhythm without altering the beat, creating a new genre: the *conga*. Even in today's *conga* one can observe the persistence of this accompaniment. In Rafael Ortiz's "Uno, dos y tres," which recently was all the rage in Havana, we see this bass line, which can be compared to its predecessor from 1856:

The popular dance forms from the beginnings of the nineteenth century were the crucible where, in the heat of black rhythmic inventiveness, Andalusian songs, boleros and verses from stage *tonadillas* (there are current songs and *sones* that remind us of bars from *El trípili-trápala* from *Los maestros de la Raboso*), and the French *contradanza* melted together to conceive new forms of expression. These orchestras of piccolo, clarinet, three violins, a bass, and a pair of *timbales* (Cirilo Villaverde), along with *güiros* and *calabazos* [similar to a *güiro*], were, give or take a horn, the same ones you now hear playing at dances in Cuba. They were the creators of a mestizo music, in which all of the pure African roots—regarding melody and ritual rhythms of percussion—had been excluded. It would take until the end of the century for the ancestral music of Africa, hidden in the slave barracks, held in the minds of slaves and those recently emancipated, to come out of its private domain and imbue Cuban dance music.

For the moment, the black musician moves within the orbit of what Moreau de Saint-Méry and Bachiller y Morales agree in calling "a spirit of imitation." But one must not forget that in Cuba, until the abolition of slavery, there were two different classes of blacks, subjected to different social climates.

In 1792, to celebrate the joyous birth of the Prince of Asturias, the black batallion of Bayamo, seconded by free blacks from the area, organized a masquerade "followed by some flageolets," exhibiting an allegorical float that represented a fortified castle with its sentry boxes drawn by two pairs of oxen. When the float arrived in front of the municipal authorities, the castle opened up like a stage, giving way to the performance of a short allegorical poem. Three black officials, "dressed as Love, Apollo, and Mars," immersed themselves in a learned discussion about a preference for letters as opposed to arms. A black Minerva closed the debate with a *loa* [a short dramatic panegyric in verse] that satisfied all, and the function closed with a "great music" by the militia band.

This colloquium of the Attic gods—without the facial profile, of course—barely a few steps from the slave barracks where, because it was a holiday, the tribal drums were beating, establishes an eloquent contrast between two black worlds: emancipated blacks and slaves. There is an unconscious materialization of long-buried longings in those disguises of Eros, Apollo, Mars, and Minerva. The black serfs were granted liberty during the siege of Havana by the British as long as they helped with the defense of the plaza; they performed stunning feats of valor, rushing forth bare-chested into the barrels of enemy canons. It was their passage to a white world of knowledge, uses, pleasures, fashions. Unfortunately, the son of the freed slave never strayed far from the threshold of his house outside of the city or the workshop or small business run by his father. Because of his skin color, he could not obtain an academic title, a priest's robe, or be choirmaster; hence, the appearance of that type of black roguishly called "professor," who would perform all the delightful things written by the authors of creole *sainetes* [one-act farces] during the nineteenth century. The "professor" is the refined black man who resorts to the most affected kind of language, the most unusual locutions, in order to say the simplest things. Deprived of a formal education, he fished for those obscure words that seemed profound and distinguished, heard in the conversation of educated whites, thereby creating a character of bungling preciosity. But the "professor" role was not limited to the *sainetes*. When his experience or innate tact removed him from such ingenuous excesses—a preciosity visible in the fledgling compositions of the first black poets who later spread their wings and took flight—he would then become a "political man." In speaking of Claudio Brindis de Salas, the father of the extraordinary violinist, Bachiller y Morales tells us: "this black Creole, a musician by profession, was a gentleman of agreeable and ceremonious ways, adhering to the norms of social behavior; he was the cream of the 'politicals' of that species, and his aristocratic tendencies made him strike up friendships with gentlemen and professors of the other race."

Independently of their behavior in popular dances, the "political men" of the musical world made an enormous contribution to the artistic life of Cuba at the beginning of the nineteenth century. The first concert player whose name appeared in the colonial press was the black Juan Peña, who played violin during intermission at theatrical functions. When Joaquín Gavira created a classical trio in 1811, it included Bartolo Avilés, a black cellist. Cuba's premier maker of musical instruments was black: his name was Juan José Rebollar and he lived in Santiago, where he died, quite old, in 1851. A cabinetmaker by profession, he had been initiated into the secrets of this beautiful profession of luthier by a French musician, Monsieur Alexis, who went to Cuba in the days of the great Haitian migration. Using Cuban wood, Juan José Rebollar made a hundred guitars, numerous basses, a few violins, and a certain cello of such pure sound that its owner, a wealthy aficionado from Santiago, "preferred it to an Amati" (Laureano Fuentes).

From 1800 to 1840, blacks were the clear majority of the professional musicians. At the end of the eighteenth century, the black militia of Santiago had a good band, which consisted of six fifes, an oboe, seven clarinets, two bassoons, two *serpentarios,* a clarion, two horns, two *cornabassi,* and military drums. Many sons of this band's musicians later formed part of dance orchestras. In 1815 there were seven black brothers with the Tamés surname, all musicians. Almost all of the good black performers of the time wrote *contradanzas.* But above all, we see a yearning to keep up with and assimilate all the musical influences brought to the island. Pedro Nolasco Boza's orchestra — he was a black from Puerto Príncipe — specialized in accompanying stage *tonadillas* when the first Spanish theater company visited Santiago. For a whole season the *Trípili-trápala* was his battle horse. There were blacks who became famous singing *tiranas* [old Spanish folk songs] and boleros. Bartolo Avilés, the cellist, wrote sacred music. Tomás Buelta y Flores composed *contradanzas* in the finest of styles. Secundino Arango, author of motets and *salve reginas,* learned how to perfectly play the violin, the viola, the cello, the bass, and the organ (as a bassist he surprised the great Bottesini). Claudio Brindis de Salas gave dance lessons to all of Havana society and had an instrumental group called La Concha de Oro [The golden shell]. Ulpiano Estrada, director of a reputable Havana-based orchestra, was such an aficionado of the courtly minuet that he kept performing it even when it was out of fashion. The mulatto Gregorio Velázquez gave flute, violin, cello, and bass lessons. And in 1850 there was a María Gamboa, daughter of free blacks, protected by the family of the ex-superintendent of Havana, who was applauded in Madrid, Paris, and London. They called her the "black Malibrán," and she ended up in Seville marrying Mariano Martínez de Morena, an officer of the Spanish army.[4]

Indisputably, the most extraordinary of the black musicians of the nineteenth century was Claudio José Domingo Brindis de Salas, son of the teacher of the same name. Although we did not want to clog up this book with performers and concert players—a difficult judgment to make in reading the criticism that is either excessively eulogistic or irresponsible—we cannot but help dedicate a few sentences to such a unique figure, an unprecedented case in the musical history of the continent. A disciple of the solid Belgian maestro Van der Gutch who lived in Havana, Brindis de Salas had the good fortune of being able to round out his musical training with Danclas, David, Stori, Sivori, and other professors from the Paris Conservatory. An exceptional virtuoso, he was acclaimed in Milan, Florence, Berlin, Saint Petersburg, and London. He returned to Cuba in 1875 loaded with medals and decorations, "with the fantastic title of Director of the Haitian Conservatory" (Guillén), then going on to Venezuela, Central America, and Mexico. He was made a member of the Legion of Honor, and was even given the title of baron. After triumphant tours in Spain and Argentina—in Buenos Aires his admirers handed him an authentic Stradivarius as a gift—he settled down in Berlin for a while, marrying a German. Appointed chamber musician to the emperor, by the end of the century he had attained all the highest honors possible. But the era of the virtuoso was fading. The great strokes with the bow, the repertoires performed to show off phenomenal technique, the Sarasate-like flourishes, were becoming a thing of the past. After 1900, forgotten by the court in Berlin, the applause waned. His last trip to Cuba was a financial failure. Finally, in 1911, his lungs eaten away by tuberculosis, he died in a sordid hostel in Buenos Aires. Of his grand past the only item preserved is a silk corset. Once the "black loafer" was identified by his passport, he was given a solemn burial. His remains were transferred to Havana with great honors in 1930, despite the fact that he was a German citizen. Born in 1852, Brindis de Salas was one of the most interesting characters in Cuban musical history as far as concert players are concerned. In terms of repertory, his programs did not reveal very rigorous criteria. Like many of his contemporaries, he preferred the "brilliant fantasy" spiked with spectacularly difficult passage to Bach or Handel. But we cannot blame him for being the victim of one of the ills of his time. The programs of the deified performers of those days were not much better than his. In the end, he had not usurped his title of the "Cuban Paganini."

In the first half of the nineteenth century, blacks played and created white music, without enriching it further, except with their atavic rhythmic sense, where they uniquely accentuated certain kinds of danceable compositions. When they wrote a melody, they did not seem to remember for the moment the rich treasure of their ancestral African heritage. The *batá* beat, the Yoruba hymn, the totemic survivals observed in the carnival parades *(comparsas)* held on Three Kings Day, the invocations in "native tongue" transmitted in the oral traditions of black slaves, would take a long time to leave the confines imposed by the colonial social system. When the *comparsas* are let loose on the streets on January 6, with their *diablitos* [little devils], kings, and *culonas* [big-bottomed women], the "political man" draws back, letting pass, just like whites, that carnival tolerated by the authorities, respecting an old custom. If the drum made the innermost fibers of his heart resonate in sympathy, he did not admit it. It is possible that at times blacks would attend the ritual drum beating of the Carraguao neighbor-hood. But in the dances where he performed his professional du-ties, he played the courtly minuet. After he had slowly modified elements received from Spain and France by modalities of execu-tion, the black musician waited for whites to draw closer to their more secret world and bequeath to them the melodic material that they potentially carried within them. In this initial phase of his def-inition as an individual, subjected to a new social climate, he was at the stage that led North American blacks to stress the offbeat of ragtime, creating the oompah rhythm, before multiplying (always within the same beat) the syncopations of the blues, or inventing the unremitting movements of boogie-woogie. After creating the conga, by linking two notes in the traditional bass line of the *con-tradanza*, Cuban music would totally modify one rhythmic aspect of the tango (if we accept that term) by diplacing only some of the stress, using a procedure that undermines the strong rhythm that Stravinsky deftly exploited in the second part of *The Rite of Spring*. An example of this, which in itself is enough, is seen in a *contradanza* by Juan Bendetti, titled "Los merengazos":

Despite his yearning to draw closer to whites, to emulate their good manners, to raise his cultural level to that of whites, the black "political man" was not above suspicion. With the liberation of Haitian slaves and the abolition of the slave trade in the British colonies, the great bourgeois of the era were always afraid that black aspirations would become too excessive, putting their wealth in danger. When the colonial authorities undertook the barbarous repression of the Escalera Conspiracy in 1844, all the whites in-volved were absolved, with one or two exceptions. Blacks, how-ever, paid for all the supposed faults. The poet Plácido and the mu-sician Pimienta were executed. The composer Buelta y Flores was tortured before being deported. The poet Juan Francisco Manzano, despite his good relationships with intellectual circles, was thrown in jail. After dedicating his best compositions to high-ranking Spaniards and writing sonnets to aristocratic ladies, Claudio Brindis de Salas, the father, was arrested and tortured by O'Donnell. After being amnestied, when he wanted to reorganize his old orchestra he found out that almost all of the musicians had been executed.

A black could dress up as Apollo or Minerva. But when he was deemed too demanding, his back was lashed with the same whip used in the slave barracks.

8. The Beginning of the Nineteenth Century

The small creole bourgeoisie, more conservative and timid than aristocrats, regarded art-related matters with a certain amount of mistrust. An article published in the *Papel Periódico de La Habana* in 1802—"On the Necessity and Manner of Imparting Mores to Children from Infancy"—clearly informs us of an attitude one could observe years earlier in the bosom of old provincial families of France or Spain:

> One sees some parents who themselves take their children to public spectacles and other diversions with no other effect than to elicit disgust for the serious and well-spent life toward which the same parents prefer to steer them. With this they are mixing poison with nourishment. They speak to their offspring only about wisdom, but at the same time they are familiarizing the volatile imagination of children with the violent impressions of passionate representations *and of music;* after which they no longer have to think about applying themselves.

In short, it was the same manner of thinking of the bourgeois in a Moratín play.

However, a slow, top-to-bottom transformation was occurring, the example of the salons. Don José María Peñalver, a great music lover, organized philharmonic soirées, garnished by the presence and artistry of clavichordist María Luisa O'Farril, of Asunción Montalvo, countess of Fernandina, and of Dolores Espadero, mother of the future composer and an excellent performer of Mozart. Haydn, Pleyel, Gossec, Méhul, Pergolesi, Cimarosa, and Cherubini were the favorite composers of these rich aficionados who were orienting musical tastes. Formed in 1811, the classical trio of Joaquín Gavira had little success, and ceased its activities after only a few sessions. Nonetheless, chamber music gained ascendance again in 1816, the year in which the violinist from Valencia [Spain], Toribio Segura, violist Hilario Segura, and Enrique González, cellist, disciple of the great Brunetti, arrived in Havana, entrusted to the generous music enthusiast Don Francisco Montero. In the house of their benefactor, and with the cooperation of local musicians, they established well-attended Thursday and Sunday public performances of trios, quartets, and quintets. The concert, removed from the miscellaneous happenings of the theater, had been born.

Many more homes were hosting musical events. It was an annual custom to invade the salon of the Sollozo ladies during Holy Week to hear Pergolesi's *Stabat Mater*, performed by amateur musicians with a kind of charming solemnity. A malicious quatrain made the rounds, alluding to the voices of the Sollozo sisters, stripped of any pleasant veneer:

Tocan ¡pero cómo tocan!	(They play, but how they play!
Cantan ¡pero cómo cantan!	They sing, but how they sing!
Con las bocas y manos provocan,	With hand and mouth they provoke,
Pero con las caras espantan.	But their faces frighten.)

The small musical world of Havana was livening up. In 1812, the irascible Joaquín Gavira published a now lost pamphlet, *La zurra musical* [The musical thrashing]. It must have been rather violent, judging by the author's character. The same year, Esteban de Boloña's press, creator of lovely vignettes, gave light to the first music newspaper in Cuba: *El Filarmónico Mensual* [The monthly philharmonic]. Its first issue contained a "primer of principles to learn the art of music." Beginning in 1803, considerably in advance of almost all other Latin American nations, musical compositions were published in Havana. The publications gathered many songs that had been in fashion at the end of the eighteenth century and that still held sway in people's memory. In 1810, the first pianoforte brought from Paris was a sensation when it appeared in Santiago de Cuba, putting the ex-capital on a par with Havana, where monochords, spinets, and clavichords, mutilated by termites, were long falling apart in garrets.

With this environment, musical instruction was progressing. The first Academy of Music on record was created in 1814, in the house of Don Antonio Coelho,

> who with the corresponding permission of His Excellency the Governor will be directed by D. Carlos Antonio de Acosta, who offers his services to all those young men and women who choose to employ him, either in the academy or in their private homes, and will impart to them all of his knowledge, both of vocal music, according to the most modern Italian style, and of violin and piano, the latter being his favorite instrument.

That same year, the following ad was published in the *Diario del Gobierno de La Habana:* "In the house at 97 de Luz Street, an intelligent lady teaches beginners to play by using the harp; and in a few days expects to receive six harps, which, with preference given to pupils, she intends to sell at moderate prices."

New instruments, new demands, and a new market become manifest in the gazettes of the time: "A dulcian (double bassoon) or bassoon with its case; six mouthpieces; the great method for bassoon by the composer Ozi; a concert for bassoon by Stamitz; three concert duos by Ozi; six concert quartets, bassoons, alto, and cello [quartets?] by Blasin..." (1818).

In 1816 the Saint Cecilia Academy of Music was founded in Havana.

A music publishing house published the *contradanza* titled "San Pascual Bailón" in 1803. This piece, one of the first, was followed by older ones such as "La Guabina," and novelties such as the bolero "Nadie siembra su parra junto al camino," "La cachucha," or the Cuban *guaracha* "El sungambelo":

De los sungambelos	(Of all the sungambelos
que he visto en la Habana,	I've seen in Havana,
ninguno me gusta	There's none I like better
como el de tu hermana.	than the one your sister has.)

But now new and wider margins of expression open up for the sentimental ballad, copied from the ones sung in the salons of Paris. Madame de Staël inspired romantic songs among certain Havana musicians. In 1820, "La Corina" was published, with delectably ingenuous lyrics, seeking to prolong the emotions of a tearful moment:

. . . tiernamente de Roma obsequiada
entre amigos dichosa vivir,
mas ¡ay! triste, de amor el veneno,
por mis venas discurre inclemente.
Yo vi a Osvaldo y le amé de repente,
Ay, Corina, ya debes morir,
Ay, Corina, ya debes morir.

(. . . tenderly from Rome, bequeathed
among friends with good fortune,
but oh! sad, the poison of love,
that inclemently roams in my veins.
I saw Osvaldo and suddenly loved him,
Oh, Corina, it's time for you to die,
Oh Corina, it's time for you to die.)

After Madame de Staël, Chateaubriand and Lord Byron were the great inspirations for romantic songs. "La Isabela," by Ramón Montalvo, still sung by our grandmothers, with its melody so full of unexpected chromaticism, was written using a version of Byron's "To Jenny." The title of the ballad "Dulce Chactas" reveals its origin. Plácido composes the poetry that, based on the plot of the famous novel, will inspire "La Atala," one of the great successes of the time. Songs with a more local flavor also appeared, such as "La bayamesa," destined to transform itself, in the heat of events, into an important patriotic song à clef. Logically so since the verses intended for a "gentle woman from Bayamo" before the revolution of 1868, took on an unexpected meaning years later, by a tacit allusion to the days when Bayamo had been free of Spanish domination:

¿No te recuerdas, gentil bayamesa,
que tu fuiste mi sol refulgente?
¿No recuerdas que un tiempo dichoso
me extasiaba en tu pura belleza,
y en tu seno doblé mi cabeza,
moribundo de dicha y amor? . . .

(Don't you remember, gentle woman
from Bayamo, when you were my radiant sun?
Don't you remember a fortunate time
when your beauty bathed me in ecstasy,
and on your breast I bowed my head,
dying of joy and love? . . .)

It is very rare for one of these sentimental ballads to offer the slightest local character, melodically or rhythmically. If today we can find a certain Cuban accent in the melody of "La bayamesa," it is by way of retroactive valorization; that is, since this type of melody has created a kind of genre, multiplying its expressions in the domain of creole songs, and being accustomed to this genre, we attribute a Cubanness to the initial type. But in reality it is only a reflection of what was sung in the European salons of the time. Many of these songs are written in triple time over a waltz accompaniment, barely disguised by random figures, embellishments, and removed from dance forms. Others, with greater pretensions, such as "La Isabela," look for their atmosphere and type of accompaniment in the German lieder. Truly, a certain Romanticism — more literary than musical — was being introduced to the island through these ballads, which salon society preferred to the uncouth ribaldry of the *guaracha*. It offered the harp players a greater showcase for their swooning gestures. But, as always happens with imported foreign fashions, these ballads ended up adjusting to the environment, turning the *mal du siècle* into tropical languidness. The custom of singing in "primary" and "secondary" manner, a Cuban tradition of Extremenian and Canary Island origins, and completely unknown to the Germans and the French, imposed its unchanging thirds and sixths on the melodies. As a last resort, the harp would sound like a guitar or a treble guitar. And slowly, absorbing the rhythmic patterns of popular dance forms already in place, the accompaniment was modified giving rise to that Italian-tinged genre, always with a sentimentality or melancholy intimately linked to the Colombian *bambuco* and the Mexican song. Nonetheless, it is very native to domestic ears, more than the ones "troubadours" of today—a Sindo Garay—sing at half voice, closing the eyes, suffering and sighing over the strings of their guitars, which is called a Cuban song. Furthermore, observe that, faithful to its origins in the 1800s, the Cuban song is (along with the bolero with which it has often been confused) the only type of insular music that, by tradition, uses foreign lyrics or poems far removed from local concerns. Just as the *guaracha*, the *son*, the conga, the *rumba*, the *clave*, and the *punto guajiro* draw from their surroundings, taking words joined together to the beat of the music, the song and the bolero take over verses by Luis Urbina, Amado Nervo, and Pedro Mata without the slightest difficulty, that is, when they were not strolling through the Verlaine-esque gardens of the minor imitators of Rubén Darío.

When the newspaper *La Moda o Recreo Semanal del Bello Sexo* [Fashion or the weekly recreation of the fair sex] was founded in 1829—its principal editor being Domingo del Monte—the musical supplements exclusively covered two types of local music considered safe enough to cross the threshold of bourgeois households and their female readers: the *contradanza* and the song. It is the same when one peruses the *Apolo Habanero,* a weekly music magazine that appears in 1835 and lasted twelve issues: alongside the inevitable *contradanzas* appear melodies whose titles are in themselves quite explicit: *Canción de la rosa* [Song of the rose], *Recuerdos de Bellini* [Memories of Bellini], and so on.

The truth is that the demand for music was sufficiently regular to foment societies, sustain professors, create newspapers, and encourage a business that in 1831 already announced the following: "drums, horns, *buisines* [medieval herald trumpets], *cornabassos,* trumpets of all modes, clarinets, piccolos, fifes," as well as pianos, violins, cellos, and harps. In 1829, when he visited the Angerona coffee plantation, the reverend Abiel Abbott chanced on an orchestra of forty black musicians, formed and trained by a Havana maestro specifically hired for this purpose and paid by their master.

In 1810, a Spanish company arrived in Havana that would perform in Cuba—with slight cast modifications—for more than twenty-two years. The company had artists of serious merit, such as the famous Andrés Prieto, a disciple of Isidoro Máiquez, Manuel García (who played the villain), the singer María del Rosario Sabatini, Antonio Hermosilla, and others. A few months later, the group was reinforced by talent of some renown in Spain: Mariana Galino, the ballerina Manuela Gamborino, and her sister, the famous *tonadilla* singer Isabel Gamborino. A Cuban actor, the basso buffo Covarrubias, author of *entremeses* [one-act farces], zarzuelas, and *sainetes*, was featured prominently on posters. The dance ensemble had eight members.

The presence of this company, as could be expected, gave a new boost to the stage *tonadilla*. But the spectacle divested itself of its monotonous structure based on comedy or drama, becoming more *tonadilla*, more *sainete*, following the new norms that director Isidoro Maiquez had imposed on the Teatro de los Caños in Madrid. Greater attention was given to music and dance. The *tonadilla*'s hypertrophy, transformed into a difficult to execute comic opera (like *La ópera casera*), was a favorable development for Havana audiences, putting them into contact with more talented singers capable of performing a serious repertory. Hence the new company staged many dramatic and comic operas from 1812 to 1816. There was one month in which *La belle Arsène* of Monsigny was performed three times—previously sung by a visiting French company. The scores performed were worthy of respect: *Les deux prisonniers* [The two prisoners] by Dalayrac; *Il matrimonio segreto* [The secret marriage] by Cimarosa; *Il barbiero de Seviglia* [The barber of Seville] by Paisiello; *Michel-Ange* [Michelangelo] by Méhul; *Le calife de Bagdad* [The caliph of Baghdad] by Boieldieu, various operas by Nicholas Isouard, without forgetting *El poeta calculista* [The calculating poet], *La gitana por amor* [Gypsy for love], *El tío y la tía* [The aunt and uncle] by Manuel García, and a great many Spanish operas of lesser importance. With an "adaptation of the music" — according to custom — a new opera, *El mejor día en la Habana* [The most beautiful day in Havana], was staged. However, it does not appear that the audiences of the time were interested in subjecting their minds to such arduous tasks. A prudent warning, which accompanies the ad for the premiere in 1816, advises that "there is nothing moving about the music." Grétry's *Richard Cœur de Lion* [Richard the Lion-Hearted], luxuriously presented to show off Galino, is touted as a "work full of charming, witty remarks."

As the *tonadilla* began a slow exile from programs, dance was brought to the fore. Manuela Gamborino, an agile and luscious bombshell, had the men of Havana in a spell. Prudently concealing themselves behind pseudonyms or asterisks, respected judges, militia officers, austere members of the Examining Board of Physicians versified, and sent laudatory poems, covetous of being the leading suitor, to the *Diario de La Marina:*

Con tu gitano adorno haces cautivos,
a cuantos en ti miran las destrezas:
Los ánimos se quedan semivivos,
Mientras que cabriolan tus gentilezas.

(With your gypsy ornaments you captivate
all who admire your skills:
All spirits are stunned
as your graces prance about.)

In that society of provincial habits, women with theatrical talent could become gold diggers to great advantage. In 1812, an adventure of this sort degenerated into a tragedy worthy of Calderón de la Barca. In a house adjoining the Teatro Principal—at 1 de Luz Street—the actress Mariana Galino was stabbed and left for dead, having provoked the legitimate jealousy of the actor Antonio Rosal. He slashed opened his veins, dying as his wife struggled back to life with various wounds on her body. Needless to say, for thirty years Havana residents commented on the event.

Manuela Gamborino, seeking personal success, paraded on stage a true anthology of European and American dances: boleros, courtly minuets, gavottes, minuets with a fandango twist, German minuets, *boleras*, polkas, *folías* [dance from the Canary Islands], *cachuchas* [an old Andalusian solo song and dance], *manchegas* [dance from La Mancha], *el pan de xarabe, el caballito jaleado,* and other diverse little dances, as substitutes for the fading *tonadilla.* Many of these dances were taught at dance academies—Havana already had some—feeding passing fashions that made hardly a dent in the *contradanza*'s popularity. Simultaneously, the waltz gained greater numbers of adherents on the island. Two years after having survived her husband's repeated stabbing, Mariana Galino introduced into Grétry's *Richard the Lion-Hearted* a "beautiful baltz [*sic*] proper to the occasion." As in other Latin American countries, the waltz was a genre cultivated successfully by local composers, even into the twentieth century. However, the tropical waltz did not create a lasting tradition on the island. Cuba did not produce a world hit in triple time comparable to the *Vals sobre las olas* [Waltz over the waves] by Juventino Rosas—who died in Batabanó. The popular music being created was so strong that it swallowed the patterns imported from afar, making them its own. Buenaventura Pascual Ferrer keenly noted, speaking of the dances of the time:

> There is nothing strange that the French-style *contradanza* be adapted with *our rhythm* (there's the word!), just like salon pieces, foreign to our soil. . . . Nor is it strange that the figures in which they were practiced, called *pantalon, été, galop, pastourelle, trévisse* and *chassé-croisé,* were substituted for *la bajada y la subida* [going down, going up], *la cadena y cedazo* [the chain and sieve] of our own.

Ferrer already sees two kinds of *contradanzas:* a *foreign* one and *ours* (characterized by *our rhythm*), without acknowledging that the second is born of the first. But it is also true that in less than twenty years, the *Cuban contradanza* had devoured its progenitor.

In 1821, the Spanish company suffered a moment of crisis. Its prolonged stay in Havana, its repertoire too loyal to a certain kind of opera, drew the public's attention toward any kind of new passing spectacle that presented itself. The Pautrets—Andrés and María Rubio—with their great choreographed pantomimes (*Macbeth, Ayder Ali-Khan, Las bodas de Camacho, Las ruinas de Palmira*), were successful in a way that predicted their future triumphs in Mexico. In those conditions, the alderman of the municipal government had to assist the comic actors of the Teatro Principal, albeit imposing conditions:

> ... we cede to the twelve comic actors the use of said theater, rent-free.... They are committed to ten public performances monthly in verse and seven operas, and a season benefit performance for the shelters as well as five for the municipal government.

Faced with the imperative need to refresh the repertory, the artists relied on Rossini. Under the baton of Don Manuel Cocco, the company's arranger and teacher to many of Havana's future musicians, audiences heard *Semiramis, An Italian in Algiers, The Thieving Magpie,* and *Tancredo. The Barber of Seville* (already well known from Paisiello's version) astonished Havana operagoers in a Spanish version by José Trespuentes, then the cathedral organist. In 1820, the same opera had been produced in a new translation, made in Havana and edited by Doctor González del Valle.

But, in 1831, audiences were saturated. Galino and Andrés Prieto, worn out from twenty-one years of acting in Havana, frankly bored the spectators. A patron who had withdrawn his subscription publicly requested hiring new singers. Romantic opera had already permeated the salons — the sentimental ballad having paved the way. Attentive to public pleas, the municipal government hired an excellent Italian company, which debuted in 1834. Bellini, Donizetti, Mercadente, and Meyerbeer made their appearance, foreshadowing the young Verdi, sweeping away eighteenth-century composers who had contributed so much to creole musical culture. But for public tastes this did not mean a rise in quality. On the contrary. The programs of the Saint Cecilia Philharmonic Society, which had featured the symphonies of Mozart and Haydn, were invaded by opera. Fragments of *The Magic Flute,* and the delicious baroqueness of Rossini, were followed by arias from *I Puritani* [Bellini], *Gemma de Vergy, Parisina* [Donizetti], or the overture to *Il Pirata* [Bellini]. Year in and year out at the Tacón Theater, at the Artistic and Literary Lyceum of Havana, and at the house of the count of Peñalver the same titles were repeated: *Norma* [Bellini], *Lucia di Lammermoor, La Favorita, Linda di Chamounix* [all by Donizetti]. A performance of Rossini's *Stabat Mater*, at the Lyceum, constituted a noble exception. Italian Romantic opera, with its concession to "feelings," its opportunities for showing off amateurs with ample voices, its implicit indulgence for *à peu près* correct performances, also invaded the programs of the Philharmonic Society of Matanzas (founded in 1829), of Santiago (1833), of Puerto Príncipe (1842), of Cienfuegos (1850), and of Santa Clara (1852). In those days, only the San Carlos seminary student orchestra maintained the cult of classical music and of the loftier and stronger expressions of musical Romanticism.

This love for Italian opera shaped a regression in creole musical culture. Mozart, Haydn, Beethoven, Schubert (some of his melodies had already been sung in Havana) became "difficult musicians," composers for those in the know, authors of sonatas not attractive to vulgar listeners. When a musician wanted to shine in society or at a given concert, the best way to do so was by executing a "brilliant fantasy" based on motifs from an opera, as was done by Hünten, Thaberg, or Le Carpentier — since the way Liszt chose to do so, at least in that type of production, was too difficult and demanded, after all, a certain gift for re-creation. The notable pianist Pablo Desvernine incurred the same sin, so admired then, of composing "fantasies" and paraphrases, just like the editor and pianist Ernesto Edelmann. For many years, the truly great music became a pleasure reserved for a select minority. Beethoven made way into the listeners' purview enveloped in an atmosphere of a small cabal of initiates, of those who knew the password, similar to the reaction in Paris surrounding the work of Wagner. At the beginning of the twentieth century, certain conservatories, anxious to "please" and seduce their bourgeois clientele, still included fantasies by Leibach as part of student exams. The difficult material odds against the endeavors of serious and disinterested art even only twenty years ago owed much to the staying power of Italian opera. During almost a century, the music scene lived under its tyrannical dominion. Fortunately, certain circumstances were able to protect the output of numerous Cuban musicians, both cultured and popular, from its influence.

9. Antonio Raffelin–Juan París

The continued practice of high-quality music was initiated in Cuba, as we have seen, with the work and example of Esteban Salas. The models offered to a Cuban in forming tastes were those of the eighteenth century: the Neapolitan school, French opera, Haydn's symphonies, and, at a less advanced level, Pleyel, Gossec, and others. This is of utmost importance, since it explains the persistence of modalities of style, classical and baroque, in the artistic production of almost all the Cuban composers of the nineteenth century. Countries of the Americas, such as Brazil and Mexico, that were strongly under the sway of Romantic opera and the European salon romance in the initial stages of composing cultured music would take a long time to shake off that influence. In Cuba, even though Italian opera enjoyed the favor of an audience quickly seduced by its direct and facile sentimentality, this preference did not weaken the resistance of musicians closely linked to the classical tradition by training and habit. Willingly or unwillingly, when a young man sought to study composition, it was the symphonies of Haydn and not the overtures of Bellini that were offered as an example. In Santiago, Juan París luxuriously bound many of the classical masters' scores, making his disciples study them. The best piano teacher in Havana during the first half of the nineteenth century was Edelmann, son of the clavichordist and pianist Juan Federico, of the same surname.

Antonio Raffelin was the composer who bridged music made and heard in Cuba at the end of the eighteenth century and a certain "Cuban classicism"—a nationalism born within the norms of classical writing—and which would later manifest itself in the oeuvre of a Manuel Saumell.

Antonio Raffelin was born in Havana in 1796, the son of a French dragoon captain whose name appears in the chronicles of the English occupation. The mulatto Gregorio Velázquez gave him cello and bass lessons. Quite precocious, he wrote a melody at the age of nine, "La boca" [The mouth], published later in New York. Don Manuel Cocco, director of the Spanish opera company that performed in the Teatro Principal, initiated him into the practice of counterpoint and the fugue. Thomas Tlown, an excellent British musician, gave him violin classes. A master of his craft, Raffelin devoted himself to the noble task of intensifying Havana musical life using all means within his reach. He gave free lessons to recruit the greatest number of aficionados to swell the ranks of an orchestra he directed. He founded the Philharmonic Academy of Cristina, to which Manuel Saumell later belonged. He could not have been a bad violinist—even with all the mistrust that exaggerated accolades of the era inspire—because everyone considered him a superlative performer worthy of great respect.

In 1836, at the age of forty, he achieved one of his greatest ambitions: he moved to Paris—where he arrived with an abundant and mature oeuvre, judging by the fact that he almost immediately handed over three symphonies to be printed. He surveyed the artistic panorama of the moment. The ambience was still permeated with the memory of the worldly triumphs of his compatriot Mercedes de Santa Cruz y Montalvo, the countess of Merlín, an acceptable singer,[1] a great friend of Alfred de Musset and Rossini, very sought out by Balzac, who had transformed her into one of the heroines of his novels, and whose salon was still a meeting place for European celebrities. At the time, Paris did not offer a very hopeful environment for a musician who was as profoundly unworldly as Raffelin. The bourgeois class, paradoxically forged by the Revolution, solidly entrenched in its power by Louis-Philippe, displayed the appetites of the nouveau riche. Monsieur Poirer could pay off the debts of his son-in-law, whose ancestors had landed in Azincourt. But this is not the reason the bourgeois did not inherit the hand-me-down good taste of a nobility that was ingloriously drifting toward the total spiritual emptiness of a Duke of Guermantes.

Times were difficult. Auber, Adam, and the repertoire of Boieldieu and Halévy satisfied the tastes of the day, as far as national production was concerned. Berlioz, unappreciated, was struggling against all odds and against everyone. Rossini had stopped composing. Meyerbeer was the kingpin of the opera stage. It seems as though French audiences had lost all love for the great musical genres. Raffelin, however, did not pretend to reap his laurels by stooping low. He did not stand in line, like so many others, at the doors of the Théâtre des Italiens with a score underneath his arm. In 1845 a quartet for strings was performed, which was published soon afterward. *La Presse* praised the work. In 1848, one of his symphonies was performed, probably the third. The quality of musical criticism of the time can be judged by phrases like this, gleaned from the column of a Parisian daily: "The symphony of Havana violinist and composer Don Antonio Raffelin was applauded with enthusiasm. This symphony modulates with sufficient naturalness [sic], its singing is precise [sic], and as a whole is very brilliant." What is interesting is that Raffelin, in that environment where the lust for theatrical success made the air unbreathable, remained loyal to chamber music and the symphony. This fact indicates a certain strength of character, an uncontaminated will, which would never abandon him.

Back in Havana toward 1848–49, the composer engaged Cuba's musical culture with renewed effort. He organized concerts. He trained new students. He toured through the provinces, and was triumphantly celebrated in Remedios. A little later he suffered a mystical crisis that made him devote the rest of his life's work to religious music. He moved to Philadelphia, where he published a musical newspaper called *La Lira Católica* [The Catholic lyre]. From that moment on, he composed nothing but hymns, motets, Masses, and Passion songbooks. He was responsible for overseeing sixteen dioceses. In 1862, he was in Rome presenting a Mass to the pope, to be sung in the chapel of Saint Ignatius. The same year he offered another Mass to the queen of Spain, with such good fortune that one of its parts was incorporated into the daily Mass of the royal chapel. From Cádiz he went to the United States. In 1867, already aged, he returned to Havana, where the most famous living poets collaboratively edited a *Ramillete* [Bouquet] of songs in his honor. He died in Marianao, near the capital, in 1882.

Although it is difficult to find the works of Antonio Raffelin, since they are dispersed in different North American dioceses, churches of Italy and Spain, or European publishing houses whose collections have disposed of forgotten scores, it can be said that the Havana musician remained loyal to his classical training until he died. When referring to the religious compositions of his last period, certain critics evoke the name of Cherubini. Our efforts have been able to unearth his Third Symphony (edited in Paris). While many Cuban musicians of the time—Laureano Fuentes, among others—tried to spruce up their catalog of works with symphonies that were no more than an overture, Raffelin composed real symphonies, in the tradition of Haydn. From this point of view, he was an extraordinary American precursor of symphonic writing—in the same category as his contemporary, the Argentine Juan Pedro Esnaola, who wrote two symphonies at the beginning of the century.

His Third Symphony in G (opus 26) is simply delectable, constituting living testimony to the excellent cultural level and technical prowess attained by a Cuban musician of that period. The work has four movements: an Allegro (with its well-known *grave*), an Andante amabile, a Minuetto, and an Allegro. It has the exact proportions of a symphony by Haydn (if we take as a general model the proportions conforming to established patterns) and the same kind of orchestration. To give an idea of the musical material it deals with, we will quote from the first theme of the initial Allegro, with a frankly popular flavor:

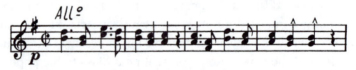

The second motif of the same movement has a charming Rossini-like air to it:

Only in the Andante amabile is there a hint of a discretely Romantic accent. A Romanticism that does not go far beyond a Cherubini—always looking back toward the eighteenth century, typical for a Cuban musician, even when the ambience of the era began filtering through into the composer's inspirations. The finale (in 6/8) constitutes a *saltarello* filled with eloquence and good humor, conceived in the most authentic Haydnesque spirit.

Haydn, who had entered the island through the cathedral doors of Havana and Santiago thanks to Salas and Goetz, continued to be a strong spiritual presence for Cuban composers.

It has been said of the priest Juan París (born in 1759), successor to Salas in the cathedral of Santiago, that "he did not compose works of music."[2] Not only was he an important and productive composer, he also turned out to be the most loyal artistic heir the Havana maestro could have dreamed of. Thanks to París, the church became an academy, a concert hall, a rehearsal space, a library, encouraging continuous and diverse musical events. The purest traditions of the eighteenth century remained intact in the shadow of his teaching, until his successors brought the repertoire of Hilarión Eslava y Mercadente, not to mention the Masses written in an operatic style, to the choir.

After demonstrating his competence by "composing a motet honoring the Holy Trinity" sung with bass and violins, París began his work in 1805, after the Goetz incident. The same year, he handed over to Matías Alqueza, horn and bassoon player in his orchestra as well as the printer of the Colegio San Basilio el Magno, some "lyrics for *villancicos* for four voices, with violins, violas, basses, oboes, flutes, and and other pastoral instruments, to be sung for the solemn matins of the Nativity of Our Lord Jesus Christ." His life was entirely given over to art. When Karl Rischer and Madame Clarais founded their orchestra in Santiago, París lent them his utmost support, offering them scores and performers. In 1812, feeling that his religious duties would not suffer, he began giving piano classes to amateurs in the city, to whom the instrument embodied a true revelation. His music disciples underwent thorough study of works by Porpora, Pergolesi, Paisiello, Cimarosa, Haydn, and Cherubini. He was the first to sponsor a performance of the Beethoven string quartets. In 1837, almost an octogenarian, the priest widened his didactic endeavors, opening the doors to all those who loved music. Anyone who could play an instrument could go to the temple after hours, to read, study, or play the archived scores. There were moments when four groups were working simultaneously in different parts of the building. Bound with iron-gilded covers, the works were available to anyone who requested them. The admirable maestro died on June 11, 1845, leaving, aside from a copious muscial production, a poem in Latin titled "Ad Parnassum." He had trained a generation of musicians.

We have found the following París works: a *Misa a tres, con violines, flautas y bajo* [Mass for three voices with violins, flute, and bass] and a *Villancico de kalenda,* of unusual proportions for this genre, "for four voices with violins, viola, bass, oboes, or flutes" (*¿Hasta cuándo . . . santo cielo?*). Both scores are from 1806 and are highly representative, since the composer had opportunities to reveal his creativity in a score that is amply developed.

París was not endowed with the prolific talent of Salas. In a written document to the town council from the year he was appointed, he complains of excessive work, stating that the labors imposed left him no time for composing *villancicos* and motets — a task "to which I was obligated." When he saw the holiday season approaching and his work was not ready, he was in the habit of resorting to a puerilely disloyal trick: putting new lyrics to *villancicos* left by Salas. The Havana composer had churned them out by the dozens! Were the good canons going to find out about this innocent deceit? At times, to dress them up a bit, he would modify their tonalities, or add a part for viola, or two parts for flute or oboe. In many cases he was content to glue strips of paper over the original lyrics, and would trace the new lyrics with a nervous hand, crossing out an eighth note here, a whole note there, linking or erasing notes in order to reestablish the correct rhythm. Weren't the *villancicos* of Salas excellent material? . . . Let's not mince words: these maneuvers were not the result of any lack of creativity on his part. But París, so attached to meticulous work methods, to the difficult solution, labored much more slowly than his predecessor. He took his art very seriously and was in the habit of posing complicated problems for himself. His orchestration was much more elaborate than Salas's. There was a restlessness, a searching. The modulatory process adjusted itself to new forms. If Salas admired Pergolesi and Paisiello, París had a particular devotion to Righini and Cherubini. Just as Salas tended to give the *villancico* three parts complete in themselves, París, acting with still greater freedom, would write *villancicos* with four parts, breaking any connection to the traditional pattern. The first movement of his *Kalenda* from 1806 alone has 160 bars in quiet time, comprising a true symphonic adagio. Nonetheless, París was inferior to Salas in the prosodic handling of his voices. He did not have the sovereign ability of his predecessor to make word and music a consubstantial, seamless whole. For the same reason, every time he could, he steered the focus of the composition toward the orchestration, his strength. In many cases, without taking the singers into consideration, he would mix them in with the instruments in a true *caccia* [poetic and musical genre, a texted canon for upper voices], letting the voice round out the restless labor of the oboes and violins.

Precisely because París loved difficulty, one sees in his work certain concerns that Salas seems to have overlooked. He gave greater importance to rhythm. He steered away from consecutive thirds in the Neapolitan style—although conserving the traditional sixth chord, which he found pleasing. He used syncopation, the *martellatto* [playing of bowed instruments with sharp, "hammering" blows of the bow to the strings]; he diversified the function of the violin parts. He was much more demanding with the *basso continuo*, clearly indicating his intentions. There are whole passages in which the bass plays an autonomous role, imposing on the performer a precise task, far from any rhythmic improvisation.

As far as musical ideas, París differs appreciably from Salas. Certain passages of his *Villancico de Kalenda* have a frank Mozartian flavor:

The Introit of the Mass that we have found begins dramatically with a brief instrumental prelude that seems a direct copy of Beethoven. But let's not get too carried away. It is the "Beethovian tone" before Beethoven, a tone we can find in the Allegro of Mozart's *Fantasia* (and if one wants to cite a unique case, in the introduction to the *tonadilla* "Los ciegos fingidos" [1774], whose themes and harmonies already foretell, in the most unexpected manner, the Pathétique piano sonata). More inclined to dramatic expression than Salas, more driven to use *tremolos,* creatively and spiritually, París nonetheless remained quite loyal to the norms of his teachers. Antonio Raffelin, this musician from the Santiago cathedral, contributed to maintaining the classical tradition in Cuba until mid-century, despite the frightening presence of Italian Romantic opera.

10. Saumell and Nationalism

On July 17, 1794, the Alsatian composer Jean-Frédéric Edelmann was guillotined in Paris, as a result of a *ténébreuse affaire* [shadowy affair], still unclear, which led to his condemnation by the revolutionary tribunal. A friend of Rouget de Lisle, present in the famous painting *La Marseillaise*, Edelmann was the author of fifteen volumes of sonatas, quartets, and concertos. Some of his works drew Mozart's praise. This musician had been one of the last European clavichordists, before fully devoting himself to the new art of the piano. His son, Jean-Frédéric, was born in Strasbourg, seven months after his father's execution. A student at the Paris Conservatory, he attained first prize in harmony at the age of seventeen. At eighteen he was a first-rate pianist. His father's tragic fate probably made him an expatriate by the end of 1815. The One Hundred Days, Waterloo, made him fear the onset of a new tortuous epoch, like the one his mother would at times evoke with legitimate horror. With her, he embarked for the United States, going through Mexico, the British and Dutch Guyanas, and the Lesser Antilles. After many years of wandering, Jean-Frédéric Edelmann arrived in Havana in mid-1832. His first concert, given at the Teatro Principal, ended with a profusion of ovations. Extremely flattered by his Havana reception, the artist decided to stay in Cuba, forgetting everything that might still tie him to Europe. Soon he was promoted to an important position in the management of the Saint Cecilia Philharmonic Society and, in 1836, he opened a storehouse and musical publishing firm, which would for a long time be a haven for local composers.

Shortly after settling in Havana, he began to give lessons to a self-taught young musician of meager resources, reading, studying, and analyzing the Mass in F by Cherubini, guiding himself with texts by Fétis and Hilarión Eslava. This young musician was Manuel Saumell Robredo.

Born in 1817 into a destitute family, Saumell was destined to die relatively young, after leading a peripatetic, sorrowful existence. An acceptable but not brilliant pianist, he knew the kind of turmoil experienced by those who try "to live by their art" in a meager milieu, where the gift of ubiquity had to make up for slim earnings. He went anywhere to play an instrument. Sweating, huffing and puffing, he ran from the Philharmonic to the Lyceum of Cristina; he gave lessons; played indiscriminately at dances and concerts; or joined the Italian lyric opera company. He performed Beethoven trios with Torinio Segura and Enrique González; he played cello when it was necessary to fill in for a musician; he orchestrated and "arranged" pieces; he would leave the palace of the count of Peñalver, where he had sung parts of *Il pirata,* to take sheet music of a *contradanza* to Tomás Buelta y Flores, director of the dance orchestra at the Tívoli. When the organist at some church was sick, Saumell was there to run his worn-out soles over the pedals. He organized musical gatherings that applauded the phenomenal bassist Bottessini, at the time a guest in Havana. And he still had energy left to work on the piano with Edelmann—although not seriously—and study harmony, counterpoint, fugue, and orchestration with Mauricio Pyke, arranger for the Italian opera company. He was a man with a sense of humor, witty, very creole and quite disinterested in money for someone so poor. Saumell would play for free when he was invited to some benefit concert, even though he was not sure if he could pay the rent. Because he did not attract attention to himself, Espadero and Desvernine treated him with a certain condescension, giving scant importance to his work. Nonetheless, Saumell did not have a bohemian mien like Joaquín Gavira. He was, on the contrary, a truly hard worker, sensitive, generous with others, demanding of himself; he was eager to achieve great things, inspired to great projects, but he was the perennial victim of the lack of time to compose, affecting anyone who attempts to wed dignity and decadence with the dearth of lucrative work.

About 1839, Saumell was hopelessly in love with a splendid woman, Dolores de Saint-Maxent, a singer with an admirable voice who had introduced Schubert's work into Cuba. Unfortunately, the beautiful and much sought out maiden was the daughter of a good family—a wealthy family that in no way wanted to hear of Saumell as a possible son-in-law. Nonetheless, for a time, Dolores encouraged the passion of the young musician. Domingo del Monte allows they must have been boyfriend and girlfriend despite paternal opposition. This romantic situation would have amorous repercussions in Saumell's spirit. Scorned by rich creole lovers of music, who accepted his art as long as he stayed in his place, he dreamed of undertaking a huge enterprise, something capable of crowning him in the eyes of Havana society; something, in any case, that no one had done before in Cuba: to write a national opera.

This fact, overlooked by all those commentators on the life of Saumell, turns out to be highly significant: the composer wanted his opera to be truly Cuban, for the action to take place on the island, and that popular elements of local life be integral to the plot. That is to say, in 1839, only three years after Glinka premiered *Zhin za tsarya* [A life for the czar], inaugurating musical nationalism in Russia, the Cuban intended to write a nationalist opera. In February of that year, the novel *Antonelli,* by José Antonio Echevarría, had been published in *La Cartera Cubana,* which he read and reread, now with fruition. It was a well-written story, but laid out in the pattern of novels by the Viscount of Arlincourt; the plot was not all that bad, but it closed with a pretty detestable denouement. From it a libretto could be extracted, neither better nor worse than those written for *Linda di Chamounix* or *Gemma de Vergy,* which drew applause in the Teatro Principal. *Antonelli,* on the other hand, provided all the qualities of place and atmosphere dreamed of by Saumell.

Quickly, the opera took shape in his mind. The action takes place in Havana in 1590. First scene: a workforce of black slaves labors to set up the machinery of one of El Cerro's first sugar mills. Juan Bautista Antonelli arrives, an Italian engineer, a protégé of Philip II, who had just begun the construction of El Morro Castle. He is accompanied by Hernán Manrique de Rojas, an Extremenian

(Spain), married to an Indian woman, father of a daughter called Casilda, a Siboney quadroon, with whom Antonelli is hopelessly in love. A duet. Antonelli tries to garner Manrique de Rojas's support to conquer the beauty's heart. The father confesses that it is futile: Casilda loves Captain Lupercio Gelabert, nephew of the governor of Havana. Second scene. The Indians play a ball game in the plaza of the Campeche neighborhood, in Antonelli's presence. Captain Gelabert appears, and runs over an Indian, Pablo, whom he hates for some obscure reason. The mistreated Indian approaches Antonelli: "What would you have done in my place?" "I would have driven my sword through him!" "I am not a nobleman; I don't have a sword," says the Indian. "But you do have a knife!" insinuates the engineer... Curtain falls. Second act. First scene: Antonelli dreams at night strolling on the esplanade of the castle La Fuerza. Gelabert appears with a guitar, confiding to him that he is going to serenade a woman. He makes him read some passionate verses, written for her... Second scene. The serenade and love duet of Gelabert and Casilda on a Havana street. Antonelli, hidden, partakes of the scene. Pablo, the Indian, leaps out from the shadows. He is going to wound Gelabert. Antonelli, overtaken by the instilled habits of nobility, stops the homicidal arm. Third Act. First scene. Enclosed in his room of the castle La Fuerza, Antonelli rereads, in tears, the episode of Paolo and Francesca from *The Divine Comedy*. Second scene. A soirée on the upper terrace of El Morro Castle. After the dance, the lovers are alone, contemplating the sea. Pablo, the Indian, quickly appears, and mortally wounds the captain. His body falls into the abyss, dragging Casilda with him. Antonelli, responsible for this double death, collapses "as if struck by lightning," while the Indian, silently, with arms crossed, contemplates the scene.

As one can see, it is an opera of the likes to be conceived in the Havana of 1839. Frankly, the first act could have been good in terms of the action. The second act, done without confidantes and chorus, was a lot better than those that inspired a Donizetti, a Bellini, or even the young Verdi. The third was of a hackneyed Romanticism, with all of the vices of the genre. But something endures: that will to have blacks and Indians sing; that Extremenian married to an indigenous woman; that sugar mill of El Cerro; the ball game; the streets and fortresses of Havana, and the Indian, the native, and the callous abuse perpetrated by a conquistador's son. Domingo del Monte wrote the following in those days to J. L. Alfonso:

> We have here a young Havana resident called Saumell, with a brilliant disposition for music, according to those who know, who, after having made helpful studies of counterpoint and composition, is extremely desirous to undertake the task of writing an opera; but he has no libretto and furthermore he wants it in Italian, and even further it should have a Cuban plot, and, if possible, to be adapted from that beautiful Echevarría novel titled *Antonelli*. . . . So, if you want to write it or have some poet friend of yours do it, and send it to me six months after receiving this letter, I would be most grateful and you will have done a great service to homeland and art.

J. L. Alfonso deemed the writing of an opera based on Cuban concerns something so absurd and deliriously conceived, not to say ridiculous, that he responded with a mocking negative response, and dispatched the matter. As for del Monte, he came to the conclusion that Saumell was in error, contributing, in the end, to discouraging him from the endeavor. But now a powerful reason would finish destroying Saumell's idea of writing a nationalist opera: the splendid Dolores de Saint-Maxent had just finished breaking off with him, opting to romantically pursue the writer Ramón de Palma. His ambitions dashed, profoundly hurt, Saumell went back to his scattered life.

Thinking of Saumell as the father of the nationalist tendency in Cuban music makes this story of a frustrated opera highly interesting. His attempt was without precedent anywhere in the Americas. Demanding a libretto in Italian can easily be explained: the only company that could stage the opera in Havana was an Italian one. In Cuba, it was inconceivable, until the end of the century, to write one in any other language than Italian, and there were even musicians, for lack of their own "bard," who wrote their own texts in a truly macaronic verse. Now, it is worth asking up to what point Saumell would have been able to write ideas of surprising quality on a larger operatic scale, building on his exquisite gifts as a musician accustomed to writing on a smaller scale, within the limited framework of the *Cuban contradanza*. Aside from his locally inspired compositions, he had written little: a "Plegaria" for soprano and organ; a piece for cello and piano; an "Idilio" for violin and piano; an Ave Maria for voice and orchestra. The closest in this type of production to a dramatic score is his "Melopea" (fourteen pages of music), based on a poem by Francisco Blanchié. Every time one goes back and breathes in the atmosphere of the *contradanzas* in this work (in the initial Andante; in the Allegro risoluto), and sees phrases and harmonies marked by a Cuban air, one encounters an enchanted realm. The dramatic-descriptive episodes, however, are written with a tremendous ingenuousness. In the marching part that ends the poem, and which attempts a certain pathos, one can observe the barely disguised proximity of the funeral march of the Eroica Symphony. Saumell, by temperament, was not a Romantic. When he approached the Battle of Hernani with something of his own to say, he adopted a delectably Schubertian tone (the first bars of "The Beautiful Maiden" "La Niña Bonita"). And even then, this is an exception. One of the few times he tried to fit a foreign accent into the *contradanza* genre he had created (*Contradanza-estudio*), he wrote an operatic concertante. He did not know how to deepen the voice. Luckily, in more than fifty *contradanzas*, we have him in full-bodied form.

We should not linger, at times somewhat disappointed, over certain *contradanzas* of Saumell's, written on the fly, God knows under what circumstances, to be premiered at dances. They are not all that bad, but they are put together formulaically, without greater ambition than stimulating the dancers and pleasantly marking the beat. One must go further, reading and selecting. One then penetrates into a zone of more profound concerns, filled with tender pages, emotional, refined, or, on the contrary, dramatic, agitated, nervous, where the presence of a good composer prevails. Many of his *contradanzas* — this group is among his best — were not composed for dancing. Obviously, *Recuerdos tristes* [Sad memories], *Lamentos de amor* [Love's laments], *Toma Tomás* [Take it Tomás], and others, were written to be played and listened to, and as such reveal that, for Saumell, the genre turned out to be a form that suited his sensibility, which he had proposed to exploit under every conceivable angle, exhausting all its possibilities. It is possible to claim that Saumell revealed a weakness in adjusting his ideas to a pattern of eight plus sixteen bars, or of sixteen plus sixteen (with some irregular applications of the rules). However, Saumell's rhythmic and melodic inventiveness is astonishing. In the fifty-plus *contradanzas* of his that merit close attention, *no two pages are alike*. He never repeats himself. In 2/4 time, or in 6/8, he inscribes an incredible variety of rhythmic combinations. Composed of two parts—*prima* and *segunda*—Saumell's *contradanzas* always encompass a willful contrast. The *prima* often starts off with a great air of a classical concerto ("La territorial," "La Josefina") already establishing the variation rhythmically when the initial theme is restated. Other times, Saumell's *prima* is a delicious romance that stands on its own, or an agitated page, almost with pathos, like the one that opens "La Luisiana," dedicated to Gottschalk. The *segunda*, on the other hand, is always very Cuban, of purely folkloric flavor—that is, when the folkloric element is not simply a direct expression of his musical sensibility. In this part he habitually conjoins in different ways the "tango" rhythm that nourished the *guaracha* in its beginnings, and other combinations already created by the intuition of dance musicians. The *cinquillo*, already characteristic of Cuban music from the eastern province, was unknown to him. It occasionally appears in one of his *contradanzas* ("El somatén" [The hubbub]), but so isolatedly that it seems more the product of an imagination of someone who was so concerned with searching for new rhythmic values.

Saumell is absolutely prophetic in regard to fixing certain rhythms that will be mined in the future under different names. The notion that Miguel Faílde, the mulatto musician from Matanzas, "created" the *danzón*, spawning it in 1879,[1] comes apart when one reads a popular *contradanza* of Saumell called "La Tedezco." All of the elements of the Cuban *danzón* are foreshadowed in the first eight bars of this piece. Nothing will be added to it—except some additional parts—until approximately 1920, the year in which that very Cuban dance form's dominance began to decline. But there is more: in the *segundas* of his contradanzas in 6/8, Saumell insistently uses a rhythm composed of a quarter note, two eighth notes, a quarter note (the choriamb), which in the future would be inseparable from the genres that many have claimed have a life of their own. The *clave,* the *guajira,* the *criolla,* which musicians of good popular inspiration were going to write, such as Anckermann, Mauri, Casas Romero, and others, rely on this kind of rhythm. If a difference can be observed between the *clave,* the *guajira,* and the *criolla,* it is merely superficial: the type of melody, tempo, harmonic atmosphere—simpler in a *clave,* more ambitious in the *criolla.* But the rhythmic and tonal base is the same. Hence, Saumell is not only the father of the *contradanza,* as it has been called. He is the father of the habanera (the *prima* of "La amistad"), the *danzón* ("La Tedezco"), the *guajira* (the *segunda* of "La Matilde"), the *clave* ("La Celestina"), the *criolla* (the *segunda* of "La Nené"), and of certain modalities of the Cuban song (the *segunda* of "Recuerdos tristes"). Everything done after him would amplify or distinguish elements plainly exposed in his works.

Saumell was in the habit of writing charming notes over a bar: "con sandunga ..." [with funky grace]. But this said, he does not forget his attachment to the classical tradition. Over one of his *contradanzas* he puts the title *Los chismes de Guanabacoa"* [Gossip from Guanabacoa], but in reality he writes a minuet in lively tempo, before going on to a very Cuban idea. The same can be said of "La dengosa," with its short canon; and of "La suavecita" and "La caridad," both almost Mozartian. In Saumell there is an economy of means that the Romantic Espadero would ignore, to be inherited by Ignacio Cervantes, despite having been trained in the shadow of Chopin and Mendelssohn.

Manuel Saumell died on August 14, 1870. His work was that of a minor master, but it has great meaning for the history of musical nationalisms on our continent. Filled with discoveries, his work for the first time traced the exact profile of creole identity, creating a peculiar "climate," a melodic, harmonic, and rhythmic atmosphere that would endure in the creations of his successors. He knew how to live on the margins of the salon style — virtuoso, brilliant, superficial — so typical of Gottschalk. He remained loyal —

like Raffelin, like París—to types of classical writing, and never saw them as incompatible with a national expression. Thanks to him, the constituent elements of a "Cubanness," which permeated the environment and emerged from the dance halls, fully became "a musical fact and event" filled with implications. Saumell's work, by drawing a line of demarcation, allowed elements of popular culture to nourish a conscientious musical speculation. It was a passage from mere rhythmic instinct to the consciousness of a style. The idea of nationalism had been born.

11. Espadero, the Romantic

Nicolás Ruiz Espadero was a man whose life and death were equally strange. Living in Havana, a city of open doors, he had the minimum contact with the outside world. Only familiar with a tropical ambience—so little given to inhibitions—Espadero lived in a long romantic dream, filled with distant images, without any rapport with the sonorous reality bubbling at the foot of his window, always barred shut. However, he was the most famous Cuban composer of his time—the only one who, without having traveled, was applauded and published abroad; the only one of his Havana contemporaries who could be compared to the great maestros of the time. Little, very little, of his work has been saved throughout the years. No one has claimed his legacy. However, the historical interest of his personality is undeniable. A musical tradition does not only feed on its achievements; it is also nourished by its errors. What must be avoided is just as instructive as the model that engenders new ideas. Seen from a current perspective, Espadero's universal worth is null, but locally his case merits examination.

Son of a pianist mother from Cádiz who distinguished herself in the Havana salons around 1810 performing Haydn and Mozart, Nicolás Ruiz Espadero was born in 1832. As tends to happen in many bourgeois families, the father, Don Nicolás Ruiz, although an art lover and flattered by his wife's talent, did not want a son devoted to music in any way. He dreamed of making him a man with a future in the colony: a lawyer, a soldier, a functionary... However, that nervous and sensitive boy—too sensitive—showed such signs of ability on the piano that the father gave in and allowed him a half-hour class a day. With his mother's complicity he really played the piano for several hours daily. So that the neighbors would not hear their indiscretions, Espadero would cover the resonating chamber with thick blankets. Aside from this, in a corner of Havana, a good child of the times was being formed. He never went to school, receiving an undisciplined home education, enrichened by haphazard and anxious readings. He did not have friends his own age, living exclusively with his family, under the constant vigilance of his mother. One can only imagine what that adolescence was like, in shadows, without struggle, without outside confrontations, without enlivening emulations. He was sixteen when his father, without previous warning, dropped dead in his presence. This blow, the widowhood of his mother, the long mourning period, further reduced, if that were possible, Espadero's horizons. He would not go out, did not accept invitations, and would not frequent the promenades. He spent the days reading, drawing, composing. At twilight, he would go to a music store close to his house to play piano until eight o'clock at night. He could not tolerate a presence at his side at those moments. Espadero was a pure case of introversion. His adolescent neurosis became more pronounced with the passing of time, making him appear unsociable, sullen, or weird. He had an uncontrollable love of cats. He was flattered by the admiration of some women, with whom he was delicate, attentive, like someone who understood certain weaknesses, but he was horrified of marriage. A true loner, amorous feelings occupied a scant place in his heart: the sublimity of the feminine ideal was his mother.

When he turned twenty-two, a man came momentarily to take him out of his voluntary cloistered life: Louis Moreau Gottschalk. An afternoon in 1854 found Espadero pounding away at full force on a piano when Gottschalk, recently arrived in Havana, entered the room without being introduced. Passing by, he had been attracted by the excellent sound of what the Cuban was playing on the keyboard. Espadero, in the presence of an unknown (he had never even seen a picture of Gottshalk), pronounced his name without hesitation. From that moment on, an ardent and romantic friendship developed between the two musicians, always fueled by questions, doubts, technical advice, lyric outbursts, anathemas against critics and philistines, afflictions, rebellious acts, all peppered with quotes from Hugo, Byron, Taine, and musical passages interspersed in their conversations. Espadero's friendship with Gottschalk is even a stranger case if we take into account that it would be difficult to imagine two people with more opposed views on life. Gottschalk, a North American from Louisiana, was a man of strong temperament, with a voracious appetite for pleasure, always impelled to physical action. His gallant trysts were innumerable. A Southener from a slave state, in his trips through the Antilles he enjoyed having love affairs of a strong local color, at variance with the racial prejudices of his home state. He would make arduous excursions to a fishing village just to eat crabs. His letters, written in French, filled with sly, intelligent observations about the customs and natural beauty of the country visited, were chock full of those *gueulardises* [gutter talk] that we find in Flaubert's correspondence, when he was not speaking of art in an exalted tone. These risqué stories would set off the chaste Espadero, as when he spoke of weddings that were never formalized in church. He loved applause, receptions, low-cut gowns, perfume. Espadero, on the other hand, had an almost pathological aversion to any public event.

One has to believe, invoking a psychological process that is quite common, that Espadero found in Gottschalk the image of what he would never become. All of his inhibitions were the ones Gottschalk tossed aside. Furthermore, this man three years his senior appeared escorted by the trumpets of fame. Théophile Gautier had sung his praises. Berlioz had called him "the poet of the piano." Some were intrepid enough to put him on a par with Chopin. The queen of Spain, the queen of Portugal, the grand duchess of Russia had stuffed his pockets with letters for captain generals and ambassadors. Knighted into the order of Isabel the Catholic, he was a guest of honor in Havana. In Valladolid, the count Pierro had him inspect the cavalry batallion of Farnesio. He was published in Paris and New York. He brought all the honors back from a Europe that Espadero would never get to know.

If the friendship with Gottschalk directly resulted in having the Cuban's work published and disseminated in France and Spain, with covers that ostentatiously wrote his name "Monsieur Espadero, de la Havane," this friendship bore little fruit in the artistic realm. Gottschalk was the typical product of an era that erected altars to the virtuoso. Liszt was more admired in the salons as a virtuoso than as a composer. Virtuosos like Thalberg kept proliferating, foreshadowing the brilliant superficiality of Sarasate and his imitators. At heart, what was asked of a contemporary performer or composer was the spirit of an operatic tenor. The brilliant fantasy, the paraphrase of a concerto, the capriccio, the well-known segment, the descriptive piece, filled up too many concert programs. Formed in that atmosphere, with no need for self-doubt since he had already received the backing of world eminences, Gottschalk let himself be strung along by his triumphs, from court to court, island to island, without seeing beyond his agile fingers. Speaking of composition, he said to Espadero, putting forth a one and only axiom: "All of the rules don't consist of anything except to agreeably wound a cultivated ear (I said: cultivated)." His preoccupation with showy effects was such that he could sign his name to serious mistakes like this:

> Haydn, Clementi, Mozart, before Beethoven, Dussek, Cramer, and Moscheles a little later, wrote charming works, correct and frequently inspired [sic], but none of them could guess all of the advantage gained by using the piano pedals, of the breadth of accompaniment given the piano's unique sound, relieving one of having to solve the dissonance in the same octave, and in an act of illusion do it in any higher one, regardless of its distance from the original chord, thereby achieving an unfurling, an opulence of sonorities unknown to all the other instruments.... Despite his talent, Beethoven sometimes made mistakes with certain effects, which, on paper, seem to respond to his thought, but on the keyboard sound otherwise.

It is a shame that Gottschalk was so dominated by a spirit that would turn the great tempest of Romanticism into fleeting breezes. A shame because this musician, eminently a charming fellow, had great moments of intuition. Longing for the nights of the Sierra del Afena, filled with grasshoppers and fireflies, he wrote to Escudier, his Parisian publisher:

The only female company I found in that solitude was a really ugly black woman, but at night she would cuddle up at my feet, on the veranda, and there, in the middle of the dark, she would sing to me in that penetrating voice, wild, and yet full of strange charm, the songs of her country and the black ballads with violent rhythms and monotonous melodies. She would keep the beat, sometimes with the movement of her head, and at others, softly clapping her hands. Our ideas on dance evoke but memories of a sickly gymnastics, performed in the company of a beautiful woman; on the other hand, the dancing of blacks encompasses an entire poetic realm: shaking, serpentine undulations, a repressed passion, a feverish love; it is love, suffering, all linked up into a tumultuous and inflexible rhythm.

Gottschalk's greatest merit is to have been the first musician with European training to have generally noticed the richness of Cuban, Puerto Rican, and African American rhythms. Louisiana inspired two compositions, *Banjos* and *Bamboula;* Puerto Rico, a *Danza* and *La marcha de los jíbaros;* Cuba, aside from a fantasy based on the eastern *Cocoyé,* some ten *Danzas.* Unfortunately, hardly a strong melody or interesting rhythm are to be found in them, they were mere expositions; the "embellishments" appear, the tremolos, the appoggiaturas in consecutive octaves, the arpeggios, the chromatic scales, and everything that, because of their uselessness, would, in the near future, become synonymous with bad taste.

One exception must be made, however: two lost symphonies whose quality (or lack thereof) has not been proven. There is one fact that leads us to believe that when the musician forgot the salon, he could express himself in a more creative idiom. In 1861, Gottschalk organized a monstrously large festival in Havana's Teatro Tacón, to premiere a symphony of his (the third), titled *Una noche en el trópico* [A night in the tropics]. Unable to employ an orchestra, he mobilized forty pianos, played by Espadero, Saumell, Desvernine, Cervantes, Edelmann, Laureano Fuentes, and all of the responsible performers he could muster. One detail stands out in particular: on percussion they brought the king of a *cabildo de negros* [black self-help association], with an entire arsenal of drums.

One of these, a gigantic *tumba*, occupied center stage, played by the king himself. Gottschalk, therefore, became the first musician to use a symphonic score with Afro-Cuban percussion—a feat only to be repeated in 1925, with Amadeo Roldán's *Obertura sobre temas cubanos*. In passing, it bears saying that one of the movements of this symphony—the Andante—has recently been published in the United States by Quinto Maganini. It is the only fragment of the work that has been found, and its quality is considerably superior to Gottschalk's pianistic compositions. Above all, a certain central passage harmonically anticipates the chromaticism of *Tristan und Isolde*, revealing a fertile, creative restlessness.

Espadero, timid and introspective, was not particularly interested in this aspect of Gottschalk's oeuvre. What seduced him was the other part, which had been praised by Liszt and Théophile Gautier; that which smacked of Europe and was dear to his favorite ideas, to be found in the preface of *Cromwell* or *William Shakespeare* by Victor Hugo. When he was given the honor of ordering and correcting a definitive edition of Gottschalk's posthumous works, at the request of his editor, Léon Escudier, he wrote a prologue revealing his most intimate convictions:

> With numbing frequency we see notable works rejected or considered second-rate for the only—and truly strange— reason that they were not written within the forms mapped out by the so-called classical school, and designated by the hallowed names of sonata, concerto, scherzo, symphony, and so on, forms created by other previous geniuses, but they do not in any way obligate a composer's manifestations of genius or expression of feeling to be enclosed within these limits. Scholastic concerns are, in our judgment, the most terrible pitfall for works of art, above all the arts that express sentiments, as does music, the most ideal of all art forms.... We believe that what is great and beautiful must be draped in new, unforeseen forms, drawing on the infinite and boundless aspects of feeling. As for the rest, in matters of art, form is, in our judgment, secondary; thought is everything. What does the shape matter if the stone is precious?... The *impulse of feelings* should not be limited, prescribing to it some measure, some limit, a form that imprisons and places inspiration in chains.

Forty years after the Battle of Hernani, Espadero insists on the ideas of 1830. Gottschalk had spoken to him about *Rienzi* and *Tannhäuser* by Wagner, beginning a sudden turn in his musical views—somewhat more serious than what he had previously admired. But Gottschalk's words were ignored.

For the moment, what remained with Espadero was the bad example of the pompous and thundering fantasy based on the "Miserere" of *Il Trovatore*, of the "Hurrah-gallop" of the *Danse Ossianesque*, and of that incredible symphony for ten pianos—*El sitio de Zaragoza* [The siege of Saragossa]—that had been performed by Gottschalk, Arizti, Desvernine, and Espadero himself, with six more pianists, a few years earlier. The memory of the second triumphal period of Gottschalk in Havana, in 1857, remained, one in which the virtuosity of his fingers was teamed up with the vocal virtuosity of the girl Adelina Patti.

The spirit that animates the best-known phase of Espadero's work can be articulated by merely quoting their titles: *Vals satánico* [Satanic waltz], *Tarantela furiosa* [Furious tarantella], *El lamento del poeta* [The poet's lament], *Ossián, Canto del alma* [Song of the soul], *La caída de las hojas* [Fallen leaves], *Recuerdos de antaño* [Memories of yesteryear], *Barcarola*, two *Ballads*, *Voces de Sión cautiva* [Voices of captive Zion], written for two pianos. He did, of course, write fantasies based on *I Puritani, Norma*, and *Il Trovatore*. Titles that say a lot, too much. Titles that dangerously evoke the names of his contemporaries Ascher, Beyer, Prudent, Billema. However, the Cuban was superior to all of them, at a level above the composers applauded in the salons of Paris, London, and Madrid. In Nicolás Ruiz Espadero there was a true musician. Take the first three pages of the romance without lyrics, *Pureza y calma* [Purity and calm], published in Leipzig. It has musical content and excellent style. Rare were the cases of Latin American composers in the same period capable of writing in that fashion. The theme, with its creole nonchalance, its refined writing, fills the page with charm. There are passages in the central part of this composition that reveal a solid understanding of harmony. But turn the page. The first theme returns "enriched" with embellishments à la Gottschalk, which flaunts, implacably, a datedness exhausted by its vices. Because of a unique phenomenon that creates all the interest of this case, the

Cuban musician of the nineteenth century who was most concerned with expressing himself in a universal language—or what he thought was universal—turned out to be the most limited by phrasing and systems that were the fruits of a passing fashion. When he wrote his famous *Canto del esclavo* [Song of the slave], what he wound up composing was the song of the slave owner. Surrounded by real black people, hearing their songs, hearing the drums on Three Kings Day that must have echoed in the patios of his house on Cuba Street, Espadero never thought of utilizing pure elements at his disposal to give us a legacy of a true "song of the slave." With its operatic introduction, its grandiose finale enriched by tremolos, he wrote a *Canto del esclavo* that a French or Italian musician of 1850 might have conceived of writing.

One time Espadero turned toward Cuba's folklore, writing a *Canto del guajiro* (opus 61), *grande scène caractéristique cubaine,* published in Paris. His warning to French performers contained more than one accurate idea:

> In this composition I wanted to paint one of the characteristic scenes of creole peasants, and to make known, at the same time, one of the diverse rhythms of Cuba, whose music, far from rejecting the rules of musical art in terms of style and expression, on the contrary, demands their exact application. This is so true that the principal basis of creole musical manifestation is melody, at times tinged with languidness and melancholy, at times flirtatious and voluptuous, indolently cooing over a backdrop of a tormentous accompaniment, but symmetric. In this fragment . . . I have tried to translate local expression and color, maintaining their slightest nuances, even in cases that might be considered as rudimentary lapses of harmony.

Gottschalk had already expressed a very analogous idea:

> The difficulty in performing the music of the Antilles consists in highlighting the melody over the tormenting but symmetrical background of the bass line, with a songlike sonority and a *morbidezza* characteristic of creole music, also moving with the naturalness of the ad libitum and of the tempo rubato within the beat, without exceeding, however, its extreme limits.

This *Canto del guajiro* has thirteen pages, which hold up very well, with an interesting rhythmic insistence, until the coda. Once again, here is where Espadero succumbs under the pressures of contemporary taste, writing a transcendentally executed finale, with a luxury of brilliant chords, sudden tremolos, and a concluding phrase that has nothing to do, by its very character, with what has gone on before. A passage in eighths, "con molto impetu," is the finishing touch—as they would say in bullfighting—to a composition that could have maintained a unity of style, within a discrete folkloric inspiration. Herein lies Espadero's weakness. Liszt, lest we forget, was the only one of his time who triumphantly passed through the era of the salon virtuoso without losing his head.

However, something tells us that Espadero, in his final years, was aware of the bad examples that had marred his work. It is amazing that the man who had written the prologue to the posthumous works of Gottschalk condemning form and proclaiming freedom of expression as a supreme right would compose, among his last works, a scherzo, a sonata, various études, and a trio. These pages show a will to pare down the writing and to return and undo the many mistakes made. Espadero seemed to understand that until then he had only scratched the surface of Romanticism, without getting to the heart of the matter. His thought starts to blaze a deeper path. Form makes it a necessity for him. He recedes into himself, looking for the pure elements remaining in him. A little more searching and he would have discovered Brahms.

But it was too late. It was alarming to see neurosis completely dominate him. While Paris continued to accept his work, while newspapers in Madrid eulogized him, while Cuba did not know what to do to flatter him anymore, Espadero increasingly isolated himself, living almost exclusively with his pianos and his cats. He was embittered, faced with an environment he saw as too meager. He distanced himself from his colleagues, gruffly reproaching them for "not having created a serious institution for the teaching of music." On the other hand, he was in the habit of showing profound tenderness toward his favorite disciples, among whom was the admirable pianist Angelina Sicouret. He died on August 30, 1890, as a result of accidental burns. Almost all of his last works—the most interesting ones—remained unpublished.

The Espadero case is highly significant. It shows us how dangerous it can be for a musician of the Americas to unquestioningly accept European tendencies. One can say that it is also a matter of being more discerning. What happened with Espadero and virtuoso Romanticism, however, was repeated many times with Impressionism. It still happens with the young Argentine, the young North American, who now write music in the twelve-tone method. The truth—our truth—is not necessarily in Paris or Vienna. Poor Saumell, with all of his limitations, *found his truth* shuttling between the El Morro Castle and the dances at the Tivoli. He had an obscure and modest intuition of that great phrase coined by Unamuno: "We find the universal in the core of the local, and in the confined and limited, we find the eternal." Amadeo Roldán reasoned likewise. Nowadays, so does an Heitor Villa-Lobos.

12. Ignacio Cervantes

Ignacio Cervantes Kawanagh was Cuba's most important musician of the nineteenth century. It is possible that others — a Laureano Fuentes, a Gaspar Villate — have an advantage over him with a greater volume of compositions. But no one ranks higher in solidity of craft, innate good taste, distinctive ideas, elegance of style, a full sound, manifested even in his minor works. Even when he "arranged" a *contradanza* by someone else to satisfy a publisher's demand, he would round it out with refined harmonic traces, ennobling the piece. Ignacio Cervantes also was, lest we forget, the first Cuban composer to handle the orchestra with a modern sense of the métier.

Born in Havana on July 31, 1847, Ignacio Cervantes found no obstacles in devoting himself to his artistic vocation. His father, a distinguished dilettante, had great respect for the musical profession. For that reason, in 1859 he placed his son in the hands of Espadero — then the most expensive and highly regarded professor — who made him work on all of Kalkbrenner, Cramer, Clementi, Moscheles, Henselt, Alkan, and Dussek, before putting him in contact with the great classical and Romantic masters. As expected, Espadero included Thalberg and Gottschalk in the great repertory; but one has to believe that Cervantes, by instinct, was able to separate the sublime from the mediocre, if we are to judge by the influences on his oeuvre. Not even in his youth was he prey to the love of virtuosity that poisoned the era. With a sure hand, he went right to the bone, free of gaudy ornamentation. In 1865, at eighteen, he was sent to Paris to enter the imperial Conservatory. After honing his skills with Marmontel and Alkan, he won a grand prize for piano in 1866, playing Hertz's Fifth Concerto. In 1868 he won awards in harmony for works that are still preserved and reveal an exceptional sureness of hand. Among his student papers we have found, moreover, a magnificent fugue, and some variations on a given theme, which already foreshadow the writing of the *Danzas*.

In Paris Cervantes led the life of the busy student who wasted no time. He aspired to the Prix de Rome [Rome Prize], but was not admitted because he was a foreigner. Nonetheless, this fact shows that the young Cuban was sure of his talents. Before dying, Rossini admitted him into his intimate circle, sat him down at his Pantagruelian table, and revealed to him the secrets of an armoire filled with wigs. Liszt held him in great esteem as a pianist. After a brief stay in Madrid, Cervantes returned to Cuba. After Raffelin, he was the first local composer to have breathed the airs of Europe. He must have found the contrast cruel, if we think of how Havana had just begun to free itself from operatic tyranny, and how serious concerts of the time were in short supply and poorly financed. Beethoven's symphonies were played on a reduced scale for small groups, if not as piano transcriptions for four hands. The circle of accomplished performers was tiny. However, Cervantes was not discouraged. He gave recitals, playing various Beethoven sonatas, works by Chopin, Mendelssohn, Liszt, as well Bach preludes and fugues. He was an admirable pianist; later he was compared to Von Bulow, in the United States, and praised by Paderewski. The story goes that soon after his return, a stranger approached him with a piano manuscript, beseeching him to eliminate what he deemed superfluous. Cervantes, armed with his red pencil, imprinted on the margins a series of concise and solemn notes. After returning the work, he found out that it belonged to Nicolás Ruiz Espadero. His old teacher never forgave the deed, despite the now useless apologies that Cervantes offered him. Nonetheless, in his last years Espadero recognized on varied occasions that his disciple, as a pianist, was *"a beast"* — in the laudatory Cuban sense of the word.

Toward 1872, despite spreading himself thin by giving classes, playing in churches, offering concerts, frequenting the philharmonic societies, Cervantes's economic situation could not have been very comfortable, judging by the moving letter he wrote to his father asking for permission to get married, and at the same time begging that he make space in the family home for his future bride since they were not able to establish themselves on their own. In December 1832, the wedding took place. The young newlywed, María Amparo Sánchez Richeaux, would bear him fourteen children. Jokingly, Cervantes sometimes said that he "aspired to form an orchestra with his offspring." But in those days, other concerns profoundly troubled his heart. As of 1868, Cubans, in the *manigua* [the bush],[1] were fighting for their independence. While certain weak-kneed composers genuflected before the Spanish authorities, providing them with *contradanzas* glorifying the volunteers [pro-colonial civilian militia known for its brutality], Cervantes remained strangely silent. In 1875 he was urgenty brought to the captain general, who boasted of his admiration for him:

"Ignacio Cervantes . . . We are now certain that the money you collect in your concerts winds up in the hands of the insurrectionists. Leave before I'm obligated to throw you in jail! . . . Where do you want to go?"

"To the United States," said the musician. "It is the closest country to Cuba, and there I can continue to do what I was doing here."

Stunned, the captain general let him leave. Cervantes lived four years in the United States giving concerts. His artistic and economic situation was brilliant in 1879, the year in which he found out that his father was gravely ill. On the other hand, the Ten Years War (1868–78) had lamentably concluded with the treaty of El Zanjón. [Antonio] Maceo [pro-independence revolutionary general who rejected the peace treaty] had preferred exile instead of a peace he could not accept. The Spanish, for their part, were anxious to forget the cruel struggle that had lasted a decade. An only son, close to a father who had never opposed his career, Cervantes returned in time to see him die. Loaded down with children, he stayed in Cuba. When the war flared up again, he escaped from the horrors of the blockade and fled to Mexico, where he was given extraordinary honors. President Porfirio Díaz generously protected him and encouraged him to stay in the country. But in 1900, once the Spanish-Cuban-American War was over, and close to the birth of the republic [1902], Cervantes, who had been so Cuban in his life and work, returned to his homeland. In 1902 he made one last trip, as "ambassador of Cuban music" to the Charleston Exposition.

Ignacio Cervantes died on April 29, 1905, as a result of a strange softening of the encephalic tissue, and a perforation in the skull, caused, according to the opinion of some doctors, by his odd habit of writing music during the wee hours of the morning in almost complete darkness.

Ignacio Cervantes had lived in Paris during the Second Empire. This fact is extremely important in understanding the somewhat scattered nature of his work, dealt out among scores for symphonies, opera, salon music, and the zarzuela. Cervantes was a contemporary of Chabrier and Saint-Saëns. He had seen Chabrier tackle light music; he had seen Saint-Saëns write for the salon. In the Paris of Napoleon III, the winners of first prizes given at the Conservatory did not feel they had lowered their creative standards by writing a waltz or emulating Lecocq (and what admiration Saint-Saëns had for Lecocq!), creating a habit that endured until our times, with Milhaud and Honegger writing operettas. The fact is important when speaking of one of our composers, because it places him in a peculiar position among his contemporaries who were looking to Madrid. Cervantes was a musician formed by French training. He had little to do with nineteenth-century Spain, full of composers of light music who rarely wrote serious music because truly their world consisted of the zarzuela. Cervantes was the complete opposite: his world was comprised of serious music. His incursions into light music were episodic. He was not drawn to it for money, or because the medium suggested a practical way to utilize his skills as sanctioned by custom. His zarzuela "Los saltimbanquis" [The mountebanks] was never staged. His other zarzuela, "El submarino Peral" [The Peral submarine], was too carefully crafted to become popular. In an era in which his contemporaries were writing best-selling piano pieces, Cervantes composed his waltz "Hectograph," his waltz "La paloma" [The dove], conceiving them directly for orchestra. These waltzes were closer to Saint-Saëns and Arensky than current productions written by dance

musicians. They were lighthearted pieces, of course, but in the manner of Chabrier's operetta *L'Étoile,* or of Messager's in *Véronique.*

In 1879, the year of his political exile, Cervantes wrote his Symphony in C. A word of caution: this is not a symphony in the exact
sense of the word, but an orchestral overture. He adheres to a tri-
partite structure, with an amply elaborated central part: Allegro
maestoso, Andante tranquilo, Allegro vivace. The idea of the Andante tranquilo has a rare distinctive melody, free of any emotion
imposed by Italian opera. If one were to look for a point of comparison, Bizet would come to mind. The same type of inspiration
can be found in a *Romanza* for orchestra, written a little later.

The *Scherzo capriccioso* (1886) is a short masterpiece of refinement and good taste. In character, it is not far removed from the
"scherzo" of *A Midsummer Night's Dream* [Mendelssohn], being,
without a doubt, the best-orchestrated score in all of Cuba's nineteenth century. Elaborately constructed, experimenting with the
most delicate of orchestral timbres, this scherzo needs no self-
justification, as do so many Latin American scores of the last century, admissible as period pieces in terms of influences, and environment, and, for the same reason, offering more historical than
musical interest. The *Scherzo capriccioso* of Cervantes is, above all,
good music, and as such its more recent performances do not dis-
appoint new generations; on the contrary, they enhance the stature
of its composer. The orchestra totally reponds to the composer's
intentions in a very Mendelssohnian way: without clumsiness,
without any errors of balance, with no decline in the quality of
sound. As we listen to it, we understand why Cervantes, in no way
intimidated by the presence of competitors, intended to garner the
Prix de Rome in Paris. (Among Cervantes's papers we have found
another scherzo, quite interesting, although in a simpler style, written for violin, viola, and cello.)

In 1895, Cervantes took on the task of writing an opera: *Maledetto.* Unfortunately, the eagerly awaited text by a certain Da Costa
was so at odds with his temperament that we cannot imagine how
he could think of using it. *Maledetto* has erroneously been called a
zarzuela.[2] It has nothing to do with this theatrical genre. It is a
comic opera (copied from the French *opéra comique*) in three acts,

with tumultuous action constantly tending toward tragedy. But if the structure of the libretto is French, the story line is Italian, of an aesthetic that was already very outdated when it was conceived, reminiscent of *La forza del destino* or *Il Trovatore*. The drama takes place in Rome and Madrid in the sixteenth century. It is a somber work with hidden motives that deals with two twins unaware of their relation. Thinking himself the identical likeness of a Spanish gentleman, Maledetto kills him, taking his place. It has an ending in which the theme of being identified by a mark on the body conventionally closes the third act, with the unexpected return of the victim and the death of the criminal brother. The environment of the times must have had great influence on Cervantes—it had been sixteen years since he had returned from Europe—for him, who was so informed, so skillful, so intelligent in the conception of his music, to begin working on that text. Who knows what he could have accomplished if he had tried to make a reality of Saumell's dream of writing a national opera!

But if the opera libretto gave off a terrible whiff of mothballs from an Italian closet, the music, on the other hand, is at a different level. The first two acts are finished, complete with orchestration. From the third act, only two or three final numbers are missing. Here, no one lives in a castle made of cardboard rocks. The orchestra authoritatively moves with lightness and grace. The introduction to the first act, with its Roman festival atmosphere, makes one think of Bizet's best moments. It is the type of sonority from the interludes and quintet of *Carmen*, with a more honed writing in the string quartet. The style is vivid, alert, nervous. The strings and woodwinds overlap each other, support one another, avoid each other, moved more by a chamber-type writing than the dramatic effects of Romantic opera. Cervantes has not forgotten his *Scherzo*. Here, once again, one can observe the modernity of a musician who had already returned from and left behind many commonplaces. Unfortunately, a libretto tends to impose its own will. Certain episodes obligate the the musician to deepen the voice. But, curiously, in a particularly tragic moment—the aria where Maledetto discovers the identity of his victim—there is a phrase with a peculiarly Cuban flavor. In trying to find operatic pathos,

Cervantes, by some obscure interior process, suddenly expresses himself in a language reminiscent of the melancholy of certain sad *criollas* speaking of deaths and betrayals.

The truth is that Ignacio Cervantes, if we momentarily forget what his *Scherzo* achieved, was particularly gifted in speaking the language of his island. Hence his celebrated *Danzas* for piano comprise the most authentic expression of his temperament. Like certain Norwegian, Spanish, or Slavic musicians, Cervantes always ended up returning to the cadences of his native soil, finding in it his most profound truth, even when he aspired to express himself in an idiom free of localisms. To start with, note that in Cervantes's nationalist work—that which is centered on the *Danzas,* with an *Intermezzo* for orchestra and some piano compositions of minor importance—he does not swerve from a firm tradition in Cuba, via the work of Saumell and of the lesser authors of *contradanzas,* of always remaining loyal to the procedures of classical writing. It is the logically direct result of a kind of music that acquired its form and style in the shadow of the great masters from the end of the eighteenth century and of the composers of stage *tonadillas.* If Cervantes took something from Romanticism, it was a certain air à la Chopin that is manifested in some of his *Danzas*—but not in all of them. And it is the Chopin of the simplest mazurkas; never the Chopin of the scherzi or of the great Polonaises. Furthermore, observe that in his piano works—the most cleanly constructed by any Cuban composer—there is no room for the ostentatious virtuosity so pleasing to many in his day. A first-rate performer who played Liszt, Cervantes expressed himself with sobriety, without saturating the staffs. A disciple of Espadero, his output renounced the affected pianistic devices to which his teacher was addicted. Trained in the Paris of the *fantaisie brillante,* the musician rejects the vertiginous arpeggio, the bravura passages, the *prestissimo* scales, the "ornament." His line is always precise, clear, bare, with great airy spaces between the notes. And not only that. Despite his love for Chopin, a love that is frequently noted in his harmonic climate, but not fully in the type of writing, he reflects very little of the Romantic spirit when he writes a Cuban score. On the other hand, he maintains obvious links to the classical manner of Saumell. Although he does not so categorically obey the contrast between the *prima* and the *segunda* sections, both endure in his *Danzas* without a sole exception to the rule. The structure of 16 plus 16 bars is respected. And as for how they constructed a piece, they coincide. Let us take the initial bars of one of his posthumous *Danzas*, published in New York:

It is the same spirit found in *La suavecita* by Saumell:

There is, as can be seen, a continuity with the classically rooted tradition, which is that of a highly esteemed Cuban musical nationalism. Cervantes is not a singular fruit that grew in a milieu, an isolated phenomenom like Espadero. He is inscribed in his time with profound justification. Composed between 1875 and 1895, Cervantes's twenty-one published *Danzas* occupy, in Cuba's music, the same place that Grieg's *Norwegian Dances*, or Dvořák's *Slavic*

Dances do in the music of their respective countries. And note that Cervantes, like Saumell, never utilizes a direct textual quote of a popular theme, except in his *Cuban Potpourri*, a lesser work. He does not avail himself of the folkloric document. He takes the Cuban *contradanza* as a form and he adjusts himself to it, without breaking its framework. He accepts some of its fundamental rhythms: that of the "tango" (in almost all of them), the conga (in "Danza no. 6," in the posthumous *contradanza* titled "Picotazos"). But those rhythms never comprise a *rhythmic constant*. They are elements of style. As for the rest, Cervantes works with his own ideas, owing nothing to the city or the countryside. It is interesting to point out, therefore, that Cervantes poses the question of a national character as a problem that can only be solved by the peculiar sensibility of the individual composer. His Cubanness came from within. It was not a stylized reworking of a received notion, nor speculation over what existed in the environment. Thus, he was one of the first musicians in the Americas to see nationalism as resulting from idiosyncracy, coinciding in this concept with what Villa-Lobos would say later. Because of this Cervantes could be considered as an extraordinary precursor. Without having a "folkloric stage" in which the musician collects popular songs in a notebook, he had superseded that necessary crisis, envisioning the matter from a more modern perspective.

We also have to acknowledge that a circumstance favored him by not venturing far from the patterns set by the Cuban *contradanza*. In his time, the *contradanza* was at the end of its rhythmic and melodic evolution — black rhythm, European melody — which had lasted more than eighty years. When Cervantes appeared, this genre had reached the limit of its possibilities, having supported all of the rhythmic combinations that were admissible within a binary measure, since 6/8 time, abandoned by dance forms, had transformed itself into different genres, with other names. Cervantes could establish a *summa* of the *contradanza* without having to think about the folklore that had nourished it in its inception, tropicalizing the original European model. In the twentieth century, there is a reoccurrence of a folkloric stage in Cuban music, the Afro-Cuban revelation of almost pure African elements, preserved but not made manifest until then. This revelation would suddenly take on an extraordinary novelty for the cultured musician, ushering in a perfectly justified regressive process, of notebook jottings and textual citation. There was a reconfirmation of the type of evolution that led the first musicians of the nineteenth century before Saumell to take the French *contradanza* as it had come to us from Santo Domingo and bring it into their own terrain, and this is where Cervantes would find the elements of his style. Roldán and Caturla also started from the living document, from the melody fished out of its milieu, before expressing the same truth with personal themes found within themselves. Cervantes is located, then, at the end of a nationalist musical evolution that culminates at the end of the last century, within a precise genre, offering the same solution — the true and only one — that a Caturla would later find at the end of a second folkloric stage in his *Berceuse campesina* for piano, where Cubanness is a pure emanation of the individual subjected to a particular environmental formation.

That is why the *Danzas* of Cervantes that we know up to now (many have been lost) present such special interest for the Cuban musician. Whereas almost all of Espadero's output languishes in oblivion, the years have enhanced the prestige of Cervantes's *Danzas*. They are played more often now than when the composer was alive. Furthermore, and above all, these moving, ironic, melancholic, jubilant pages always differ one from another: they are small marvels of good taste, charm, élan. Nothing in them sounds false or stuffy. They have a slightly restless, feminine, and elegant bearing that emanates from everything creole. With his clean and clear style, they comprise a small sonic world — as small as one would like — that belongs only to Ignacio Cervantes. This achievement is a noteworthy feat for a musician of our continent.

13. Cuban *Bufos*

As of 1815, the stage *tonadilla* began to vanish from Havana theaters, after being in vogue for more than twenty-five years. However, its oblivion was not total. From time to time, the *tonadilla* was used for a benefit or to round out a company's repertoire on tour in the provinces. *El trípili-trápala* still appeared in functions with mixed programs until 1840. The important point is that in the precise moment that the *sainete* and *tonadilla* lost force and effect, Cuban *bufo* theater emerged out of a fusion and transformation of both.

Francisco Covarrubias, the Havana "caricaturist" [basso buffo], was one of the main forces responsible for the adaptation and modification of genres that were no longer popular in Spain, constructing with these vital elements a typical creole theater. Born in 1775, Covarrubias began studying philosophy — Dr. Romay was his mentor in Aristotelian philosophy — but then studied medicine. An even truer vocation irresistibly led him to theater. After an apprenticeship with a group of amateurs, he debuted in the Circo del Campo de Marte, in 1800, acting in comic roles. Around 1811, he joined the theater company of Andrés Prieto. For many years Covarrubias was the most celebrated comic actor on the island. Maiquez, through references, bestowed phrases of admiration all the way from Spain. But, after a long period of saturation, public tastes relegated him to the background. One time, furious with the mediocre reception of an audience, he abandoned Havana, retiring, with a gesture fit for Coriolanus, to the town of Guanabacoa on the other side of the bay. He did not understand that the times were chipping away at his mask. Certain jokes, certain attitudes, his disguises, his entrances generally done with a *tonadilla* that had long ceased to please, only amused men of his age, old heartthrobs of Manuela or Isabel Gamborino. He was a character from another era. He died, quite poor, in 1850.

Covarrubias was the father of Cuban *bufo* theater. Familiar with Spanish light theater, he immediately understood that the characters that animated the *entremeses, sainetes,* zarzuelas, and *tonadillas* could be substituted with local characters. Having played the hero in an operetta of local character, staged in 1811, titled *Los apuros de Covarrubias* [Covarrubias in hot water], the "caricaturist" knew the value of local idioms faced with audiences that were increasingly more Cuban. Sure, there were the dandies and lowbrow braggarts, the Catalans, the Galicians, country bumpkins, gypsies, Moors, and beggars from works by Laserna, Esteve, Rosales, and Misón; but all of that could be transformed into something with more immediate appeal. Realizing this premise, in 1812 the stage began to fill up with *guajiros* [Cuban peasants], hunters, carters, peons, and other popular types from the island. As Arrom points out in his excellent *Historia de la literatura dramática cubana,* Covarrubias is loyal to peninsular prototypes in the first stage of his output: "Thus, to the *Los payos en el ensayo* of Ramón de la Cruz corresponds *El montero en el teatro* by Covarrubias; to *La visita del duelo, Los velorios de La Habana;* to *El rastro por la mañana, La feria Carraguao;* and *Las tertulias de Madrid,* is mirrored by *Las tertulias de La Habana.*" But, and this is what interests us, to this process of adaptation was added a substitution of musical elements. In 1814, when *Las tertulias de La Habana* [Literary gatherings of Havana] was premiered, the Cuban melody "La Cirila" was inserted into the action. In *Los velorios de La Habana* [The wakes of Havana], Covarrubias himself sang a hit of the day: "Tata, ven acá." That is, by becoming acclimated, the traditional genres began to cast off their Spanish characters, also losing the baggage of the *seguidillas, boleras,* and *villancicos,* and to give way to Cuba's popular music.

This process of transformation became more pronounced with the productions of José Agustín Millán, whose titles speak for themselves: *Un velorio en Jesús María* [A wake in the Jesús María neighborhood], *El hombre de la culebra* [The snake man], *El andaluz y el habanero* [The Andalusian and the Habanero]. Notice the very *tonadilla*-like title of this last *sainete. El hombre de la culebra* was inspired by a local incident: the story goes that in the convent of San Juan de Dios of Havana lived a black witch doctor "with a huge snake coiled around his neck." But in Millán the heritage of the Madrid-based *sainete* and *tonadilla* still weighed heavily. He mixed in Catalans and Andalusians, conventionally profiled, with *guajiros* and witty habaneros. With Bartolomé José Crespo y Borbón, on the other hand, the characters of Cuban *bufo* theater became totally drawn out. With him, blacks entered the stage.

It is an amusing paradox that this playwright who signed his *sainetes* with the slave-with-halter pseudonym of "Creto Gangá," and wrote keen criticisms of the colonial regime, was of pure Spanish origin. However, brought to the island as a child, he studied with Don José de la Luz Caballero, and so his acclimatization was absolute. In 1847 he premiered *Un ajiaco o La boda de Pancha Jutía y Canuto Raspadura*, with a plot reminiscent of the *Entremés de los negros* by Simón Aguado in which the slaves of different ethnicities express themselves in slave-barracks argot. This argot, by curious coincidence, is surprisingly similar, despite its authenticity, to the language spoken by stage blacks of Spanish Golden Age poets:

> PANCHA AND CAÑUTO: Negrito ma fortuná
> Non lo salí lan Guinea.
> ¡Ja! Bindita hora que branco
> Me lo traé nete tierra.
> Ya yo son libre,
> Yo ta casá:
> Mi su amo memo
> Me libetá.
>
> CORO: ¡Guah! ¡Guah! ¡Guah!
> Baila, carabela,
> Meníalo la pata:
> Cañuto son libre
> Y casá cun Pancha.
>
> (PANCHA AND CAÑUTO: Little black man so fortunate
> to have left Guinea.
> Yes! Blessed the hour the white man
> brought us to this land.

Now I am free.
I am married:
My very master
freed me.

CHORUS: Guah! Guah! Guah!
Dance, slave born in Africa,
Wiggle your paw:
Cañuto is free
and he married Pancha.)

Of course, not all blacks would give their blessings to "the hour the white man brought us to this land." But with Pancha Jutía and Cañuto Raspadura, new popular types appear in Cuban *bufo* theater. When, in 1864, Bartolomé José Crespo himself premiered his *sainete Debajo del tamarindo* [Under the tamarind tree], the *tonadilla*-like characters of Covarrubias and Millán productions had completely disappeared. In their place we find Malarrabia, Juan de la Cruz, and Cañamoso, mulattoes; Serapio and Pancho Mandinga, blacks; a white hunter, a peasant, a Mexican timbales player, a Chinese man, a lottery ticket vendor, various calash drivers. In sum, it is the kind of folks that later enlivened the Cuban zarzuelas of the Alhambra Theater, with the twentieth century in full swing. When the black woman Mamá Rosa sings, she already has the percussive tone that Nicolás Guillén would bring, transformed into verbal rhythmic values, to some of the *sones* in *Sóngoro Cosongo:*

Bémbere que bémbere ¡fuah!
que frutana Dió se lo da.
Bémbere que bémbere ¡fuah!
porque nella lo meresé.

What is important in this evolution of *bufo* theater is the ever-increasing space given to the musical genres of the island. Mamá Rosa speaks in "black lingo," but she sings that way too. Ulpiano Estrada is satired for his boundless adherence to the courtly minuet. *Güiros* are played. There is always a character who appears playing the *tiple*. The *seguidilla*, the *villancico*, the *tonadilla* aria, have given way to the *guajira*, the *guaracha*, the peasant *décima*, to the

Cuban song, if not to certain freer compositions that pretend to express the character of the haughty free or ethnic blacks as well as the "black professors," set up as traditional types, equivalent to the Chilean *roto* or the Mexican *pelado*. An excellent author of *guarachas*, Enrique Guerrero, director of a *bufo* company, became a leading force in handling black themes in the theater. In 1879 he published *La Belén*, "in *clave* pitch, characteristic of Havana," for two voices, chorus, and orchestra, which is, in sum, because of its structure, a creole scenic *tonadilla*. The influence of Laserna, Esteve, Castel is felt in this production that goes from the simple duet without becoming a zarzuela and whose *parts* are rigorously written: the singers and members of the chorus cannot take their eyes off of what is written in the score, having to observe the harmonic intervals and changes with utmost care. However, the atmosphere has totally changed. Those singing are blacks and mulattoes. Previously from the Lavapiés neighborhood, the characters are now from the Carraguao neighborhood.

In those days, there were some *guarachas* heard everywhere on the streets of Havana, endowed with true charm and popular flavor:

Una mulata me ha muerto.
¿Y no prenden a esa mulata?
¡Cómo ha de quedar hombre vivo
si no prenden a quien mata!

La mulata es como el pan;
se debe comer caliente,
que en dejándola enfriar
ni el diablo le mete el diente.

(A mulatta has done me in.
Won't they arrest that mulatta?
How will any man stay alive
if this man-killer isn't arrested!

The mulatta is like bread;
you gotta eat it while it's hot,

because if you let her cool off
not even the devil will take a bite.)

The character types of *bufo* theater had passed over to the song, creating an entire slum and lowlife mythology. We have spoken of the characters that half a century later would reappear in Afro-Cuban poetry. The black woman, María Belén, "an unrivaled dancer of danzas and minuets"; Perico Trebejo, the thick-lipped black man "who leaps like a frog"; Adela, "sweet solace"; the rumberas "who, with the *tumba-tumba* of the rumba are stunning"; the *ñáñigos*, who keep "sacks, sugar cane, and roosters in their *fambá* room"; the mulatta Juana Chambicú; the mulatta María de la O; Candela, "the little black dude who cuts up and cuts loose, who flies with a knife, and with a blade cooks your goose."

No hay mulata más hermosa,
Más pilla y más sandunguera,
Ni que tenga en la cadera
Más azúcar que mi Rosa.

(There's no mulatta more beautiful,
more mischievous, and more sassy,
nor one with more sugar
in her hips than my Rosa.)

All this, without forgetting the black man José Caliente, "who, if you get in his way, will cut you in half"; the woman with the mole immortalized in the Mexican song known as "Cielito Lindo"; the handsome tough Juan Quiñones, elevated by a police incident into a kind of hero in a slum-type romance:

Lo vinieron persiguiendo
al paso de la Marqueta;
lo fueron a encontrar
a bordo de una goleta.

La mujer encinta estaba
cuando se quiso escapar.

El pobre se figuraba
que lo podría lograr.

Lo llevaron al juzgado
su casamiento a firmar
y allí juró llevar
esa cruz hasta el Calvario.

¿Quién te mandó, Juan Quiñones,
comer fruta prohibida?
Hoy tienes obligaciones
mientras te dure la vida.

(They came chasing him
a step away from La Marqueta;
they found him
on board a ship.

His wife was pregnant
when he tried to escape.
The poor soul figured
he could get far away.

They took him to the judge
so as to make him marry
and he swore to carry that cross
all the way to Calvary.

Who told you, Juan Quiñones,
to eat forbidden fruit?
Now you have obligations
for as long as you live.)

From 1850 on, titles alluding to blacks and black concerns come out of their *guaracha* enclave and pass over into the *contradanza:* "Los ñáñigos," "Tu madre es conga," "La negrita," "Quindembo,"

"Mandinga no va," "El mulato en el cabildo." Here black themes are expressed principally by certain rhythmic elements. As for melody, what already appeared from to time were carnival songs, in other words, that which whites most easily could grasp and accept, familiar with merrymaking in the streets. There was not a clear idea yet of what an "African melody" could be. And it was so for a very powerful reason: only a detailed and methodical study of the black folklore of Cuba would be able to exactly define its different roots and sources, as well as the degree to which the original songs had been preserved or changed to make them more palatable. Nobody in the nineteenth century bothered to differentiate between a Yoruba hymn and a *ñáñigo* invocation. Nor was any interest shown in ancestral practices that had survived. As a way of knowing, one went directly to the street and grabbed up in passing what could be heard on Three Kings Day. Black they all were, even if they were Yoruba, *carabalíes, fulas, minas, congos,* or *mandingas.* On January 6, they all mixed together. They played drums, shook tambourines, and struck the *claves.* From this was extracted a "general air of things African," an impression of the whole, which was later staged or brought to the dance hall in a schematic and superficial way. We cannot find in the first manifestations of musical "Afro-Cubanism" the slow and profound melodies sung in chorus in the heart of the Yoruba *cabildos,* in the noble "farewell to the sun" that closes the *plantes* of the *ñáñigo* spirits. In this phase, the *contradanza* takes from blacks in the most superficial fashion: the obsessive repetition of a phrase, marking a rhythm to the beat of a *comparsa;* a brief and well-marked theme, which returns again and again to the point of saturation, creating a kind of physical euphoria in those who charge forward following its beat. It is no mere coincidence that all of the new *contradanzas* of this period alluding to blacks are marchlike.

But, in any case, something would be added to the already-known elements. The *contradanza* was brimming with rhythmic innovations. In a great many of them, the basic rhythm of the tango, with its derivations and subdivisions, was substituted with a formula—new in Havana, though already known in the east as *Cocuyé*—intelligently employed by Gaspar Villate in the *contradanza* titled "Como tú quieras" [However you like]. The influence of the black *comparsa* [carnival parade music] is quite visible in this fragment:

More and more, the norm became ingenious experimentation. Lino Martínez would define the *danzón* as a classically constructed *contradanza*, with its *prima* and *segunda* of traditional lengths, which began in this manner:

As set forth by Saumell, the *danzón* would become enshrined as the new type of dance by Matanzas native Miguel Faílde, who in June 1877[1] composed four *danzones* titled "El delirio" [Delirium], "La ingratitud" [Ingratitude], "Las quejas" [Complaints], and "Las alturas de Simpson" [Simpson Heights]. It has been said that Faílde invented the *danzón*, without taking into account that *danzones* were published—and already called that—at much earlier dates. What happened is that, from the beginning, musically the *danzón* scarcely differed from the *contradanza*. In what was called *danzón* the couple dances arm in arm, which came to replace the dance with figures that was the trademark of the *contradanza*. As for the rest, the *prima* and *segunda* sections persisted, with all of their characteristics. Already in 1878 the spread of the *danzón* must have been considerable, to judge by the contest organized in the Albisu Theater by the Center for Coach Drivers, Cooks, and Bakers of the Colored Race. Faílde's orchestra from Matanzas and Raimundo Valenzuela's from Havana performed rumbas, *guarachas*, boleros, *puntos de clave*, and *guajiras*, in addition to *danzones*. At last, in 1879, the Matanzas Society gave its official acceptance to the dance that the general populace knew all too well, in a party thrown at the Lyceum.

The adversaries who refuse to recognize any black influences in Cuban music have repeatedly declared that with the *danzón* "a national genre was created," free of any African influence. ¡*Voire!* [Look again!], as Paniurge would say. What first strikes one's attention in Faílde's *danzones* is the abundant and deliberate use of the *cinquillo*, which came from the French blacks of Santiago, and had slowly blazed its path throughout the island, obliquely going past the Havana *contradanza* without leaving a mark before suddenly affirming itself, with the right to call itself Cuban, in this new dance. The truth is, the *danzón*, as it was played in 1880, is a mere amplification of the *contradanza*, with an open-door policy for all the musical elements swirling about the island, regardless of origin. There is a clear Saumell-like accent in its eight-bar introduction (repeated), which often begins with a classical theme — exactly corresponding to the *prima* of the *contradanza*, despite having a new title, *introduction*. In the second part, or "clarinet part," the piece works almost always over the *cinquillo* rhythm. It returns to the *introduction*, and then goes on to the more melodic "violin part," which functions as an Adagio before closing with the initial bars. In Faílde's first *danzones*, this formula is fully defined, the *contradanza* thus taking on a new period of sixteen bars. This scheme is adhered to until the beginning of the twentieth century, in which the *danzón* was enriched by a very fast coda (or fourth part), generally taken from a rumba, from some street vendor's cry, or from an Afro-Cuban song.

Until about 1920, the *danzón* was Cuba's national dance. There was no event, for forty years, that was not glossed or honored by way of a *danzón*. There were *danzones* to greet the birth of the republic, and political *danzones*, such as El triunfo de la Conjunción," or "Zayas no fue" [Zayas wasn't the one]; patriotic *danzones*, such as the one taken from the *clave Martí no debió morir* [Martí shouldn't have died]; *danzones* from World War I, such as "La toma de Varsovia" [The taking of Warsaw] and *Aliados y alemanes* [Allies and Germans]. There were *danzones* based on opera or zarzuela themes. Starting in 1910, one could say that any musical material that could be taken advantage of was used in the *danzón*. Fashionable boleros, American ragtime, Tipperary, street vendor cries, Rossini arias, Spanish ditties, even Chinese melodies, such as the one that opens the long famous *Bombín de Barreto* by José Urfé. This acceptance of things Chinese — so linked to popular life in Cuba — was not circumstantial. Cuban listening habits included a clear notion of Chinese pentatonic scales, which often appeared in slum dances. To stick to just three typical examples, we find entire refrains written in the pentatonic scale, in *Los chinos* of Raimundo Valenzuela, in the *Espabílate* of Eliseo Grenet, in *El dios chino* by José Urfé. (Because of its strident sound, the five-note Chinese trumpet has been used many times in Havana political rallies.)

As can be seen, the English country dance, by way of France, taken to Santo Domingo, introduced to Santiago, rebaptized and amplified in Matanzas, enriched in Havana with mulatto, black, and Chinese elements, had acquired a level of *mestizaje* nothing short of vertiginous. And yet the *danzón* maintained its character and unity, remaining faithful to its origins as far as form and writing. It conserved its traditional structure, which, deep down, was that of a rough-hewn rondo (A-B-A-C-A-D). Harmonically, it remained close to the classical procedures of its progenitor, with its long passages in thirds, inherited from the Neapolitan school and of the French *contradanzas* published for violin *avec dessus de viole*. In a *danzón* published in 1892 by Jorge Anckermann in Mexico, we find this passage, which despite its triplets and quintuplets, sounds like a *Gypsy Rondo* by Haydn:

The examples of *danzón* introductions with fifths on the trumpet, and themes sporting an eighteenth-century air, are countless. You would need fifty pages just to quote the best. Even when the rhythm imbues them with a strong tropical feel, as in the following example, they do not lose the charming form of a classical concerto:

The tradition that accompanied the formative period of Cuban music is still a living presence. Even today, in current hits that stir up glorious memories of the *danzón,* such as "Almendra," for example, we can discern, over an unflappable bass line, classically conceived authentic flute variations — compositions that reflect a classicism lodged in the memories formed by a century and a half of listening habits, passed on from generation to generation, and that still maintain a certain stylistic unity.

Around 1920, Havana was invaded by the *son.* The lyrics speak of Manzanillo and Palma Soriano, with eulogies to small homelands, enclaves within the motherland:

Son de Oriente,
mi son caliente,
mi son de Oriente.

(*Son* from *Oriente,*
my *son* hot as a beast,
my *son* from the East.)

The *son* constituted an extraordinary novelty for habaneros. But it was not a recent invention, as is sometimes imagined. From the times of the "Má' Teodora," it was known as a song you could dance to in the province of Santiago. But, from the sixteenth to the seventeenth century, the word *son* alluded to imprecise forms of danceable popular music. The same happened with the rumba, which still has not been properly defined by those who play it. Everything fits in it: all of the rhythms found in Cuban music, in addition to all the black rhythms that can jibe with the melody. Everything capable of going in two-four time is accepted by this genre, which, more than a genre, is an *atmosphere*. This without saying that in Cuba there is not one rumba, but various rumbas. For the drummers, for the initiates, a *yambú* is not the same as a *guaganco*, or a *columbia*, or a *papalote*. As for the stage rumba, danced in theaters and cabarets, it is a mix of this and that. As we said in a previous chapter, there was a vast sector of the continent that had black dances, the couple dancing apart, voluptuous and even lascivious, that received different names and that were accompanied in different ways, without an essential difference between them. All were danced to a rhythmically potent music, with many percussion instruments. It could be the *resbalosa* in Argentina, the Dominican *calenda*, or the *chuchumbé* taken by Cubans to Veracruz. All were rumbas; that is, above all a fiery dance, whose rhythms served to accompany a kind of choreography that conjured up ancient sexual rites. There were no figure changes, as in the *contradanza*, for example, nor, as in the *danzón*, "parts" endowed with their own character. So we can say that the rumba, even today, is an undefined genre and yet quite present. Any Cuban recognizes a rumba without blinking. But Sánchez de Fuentes and Emilio Grenet, in their studies on Cuban rhythms, elude the problem of its definition, turning the page, so to speak. And it is because the rumba, as we said before, is an *atmosphere*. Put a mulatto out there moving his hips within the choreographic reach of a dancer, and all of those present will produce the adequate rhythms, with their hands, a box, a door, or on the wall... It is no small wonder that the word *rumba* has passed into the language of Cubans as a synonym for noisy partying, licentious dancing, boogying with loose women.

If we observe how the song "Má' Teodora" feels so remote in time, with its melody of the romance, its Castilian meter, its 6/8 time, from what today is called the *son* (not so with the *danzón*, loyal to an evolutionary development), we can deduce that for a long time it was an inchoate *sound* of voices and instruments. It began to assume a definite profile with the arrival of the French blacks in Santiago. Its development — in essentially popular environments — was parallel to that of the *contradanza*. When he quotes old *sones*, Sánchez de Fuentes transcribes the one called "Mujeres, vamos a la rumba" [Women, let's go join the rumba] like this:

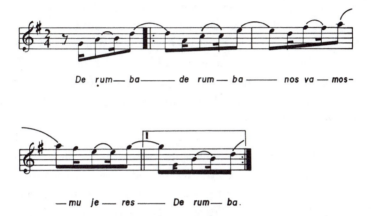

One can observe an identical rhythmic process (suppressing tied notes) of the [French] "creole" song ("Tabatié mué tombé"), collected by Emilio Bacardí in the eastern part of the country:

As for the rhythm that is frequently cited —

— it is a simple dilation of the eternal tango rhythm, altering the notes and displacing the beats. The anticipated bass line suppresses the initial strong beat, but, as in the tango, the second note of each bar is inevitably the briefest, in contrast with the note before, which is always the longest. This in reference to its roots. Regarding its performance and spirit, it has come to differ from other dances of the island, because of a series of particular circumstances.

The *son* has the same constituent elements as the *danzón*. But both became so different because of their trajectory: the *contradanza* was a salon dance; the *son* was a thoroughly popular dance form. The *contradanza* was played with an orchestra; the *son* was a song accompanied by percussion. This, without a doubt, comprises the best guarantee of its originality. Thanks to the *son*, Afro-Cuban percussion, confined to the slave barracks and the dilapidated rooming houses of the slums, revealed its marvelous expressive resources, achieving universal status. Lest we forget, dance orchestras before 1920, in terms of percussion, were only aware of the *timbales* (not the Cuban *timbal,* which is something altogether different), the *güiro* or *calabazo,* and the *claves* — from Havana. The maracas were used a lot less. An entire arsenal of rhythmic "weapons" stayed in the shadows.

We still remember the marvelous stupor with which the people of our generation greeted, one fine day, the instruments that came from the eastern provinces, and that today are heard, poorly played, in all of the world's cabarets. The *marímbula,* seen in Santo Domingo by Moreau de Saint-Méry; the *quijada,* or jawbone that Lafcadio Hearn heard in New Orleans; the bongo, on whose hide were heard the most sonorous glissandi with the palm of the hand;[2] the creole *timbales,* secured between the knees, so nervous and mischievous, as they were struck with one or more fingers; the *econes* or *cencerros* (cowbells), little bells made of dull-sounding metal, played with a metal stick; the *botijuela,* a potbellied clay jar, with a narrow neck, from whose lips pour forth a sound analogous to the pizzicatto of a bass; *el diente de arado,* shaped like a pipe, with its obsessive sonority of deep-sounding cowbells . . . Emile Vuillermoz said the following when he was placed before all of the Afro-Cuban percussive instruments:

> With any kind of object, the long dry fingers (of Cuban blacks) find a way to produce unexpected sounds, discrete or violent, sharp or dull, soft or cruel. Wood, metal, baked clay, dried hides, they offer an inexhaustible range of delightful timbres, from which they extract a true orchestration of sounds. Cubans

have especially discovered a certain quality of wood that produces the clear and metallic sound of an anvil (the *claves*). With them they obtain notes that have the luminescent and melancholic purity of the frog's nocturnal song. Add to this a series of mysterious whisperings, produced by friction, hummings, percussive sounds, hand clapping, or of fingers over small *timbales*, the rubbing of a little stick over hollowed-out gourds, and the silky palpitating of pellets (actually small stones or seeds) inside a dried fruit. With them, an orchestration close to the life source is obtained, evoking the universal consent of things moving to the rhythm of the dancing. Tell me: what worth do our timbales, our tambourines, our triangles, our cymbals, our resonance boxes have when faced with Cuban percussion instruments, so full of nuance, so poetic, with their spellbinding hums, their caresses of torn silk, and their small silver anvil?

And let it be known that when the *son*'s percussive instruments appeared, blacks still did not come forth with their ritual drums that accompanied initiation ceremonies in secret societies, witch-craft practices, and syncretic religious celebrations, in which invoca-tions to the Virgin are mixed in with more or less profane dances, or danced for the simple pleasure of moving their bodies in a sea of rhythms. The great revolution of ideas instigated by the *son*'s percussion was in giving us *the sense of a polyrhythm subjected to a unity of time.* Up until then, one spoke of *the* rhythm of the *con-tradanza, the* rhythm of the *guaracha, the* rhythms of the *danzón* (ad-mitting to a plurality within that succession). The *son*, on the other hand, established new categories. Within a general tempo, each per-cussive element assumed an autonomous existence. If the function of the *botijuela* and the *diente de arado* was rhythmic regularity, that of the *timbales* was to enact rhythmic variation. If the *marímbula* worked on three or four notes, marking the harmonies with the in-sistence of a basso continuo, then the *tres* furnished a cadence. The bongo acted more freely, using a more direct percussiveness or a glissando technique. The other percussive instruments would man-ifest themselves according to their tonal registers and possibilities, according to the performer's imagination, as long as the singing—

all of the musicians sang—was sustained by the percussion. The Cuban *son* in its pure form of 1920 brings to mind a rudimentary *Les noces* by Stravinsky. It would be hard to find two types of music adhering to such similar norms, despite their enormous differences. It is seen in the melodic material entrusted to the human voices, and the sonorous climate and rhythms produced by a group of percussion instruments.

Furthermore, the *son*, in its maturity, came to us with a definite form: a *largo* and a *montuno*. The *largo* was the initial recitative, the exposition of the ballad, anciently rooted and Santiago-based, in a deliberate time, sung by one voice:

Señores,
Señores,
los familiares del difunto
me han confiado,
para que despida el duelo,
del que en vida fue
Papá Montero.

(Listen all,
listen all,
the relatives of the deceased
have entrusted me
to say good-bye, as we mourn
him who in this life
was Papa Montero.)

Enter the nervous reaction of the percussion. And then the voices came in, all together, establishing in the *montuno* the old call-and-response form, already observed in the "*Son* of Má' Teodora":

coro: A llorar a Papá Montero,   (Let's cry for Papa Montero.
        ¡zumba!   Zumba!
        canalla rumbero.   Roguish rumbero.

solo: Lo llevaron al agujero.   They took him to the grave.

```
coro:  ¡Zumba!                            Zumba!
solo:  Nunca más se pondrá sombrero.      No longer will he don a hat.
coro:  ¡Zumba!                            Zumba!
       Canalla rumbero.                   Roguish rumbero.)
       etc., etc., etc.
```

With a minute acceleration of the tempo, the variations could be endlessly improvised within a general rhythmic framework. The instruments embroidered, designing "filligrees," subdividing the basic notes, working in tandem with the growing excitement of the dancers, who, in turn, made their steps more intricate. The choreographic moves of Africa were present in this rudimentary *allegro with variations*, which the musicians and singers sustained by going all out, until it became physically necessary to pause. "Los hombres no lloran" [Men don't cry], "Maldita timidez" [Darned bashfulness], "Esas no son cubanas" [Those aren't Cuban women], "Papá Montero," "Mujeres, no se duerman" [Women, keep your eyes open], "Las cuatro palomas" [The four doves] constitute the cornerstone of that repertoire, representative of that great era of the *son*, the decade of 1920–30.

Until now, one could not say that Cuba—aside from some bass lines of the *guaracha* paired up with African percussion—had invented a rhythm. It had assimilated certain rhythmic formulas, subjected to a wide process of intermigration throughout the continent, modifying them through performance. But if the tango differed in Cuba—by serving as the bass line for the *contradanza*—from the applications of that same rhythm in Paraguay or Argentina, it was simply a matter of "local color," of tempo, of inflection, imposed by Cuban idiosyncracies. Carlos Vega underlines, quite correctly, this matter of "local color," which tends to mysteriously differentiate itself and create two types of music whose outline can be quite similar. In the folkloric collections of Argentina, there is a *candombe* melody that is absolutely identical to the song "La paloma azul" [The blue dove], which passes itself off as Mexican. But it does not matter that the notes and rhythms are the same. When "La paloma azul" is sung by Mexicans, it is Mexican to the core.

Something analogous happens with the *cinquillo* in the Dominican *merengue* and the same *cinquillo* employed in the Cuban *danzón* and bolero. However, in these cases there is no *invention of rhythms*.

The *son*'s great merit is that by granting freedom to spontaneous and popular musical expressions, it favored rhythmic invention. The notes were subdivided and diversified within each measure. From a certain moment on, there was true creation. Many *son* orchestras were famous for the fact that they "played differently." They had more warmth, more novelty within the known meter; sudden flights of fancy in the percussion that elicited enthusiastic exclamations from the dancers. When trying to approximate a written notation of the *son* "La mujer de Antonio" [Antonio's wife], it cannot be transcribed as one would "Buche y pluma" [Hot air]. The insistent bass in "Galán-galán" [Lover boy, lover boy], with its three notes repeated obsessively, has little to do with the martial percussion of "A la loma de Belén" [On Belén hill]. With the *son*, an area of Cuban music emancipates itself almost completely from the rhythmic traditions characteristic of the nineteenth century, even if its history, deep down, was parallel to that of the *contradanza*. For this reason, the worldwide diffusion of the habanera was quite inferior to that of the *son*. Because one must keep in mind that all of the dances introduced in recent years in Europe, the Americas, and Asia, under the euphonic rubric of *rumbas*, were really *sones* that were long known in Cuba. The *son* is to Cuban music what "Christopher Columbus" by Benny Goodman or Ellington's "Black and Tan" is to ragtime music in 1915. In the *son* there is a richness, a precious fluid, that other previous genres were not familiar with, despite their charm and grace. It is not mere happenstance that by enriching itself with a fourth part that prolonged its life, the *danzón* ended up invariably adopting, by way of a coda, a *son* melody and rhythm.

Starting in 1850, the production of light theater became increasingly copious and diverse. The boundaries of the creole *sainete* of Millán and Bartolomé José Crespo still had *tonadilla*-esque residues. Rafael Otero, a biographer of the *bufos*, was the first to expand the *sainete* to the format of a zarzuela with "Trespalillos o el carnaval de La Habana," which premiered in 1853. The following year, An-

tonio Medina staged another native zarzuela, "Don Canuto Ceibamocha o el guajiro generoso" [Don Canuto Ceibamocha or the generous peasant], and Pedro Carreño, his "El industrial de nuevo
cuño" [A new kind of industrialist]. In 1855, M. García, a black
writer, asked black musician Claudio Brindis de Salas for a score
of a two-act zarzuela, which returned to *tonadilla* themes: "El adivino fingido o la traición de una mujer" [The fake fortune-teller or
a woman's betrayal]. But these regressive lapses became much rarer.
The genre had been created, and by way of the refined zarzuelas
of Raimundo Cabrera and José Mauri, it would become, with few
variants, what it is today. In 1868, the Cervantes Theater — father
to the Alhambra Theater — exclusively staged Cuban light opera.

It bears pointing out that, because of its popular roots, the *bufo*
genre reflected anti-Spanish sentiments during the Ten Years War
(1868–78). While many composers of *contradanzas*, flattered by salon society, dedicated their works to the colonial authorities, to the
"volunteers," or to illustrious countesses who were supportive of
repressive measures, the *bufos* were increasingly audacious in their
satires of the existing regime. Shortly after Cespedes's uprising [Oc-
tober 10, 1868], the Spanish authorities had to close the Cervantes
Theater for a while, believing it to be a "nest of rebels." On January
22, 1869, during the performance of the piece *Perro huevero aunque
le quemen el hocico* [Gutsy dog even if they burn his snout], by Juan
Francisco Valero, held at the Villanueva Theater, the "volunteers"
cowardly fired on the crowd, claiming that under the guise of an apparently innocuous plot an enthusiastic endorsement of the Cuban
independence struggle was being expressed. That night, with the
theater seats bloodied, no one danced the rumba that traditionally
closed a *bufo* spectacle (a custom created by the dances that concluded *tonadillas* a half a century before). In June of 1882, a first
Cuban *bufo* company performed in Mexico, with "Los negritos cate-
dráticos," "Juan Liborio," "Caneca," "La duquesa de Haití," and
other zarzuelas of that type.

Popular theater in Cuba had its most perfect expression in the
repertoire of the Alhambra Theater, which, for thirty-five years, op-
erated continuously. The picaresque tone of certain *sainetes* made
it a male-only enclave. However, one cannot forget that on its stage,

tons of ingenuity, good humor, and creole winsomeness were expended daily. An electoral campaign, a cabinet crisis, a police incident, the Rif campaign, or the European war inspired zarzuelas
right off the cuff, comprising a delightful spectacle. It was, in sum,
the kind of "political theater" that Rafael Alberti wanted to create
in Madrid on the eve of the Spanish Civil War. The men of our generation still nostagically remember extraordinary achievements
like "La Diana en la corte," "El rico hacendado," "La casita criolla,"
"Los grandes de Cuba," "Aliados y alemanes," "La danza de los
millones," "La Chelito en el Seborucal." Conducting the orchestra
was Jorge Anckermann, a most Cuban composer of light music,
author of innumerable zarzuelas, whose "numbers" embodied more
high-quality ideas than the pretentious and loud scores of some of
his contemporaries, who pretended they were writing for a world
audience. In "La casita criolla" and other scores of his, there are
many pages of good taste and naturalness that are simply admirable.
Always thinking in Cuban rhythms, Anckermann composed vi-
brant *danzones* that were the overtures to the performance. With
equal elegance he handled the *punto,* the *clave,* the habanera, the
guaracha, the bolero, the *criolla,* and the rumba. Since the librettos
demanded a great mobility, and the most diverse of locales, he
would not hesitate in resorting to things Afro-Cuban. So, when
the *comparsas* were prohibited in 1913, many of their songs were
brought into the repertoire of the Alhambra. In 1912, Anckermann
had mixed into "La casita criolla" a congo-style tango of his invention that would create a genre. His *guajira* titled "El arroyo que
murmura" [The murmuring stream] is one of the quintessential
songs of the island.

Bufos played a considerable role in the evolution of Cuban popular music. Thanks to them, all types of urban and rural songs and
dances were brought to light, disseminated, and mixed together.
The demands of the stage diversified genres born of the same roots.
Black culture finally took on a definite strength and relevance. The
Alhambra Theater was, for thirty-five years, a true conservatory
of national rhythms, where composers learned a great deal, especially those closer to Saumell and Cervantes than to Espadero.

14. Laureano Fuentes–Gaspar Villate

From 1830 to 1860, Cuban musical culture in Santiago de Cuba maintained a level superior to that of Havana. Whereas the capital was overtaken by Italian opera, the disciples of Juan París remained loyal to a certain number of healthy disciplines. It is quite true that when the Philharmonic Society was inaugurated in 1846, the program was made up of opera fragments. But, despite the fact that the new choirmasters, among them Antonio Bardalonga, from Madrid, were drawn to the repertoire by Mercadante and Hilarión Eslava, the scores stashed away in the archives were frequently retrieved and played. In 1849, Salas's Requiem was still sung. Haydn was not forgotten. Nor was Pergolesi. In 1851, General Enna's funeral brought together 102 performers to play Mozart's Requiem. There were numerous musicians in the city. In 1838, to open up the season of masked balls in the Salón de Oriente, an overture by Ramón Carnicer was played, written for three orchestras. The score included wooodwinds and brass with four, five, and six musicians for each. There were twelve clarinets, seven saxhorns, and five trombones. Furthermore, performances of classical works were much more frequent than in Havana.

In that environment an important composer in the island's musical history was formed: Laureano Fuentes Matons. First, it bears mention that Laureano Fuentes had the rare privilege of coming from a family of musicians. He was the direct descendant of a harpist who had lived in Santiago at the end of the seventeenth century, and of the Pérez Alaiz family, cantors of the cathedral in the first half of the eighteenth century. Born in 1825, Laureano solmizated correctly in the presence of Juan París before turning eleven.

He learned composition and harmony from Casamitjana, the Catalan maestro, to whom we owe the first band version of the *Cocoyé*.
Fuentes's life is not marked by any unique event, outside of the
tragic death of his wife, who drowned in the bay of Santiago. As
for the rest, his days were placid and serene. He never left the island. He dedicated himself totally and energetically to music. A
notable violinist, a conductor, a composer of religious and profane
music, he went anywhere his artistic efforts were needed. At fifteen he was first violinist in the music chapel of the cathedral. He
created an orchestra in 1844. He founded the Saint Cecilia Music
Academy, and later the Apollo Academy, which lasted briefly. He
left behind a great many religious works. He was the first Cuban
musician to have written an opera on the island, and also the first
to compose a true symphonic poem. Even in old age he served the
artistic community of Santiago with adolescent vigor, contributing
to the knowledge and diffusion of Beethoven's work. Bestowed
with all the honors, Laureano Fuentes died in the city of his birth
in 1898. To ensure the musical tradition of his family, he left a son,
Laureanito, a gracile and refined composer of Cuban *danzas*—two
of which would be orchestrated by Amadeo Roldán.

The work of Laureano Fuentes is probably the most copious legacy
of any Cuban composer. His religious output—the most important—is comprised of a *Misa de difuntos* [Mass for the dead], for
three voices and orchestra (1856); two Requiems; a *Responso* [Prayer
for the dead], for four voices and orchestra; *Liberame Domine*, for
chorus and orchestra (1870); a *Stabat Mater* (1873); in addition to a
large number of hymns, *salve reginas*, antiphons, and music set to
Scripture, all imbued with a sincere mystical inspiration. The catalog of his scores includes all genres, without exception; *América*,
a symphonic poem given a prize in a Santiago competition, to com-
memorate the four hundredth anniversary of the discovery; *Galatea*,
an overture that premiered in the Floral Games of Puerto Príncipe,
in 1868; various symphonies (overtures) for large and small orchestra; various string trios, and also for violin, flute, and piano;
an opera, *La hija de Jefté* (1875), lengthened later and staged under
the title *Seila*, nineteen years after the composer's death. To this

must be added four zarzuelas staged in Santiago, various marches and hymns for orchestra, and an incredible number of compositions for voice, for violin, and for piano. Among popular works we must cite the song "La candelita," well received and played throughout the island, as well as many graceful and fresh *danzas,* which merit a careful selection, since they present, given those known by Cervantes, a certain interest for the study of Cuban music, by offering all of the peculiarities of the *contradanza oriental* [from the eastern provinces].

Trained in Santiago de Cuba, far from the great artistic trends of his epoch, Laureano Fuentes was trapped between two eras. On the one hand, he worked in the classical tradition, firmly rooted in the Santiago examples of Salas and París, and eloquently evidenced by his religious oeuvre, with Haydn and Pergolesi as exemplars. On the other hand, he would receive news from Havana, scores from Europe—not always the best—which seemed to indicate a shift in public tastes toward new modes of expression. Vacillating between these two poles, Laureano Fuentes made the most laudable efforts to find a balance between the two. But his disorientation was evident. His *Galatea* overture, from 1868, was conceived with a dangerous ingenuousness. (There is in that score a progression that lasts some fifty-odd bars over the same tremolo.) Thinking he was being up to date, the composer wrote an overture à la Suppé. When his *Stabat Mater* was performed five years later, the mystical inspiration harks back to his first maestros. He uses counterpoint with severity, and avails himself of the fugue style, thinking of the religious music that contemplated him from the cathedral bookshelves. Later, his symphonic poem *América* inaugurated the genre of "program music" on the island, resorting to new orchestral techniques. In the beginning, a *Marziale maestoso* describes the launching of the three ships. Then there is the episode of the storm; we witness the uprising of the sailors. Rodrigo de Triana's yell can be heard from the top of the masts. Cannon fire is heard. The sailors kneel and pray. A finale, with potent sonorities, paints the picture of Columbus's landing.

But Laureano Fuentes arrived late to the symphonic poem (1892)—just like other musicians from the continent. Richard

Strauss was pushing the genre to its limit. Orchestral composition was undergoing a profound transformation. Because of that, the score of *América*, which would have been prophetic twenty years earlier, situating itself in a Lisztian orbit, was only destined to mark a date in the history of Cuban music. A similar fate was in store for Laureano Fuentes's opera. Primitively, this score had been a sort of cantata in one act, based on a biblical theme, in which the author had given free rein to his good melodic inspiration. The same admirers of *La hija de Jefté* (among them, Rafael Salcedo) could see in it the influence of Gounod—a very honorable influence for a Cuban musician in 1875. When the score was revised and lengthened—based on the unfortunate Italian text written by Laureano Fuentes himself—premiering with its new title *Seila* in 1917, it was a totally anachronistic work. Forty years of particularly restless music had passed him by, draining it of any universal value. Despite some enchanting traits, it was a dead score. Out of its environment, out of its epoch, its defects stand out in a cruel way. The unfortunate idea of using the lyrics of *Lascia ch'io pianga* from Handel for an aria in the second act only accentuated the contrast between a grand perennial style and a hybrid style, oscillating between the classical and the Romantic. However, the orginal cell of this opera, the first cantata, should be seen in its time; there it is an effort worthy of remembering. As a cantata writer, Laureano Fuentes revealed himself to be a precursor.

Laureano Fuentes's best efforts are in his religious music. There we find noble scores, melodies of great emotion, deftly handled choruses, with an orchestra that, while not displaying great originality, sounds very good. But, in any case, despite the fugue-like style, the accomplished handling of counterpoint, there is neither the elevated tone of a Salas nor the conceptual unity of a París. Laureano Fuentes should not be blamed for that, however. When he entered the cathedral of Santiago, religious music was in a decline everywhere. The mien and meaning of the great ordinations had been lost; it slowly became a type of mystical vocal music that one can hear nowadays in the churches of Auteuil, where the young ladies of the great world of Paris show off, by singing trills in honor of rose water in swooning and sensual voices.

It is principally in Laureano Fuentes's popularly inspired work that we find pages forming part of island musical anthologies. When he accepted the local accent, he was more in tune with the times. He lacked neither sensibility nor a sure instinct, and both revealed themselves, despite his disorientation, in precisely the compositions he considered of secondary importance, attributable to his provincial desire of wanting to be more than a minor artist.

In 1840, there was an eighteen-year-old Cuban in Paris named Cristóbal Martínez Corres. He had already written an opera *bufo* titled *El diablo contrabandista* [The devil contrabandist], a Mass, various pieces and romances. Shortly thereafter, he moved to Italy. Endowed with a surprising gift for composing, he took little time to finish the score of a new opera, *Don Papanero o la burla del hipnotismo,* another Mass, and a septet. The manager of La Scala in Milan, hearing of his talent, commissioned a serious opera from him, to be premiered in his theater. Martínez Corres, whose health was terribly fragile, and who needed long periods of repose, surrendered himself to the task with the premonitory fury of someone who feels the need to leave his mark on the world. He died in 1842, in particularly touching circumstances, without being able to finish his opera *Saffo.* Five days before, his old black servant, brought from Havana, had died, exhausted from the nightly vigils that his master's illness imposed. No works by Martínez Corres have survived. It bears saying, however, that this sickly adolescent was the first Cuban to have written scores destined for the lyric stage. He had been born in 1822.

Gaspar Villate, in a way the successor of Martínez Corres, temperamentally, produced an abundant and wide-ranging work, all centered on opera. Born in Havana in 1851, he emigrated with his family to the United States in 1868, when war broke out in Cuba. One year earlier he had written the score of *Angelo, tirano de Padua,* based on the play by Victor Hugo. Back in Havana in 1871, he composed a second opera, *Las primeras armas de Richelieu.* Sent to Paris to finish his studies, he worked diligently under the direction of Bazin, Victorien Joncières, and Dannhauser. During a new stay in

Havana, he composed extremely refined *contradanzas* and some beautiful melodies of local inspiration: *La virgen tropical*, based on a poem by Fornaris, already a habanera with all the characteristics of the genre; *Adiós a Cuba*, a romance; *Sérénade Havanaise*, based on a French poem. But Villate was a man of the theater. Soon he would hit his stride in the field of opera.

His eight waltzes, his *Soirées Cubaines*, his romances, were very much relished in the salons of Paris. Making ever greater concessions to the medium—Villate was not of Antonio Raffelin's caliber—he wrote completely trivial pieces, such as his *Marche des petits pompiers*, for orchestra. But these sins, far from damaging his career, opened the doors to a certain notoriety. His publisher, Léon Escudier, then the director of the Théâtre des Italiens in Paris, felt that Villate, a flexible and talented man, could compose a good opera. Temístocles Solera, the famous Italian libretto writer, was commissioned to write the drama. From this collaboration came *Zilia*, premiered on December 1, 1877, with Tamberlick heading the cast. Frankly, the plot was detestable. All the clichés of a second-rate Romanticism were heaped into this one piece, whose ambience was highly reminiscent of Ponchielli's *Gioconda*. It was the Venice of the cloak-and-dagger novel, with its choruses of *uscocos*, a mailbox for denunciations, and conflicts between enemy families. Amazingly, the Parisian critics gave it favorable reviews. They took into account Villate's youth and praised the best parts of the score. Only Jules Claretie treated the composer a little dryly, although he recognized that the work had a "very beautiful quartet" in it. In 1881, *Zilia* was premiered in Havana.

After that opera, Villate devoted his creative energy to the theater. In 1879, he wrote *La Czarine* [The czarina], based on a libretto by Armand Sylvestre. Four acts, seven scenes, on the well-known and beautiful story of the princess Tarakanova. First Villate wanted to premiere his opera in Madrid, because of the financial problems that had paralyzed the Théâtre des Italiens. After waiting some, the work was finally presented in the Royal Theater of Le Havre, receiving an enthusiastic welcome. In February 1885, the Royal Theater of Madrid embraced his new opera, *Baltazar*, inspired by the famous play by Gertrudis Gómez de Avellaneda.

Toward 1884, some newspaper articles announced that Villate was working on the score of a *Christopher Columbus*, an opera of vast proportions, which was to consist of a prologue, three acts, and an epilogue. The third act, which took place in Cuba, was supposed to have included some melodies of local character. But that score—if it was ever written—has been lost.

Villate had the privilege, in those years, of becoming close friends with Verdi, whom he deeply admired. Verdi suggested he write an opera on the tragic history of Inés de Castro. Villate put his mind to it. But his mother's illness and death interrupted his work. The fragments written—to which the composer made reference in a letter to Benito Zozaya—seem to have been lost. Shortly before dying, Villate began writing the score to a lyric drama, *Lucifer*, whose existence has been contested repeatedly. From this score we have found two important fragments, totally finished and orchestrated: a scene from the first act (a duo with parts written for organ and a chorus of female voices), and the entire beginning of the fifth act—a *sabbath* rondo, with a long instrumental passage, and the intervention of a mixed chorus and ballet, which is quite reminiscent, given its spirit, of an analogous scene in Boito's *Mephistopheles*. Gaspar Villate died in Paris on October 9, 1891.

Villate belongs to Cuba only because of his nationality, his *contradanzas*, and a handful of melodies of local inspiration. Disillusioned by the meagerness of Cuba's artistic milieu, the musician always lived spiritually in Europe. Despite his long stays in Havana, he was a man shaped by the atmosphere of the Théâtre des Italiens, and devoted his best efforts to those genres that could yield easy successes in Paris and Madrid. A short man, quite desirous of fame, accustomed to collecting all the articles, notes, criticism, or gazettes that made reference to him, Villate aspired, in every way, to satisfy the tastes of the day. Meyerbeer and the young Verdi were his principal models. He never thought to add anything to what drew acclaim and applause, accepting librettos that were absolutely conventional. Even though his plots were situated in Babylonia or Russia, he never veered from a strictly observed Italian operatic mode. He was talented, skillful, but he lacked genius. He could do a good job on any stage of the time without ever going beyond a safe middle ground. The recent Havana stagings of *Baltazar* and of *La Czarine*—why deny it?—harbored a cruel deception for those expecting something better. All of the commonplaces of his time are summed up in those operas, which, within Cuban music, only offer a historical-type interest. Maybe his *Cristóbal Colón* would have been a work of larger ambition. But there is no score to let us know.

In his last years, Villate himself must have realized that his manner had become passé. The found fragments of *Lucifer* reveal a will to take the orchestra toward a new terrain of possibilities, to try and achieve a greater dramatic intensity. The knowledge of Verdi's *Otello* that had made him marvel; the memory of Berlioz's *Treatise on Instrumentation,* which had been his guide in his youth; and perhaps, the revelation of Wagner had created new concerns for him. His *sabbath* rondo, with a diabolical minuet written for two English horns, backed by a string quartet, reveals a thorough knowledge of his craft. But nothing indicates that he had finished the score before his death.

Gaspar Villate, despite his European triumphs, offers very little to the new generations, especially alongside a Saumell or a Cervantes. Villate is more remembered for some delectably put together *contradanzas* than for his operas premiered in the Théâtre des Italiens, the Royal Theater of Madrid, or the Royal Theater in Le Havre.

15. A Transition Period

Let us browse through the Havana concert programs from 1850 to 1860. In the house of the Count of Peñalver one had the overture *La muda di Portici* for two pianos, played by the gentlemen Desvernine and Arizti; *Lucía Zampa*, a fantasy by Thalberg. In the Lyceum (1853), *I Puritani, Lucrezia Borgia, Marino Faliero*. Fourteen years later, in the very same Lyceum, *Martha, Don Pasquale, Rigoletto, Il profeta*, and for once, a sizable fragment from Rossini's *Moses in Egypt*. The concert continued to be an anthology of arias or fragments from operas. Nonetheless, in 1866, the Society for Classical Music was formed in Havana, in order to break with that routine. The inaugural program included a string quartet by Haydn, a trio by Rubinstein (arranged for quartet [?] by Espadero), an *Ave Maria* by Espadero, and Beethoven's Symphony no. 7, arranged for a small orchestra.

Beethoven's appearance in a program was a sign of the times. The most serious performers in Cuba at the time—Arizti, Bousquet, Carlos Anckermann, Espadero, Van der Gutch, Desvernine, and Serafín Ramírez—rebelled against the dictatorship of Italian opera. Little by little, the ambience became healthier. In 1872, the maestro Salcedo founded the Beethoven Society in Santiago. In 1885, an excellent Belgian musician, Hubert de Blanck, opened a conservatory in which musical teaching was seriously undertaken, with help from the best teachers of the time. The process of musical purification became more pronounced. In 1888, the eastern capital [Santiago] already had a Chamber Music Society. In 1893, in the same city, Salcedo organized a Beethoven festival, of crushing length, which included three piano sonatas, a symphony (for two pianos and eight hands), some minor compositions, the *¡Ah, perfido!* and the Concerto in E-flat. To mention only some titles that reveal an evolution in the public's cultural tastes, we find the following references made from 1892 to 1903: various overtures by Mendelssohn, various concertos by Rubinstein, a concerto by Chopin, works by Saint-Saëns, *The Furies* by Massenet, the overture and arias from *Rienzi* [Wagner], Tchaikovsky's Concerto for Violin, Bach's *Well-Tempered Clavier*, many sonatas by Beethoven, the Concerto for Two Violins by Bach, the Sonata, *opus 7* by Grieg (played by Cervantes). In 1897, Sarasate played the Concerto in D by Beethoven and Lalo's *Spanish Symphony*. In 1903, in the newly created Popular Concerts, a smaller-scale orchestra performed Haydn's *Military* Symphony, the *Leonore Overture* [Beethoven], and the *Danse macabre* by Saint-Saëns.

But at that moment an intelligent, exceedingly well-trained musician made prodigious efforts to familiarize Cuban audiences with unknown or little-known composers: Guillermo Tomás. Director of the Municipal Band of Havana, Tomás aspired to the quality and artistic consciousness of the band of the Republican Guards in Paris, which in those years was a true exemplar for all the *musiques d'harmonie*. Let us briefly linger on the programs fashioned by Guillermo Tomás, because they reveal an extraordinary educational activity that is almost unparalleled in the rest of the continent. From 1900 to 1903, the band engaged in an intense labor of Wagnerian diffusion, performing large parts of the *Ring Cycle*, *Parsifal*, *Tristan*, *The Flying Dutchman*, *The Meistersingers of Nuremberg*. In 1905, festivals were organized with a chorus to perform Bach's *Saint Matthew Passion*, part of Haydn's *The Creation*, the ballet from Rameau's *Castor and Pollux*, a *Siciliana* by Alessandro Scarlatti, and segments of operas by Gluck, Paisiello, Cimarosa, and Pergolesi. But that was not all. The following premieres were featured: *The Great Russian Easter, On the Central Asian Steppes* (Borodin), parts of *Hulda and Giselle* by César Franck; the overture from *Hansel and Gretel, Death and Transfiguration*, the prelude from *Fervaal* by D'Indy; *The Sorcerer's Apprentice*, large segments of the first and third acts of *Siegfried*, and, what seems most incredible, two fragments of *Pelléas et Mélisande* by Debussy (the introduction to the first act and the final scene of the fourth act), a score that had only premiered in Paris, with little success, three years before.

In 1908, Tomás organized a true symphony orchestra — which functioned irregularly — in order to widen his possibilities. In 1910 he presented Brahm's *Tragic Overture, The Moldau* by Smetana, and two movements from a symphony by Schumann, but emphasizing more the work of Dukas, D'Indy, and Debussy. In 1912, fragments of *Der Rosenkavalier,* a *Suite* by Max Reger, the finale of Albeniz's *Pepita Jiménez,* and two movements from Mahler's Third Symphony were featured … If it is true that the wider public did not always appreciate Tomás's efforts, the musicians were assimilating new ideas that in 1922 would make it possible to create the first regularly functioning symphonic orchestra that Havana had known.

Espadero's Romantic-Europeanizing tendency had its followers in Cuba. His disciple, Cecilia Arizti (daughter of the pianist of the same surname), published in New York, in 1877, a series of piano compositions: two scherzi, a *Nocturno,* a *Mazurka,* a *Reverie,* an *Impromptu,* a *Barcarola,* a *Romanza,* a *Vals lento,* a *Valse brillante,* and a *danza.* Cecilia Arizti's style was more restrained than Espadero's and ignored the virtuosity so prevalent at the time. The *Nocturno* is of a rare delicacy. Unfortunately, Cecilia Arziti, like her teacher, was a victim of her yearning to work according to "the good examples" set forth during her time. Her inferiority complex limited her possibilities. The influence of Rubinstein — then a deified performer — was too great. We see a glimpse of the composer she could have been when she writes plain and simple pages of an attenuated Romanticism which makes one think — a curious but true coincidence — of the Adagietto of Poulenc's *Les Biches.*

José Manuel (Lico) Jiménez is a similar case. His father, a talented violinist, son of a musician from Trinidad [Cuba], had begun studying in Havana with Arditi. Supported by two rich landowners, he pursued his career in Leipzig, occupying one of the top positions in the Gewandhaus [concert hall]. After a trip to Cuba, the father returned to Germany in 1869 with José Manuel, who was then fourteen, putting him in the hands of Reinecke and Moscheles. José Manuel completed his training with Marmontel, obtaining a first prize in piano at the Paris Conservatory. The talented young black adolescent was taken to the Wahnfried Villa, where he played in the presence of Wagner. Liszt, who knew him, already had praised him warmly. With that kind of technical and moral baggage he returned to Cuba in 1879, playing a series of concerts throughout the island. Fervent followers of Beethoven, the Jiménez family performed many of his sonatas. Liszt, Chopin, and Rubinstein rounded out the repertoire of the young pianist. But the Cuban bourgeoisie, which preferred black orchestras to liven up their dances, wore down José Manuel Jiménez with all the weight of their racial prejudice, denying him the position he deserved as performer and as professor with a solid overseas training. Disheartened, the musician returned to Europe for good. His younger brother, Nicasio, taught cello in Tours. Lico, who married a German woman, finished his days as a professor in the Hamburg Conservatory.

Endowed with a much subtler harmonic sense than Espadero, at times truly audacious, Jiménez, who knew the inner workings of Schumann's and Liszt's art, always showed himself to be an ingenious composer. But he lacked spirit. His emotion never went much beyond the well-written page. With *El Azra, El amor,* and *Crepúsculo,* he was the first Cuban musician to take on the lieder. The best of his output is his *Valse caprice, Solitude, Elegía, Murmullo del céfiro* [Murmur of the zephyr]. He even wrote some *danzas* with a popular feel to them. But, as for things Cuban, he does not surpass Cervantes. After he returned from Germany, he composed a sonata and a concerto for piano and orchestra. One can believe that the atmosphere surrounding the conservatory at Hamburg, where he was in daily contact with the scores of Brahms, Reger, and Strauss, would have had an impact on the evolution of his thinking, given his affinity with these composers. The war has prevented us from reclaiming these scores, which, in any case, would not add a great deal to the island's musical tradition.

In this group, the musician who maintained the greatest ties to his native land, despite his cosmopolitan life, was the great mulatto violinist José White. Although I mistrust the superlative accolades showered on Cuban performers of the past, a comparison of the criticism published in Europe, Brazil, and Havana allows one to affirm that he was an absolutely extraordinary artist. Moreover, there must have been a reason he was given the professorship previously held by Allard at the Paris Conservatory. Although his activities as a professor and a performer drew him away from composition, White wrote a Concerto for Violin and Orchestra, which premiered in Paris,[1] a quartet, and various melodies, among which is "La bella cubana" — one of the most traditional songs of the island — with a skillfully constructed melody over a rhythm that appears in the most ancient *guarachas* and Haitian merengues: three eighth notes in binary rhythm, the first two eighth notes with a point of augmentation. (We find this rhythm, of purely Antillean origin, in the bass lines of certain Afro-Cuban *sones*.) Born in Matanzas in 1836, José White died in Paris in 1918.

With the birth of the republic [1902], Cuba witnessed a phenomenon that happened in other Latin American countries: attaining sovereignty is coupled with a momentary underestimation of national values. The newly born country aspired to be part of all the great cultural currents of the day, to be au courant. Through an understandably evolutionary process, independence comes linked to a desire to apply new methods, to be "up-to-date," to sweep aside anything that smacks of colonialism or provincialism. After an eminently polemical period, in which historical events occupy the minds of many; after the heroic period, in which Martí's genius had yielded to a harvest of bullets, Cubans aspired to attain a similar cultural level to those countries offering a higher degree of civilization. Paris, after the Exposition of 1900, seemed to symbolize the pinnacle of culture. The men of the Americas, poets, painters, thinkers, musicians, would go, like larks mesmerized by a mirror, toward the City of Light. In Cuba one could hear echoes of the French Heredia, of Rodenbach, of Verlaine, and even of Jean Lorrain. The names of Léon Dierx, of Auguste Dorchain, of Paul Fort, of Mallarmé, arrived all scrambled together in the Cuban provinces, provoking the lyrical outbursts of a José Manuel de Poveda.

Guillermo Tomás, as we have seen, was one of the maximum promoters of this universalistic movement within his milieu. Even though it is absolutely necessary for a culture to be up-to-date, this catching up was a double-edged sword. Faced with the presence of glowing, unexpected, unique, examples of art, overwhelmed by the impression that for a long time a throbbing new world had passed them by, artists tended toward cosmopolitanism, trying to reach by imitation the high culture of the time. No longer did we see composers like Espadero, who simply tried to adjust to the models that were successful at a given moment. Now artists wanted to assimilate the best of an era, were anxious to avoid mistakes, and desperately sought entry through the narrow door of salvation. In short, one had to avoid the error committed by Laureano Fuentes with his [symphonic] poem *América*.

Dazzled by Wagner, by the fin-de-siècle spirit, by the great affective myths of poetry, Guillermo Tomás composed a *Sakuntala*, "a musical dialogue in four acts based on a Sanskrit drama of Kalidasa," writing *its* poem and *its* music. *The Prayer of the Believer*, another work of his, quite sparely conceived (a cantata for soloist, chorus, and band), dwells in the atmosphere of the Holy Grail. Surrendering to less transcendental exercises, Tomás thinks of Pierné, of Guy Ropatz, while writing his impressions for orchestra *Veillée de fête, Ronde interrompue*. Of similar inspiration are his *Scenes from an Imaginary Ballet* (in four movements). These works would have been well regarded had they been on a good program of European symphonic music. Furthermore, they signaled a necessary transition toward the practice of newer techniques. But they added nothing to a living music. His *Chorale and Fugue for Orchestra* was an exceptional score in an ambience in which few could claim to be doing anything better. But in the Schola Cantorum of Paris they were already writing chorales and fugues as a pretext for obtaining new objectives within the form. On the other hand, his functions as a band director took away much of his energy, imposing on him civically minded musical obligations. A man of great moral rectitude, Tomás had already dedicated a *Canto de guerra* to the liberators [pro-independence revolutionaries] in 1896. In the first years of the republic he would have to compose many marches and fanfares of circumstance, serving the commemorative needs of an incipient nationhood.

Tomás, however, spoke in a Cuban idiom with three *Danzas íntimas* for band; *Esbozos de mi tierra* [Sketches of my land], for piano and orchestra, and *Páginas de mi breviario* [Pages from my breviary]. They are all highly laudable scores. But in those days, new winds were blowing. The knowledge of folklore posed problems that went beyond a correct interpretation of melodies and rhythms. The *contradanza* and the *danza* were already academic models that Cuban music had left behind, like a snake shedding old skin. It was only possible to return to them with a vision that nobody in the Americas could have at the turn of the century. This explains how a man who was wise, rigorous, and musically endowed could not express his true artistic worth in his own milieu. If it is true that Tomás's Cuban-inspired work embodies a true, high-quality contribution to the island's music, he did not exercise any influence on others, nor did he serve as an example for the future.

Eduardo Sánchez de Fuentes (1874–1944) was the most representative musician of this transition period. Molded in the bosom of an intellectual family, son of a poet, he had Ignacio Cervantes as one of his first teachers. At the age of sixteen he had written the most famous habanera, "Tú," a perennial piece, like Ponce's "Estrellita," with extraordinary success in Spain and Latin America. Today it is the quintessential habanera, and it has wiped out the memory of previous habaneras. The truth is that the habanera never embodied a type of music that was peculiar to Havana. It shared the same fate as Cubism, never baptized as such by the painters who created it. Decades had passed since the Cuban *contradanza* had been assiduously exported as a musical product of the island, republished abroad under the title *Danza habanera*. We have Mexican editions of old Cuban *contradanzas*, of Fernández de Coca and del Infante, presented under that same rubric of *Danzas habaneras*. In Spain they were presented as *Danzas americanas* or *Americanas*. To show how widespread the designation of habaneras was, we see the term used by Bizet in *Carmen*, where he borrowed, without the slightest malice, the theme and rhythm of a song by Sebastián Yradier, erroneously attributing it to folklore. The habanera "Tú" only comprised a novelty by exhibiting a greater liberty in using the *danza* form (the traditional *prima* section included an introduction of six bars) and in its tempo. Its long and voluptuous melody could be sung like a ballad, in contrast to the traditional *contradanza*, almost unsingable because of its vivacity. As for the rest, there was no hint of any rhythmic innovation: *cinquillo* and tango. It is not by mere chance that this habanera was baptized tango-habanera when it was republished in Paris. Thanks to a spiritual affinity easy to explain, this song became greatly loved in Buenos Aires. In passing, these historical references should not detract from the fact that this is a fine and delicate melody, and that it figures as a centerpiece of Cuba's traditional music.

In 1898, after having written a good many songs, Sánchez de Fuentes, at the age of twenty-four, undertook the enterprise that Saumell had left on the drawing table: to write a national opera. The score of *Yumurí* premiered in October of the same year, in the Albisu Theater. The libretto, by Rafael Fernández de Castro, was written in an excessively rhetorical language, with a palpable ignorance of the rigors of the sung word. One shudders to think how the public must have received this strophe to be sung by a female chorus:

¿Por qué te encuentras triste, bellísima princesa,
Encantadora sílfide del valle de Nathlan?
Desecha tus penas, disipa tu tristeza,
Que Caunabaco viene tu dicha a realizar.

(Why are you so sad, beautiful princess,
Enchanting sylph of Nathlan Valley?
Banish your sorrows, dissipate your sadness,
for Caunabaco will bring you good fortune.)

The plot, on the other hand, with its earthquake finale that sculpts into the ground the fissure made by the Yumurí River was good operatic dramaturgy. Two very moving acts with five scenes. The characters: Yumurí, the daughter of an Indian chief; Alonso de Pineda, a conquistador; Caunabaco, a chief of the tribe; the cacique, a confidante, and a priest who responded to the overly Wagnerian name of Waltunka (one thinks of Waltraute). It is the classical story of the white man and the Indian woman, held back in their idyll by the religious traditions of the tribe. Everything ends under a collapsing mountain.

The libretto moves along a tight and concise plot, offering the composer a succession of arias, duos, and concertantes, which logically flow one from the other. Sánchez de Fuentes was able to pull off a good beginning, with a great melodic power that would never abandon him. It was, lest we forget, the first opera written on a national theme or story. The youthful musician had been trained in an environment bereft of solid guidelines. Nonetheless, his thematic choice points to an error that would later beset a large part of his work: an unjustified admiration for the aboriginal world, the only element of Cuban culture that could not offer him anything in a pure state, not even through archaeological materials. "Indian music" had to be made hypothetically. Thirty years earlier, the Mexican Aniceto Ortega had written a *Guatimozín*. But he had allowed himself the luxury of peppering the Italianisms of his language with his truly authentic *tlaxcalteca* dance, based on existing musical documents. If *Yumurí* reveals a musician endowed with a theatrical sense and of generous inspiration, in terms of musical nationalism, his conceptual premise is erroneous.

In 1901, Sánchez de Fuentes returned to the theater with *El náufrago* [The castaway], an opera in two acts. This time he made his contribution to try and "civilize" the language, a concern of many Cuban artists in the period following independence. The plot was taken from Tennyson's *Enoch Arden* — an excellent subject for a lyrical drama by an English or French composer imbued with the spirit that could later animate *La complainte du pauvre matelot* by Darius Milhaud. But the twentieth century had just been born. Only two paths, both equally dangerous, were then open to the opera composer: post-Wagnerism or Italian verismo. Sánchez de Fuentes opted for Italian verismo, achieving an indisputable success with the public. This success set a bad precedent and led the composer to premiere *La Dolorosa* in 1910, an opera that would become the most accomplished, terminal expression of verismo [realism] in the Americas. A very poor libretto by Federico Uhrbach had contemporary characters on stage dressed in tails, in U.S.-style apparel, or sports clothes—an aesthetic akin to Leoncavallo's *Zazá* or to *Louise* by Charpentier. But at least, in *Louise,* the blouse and the corduroy trousers have a polemical value and are accompanied by street vendor cries. On the other hand, with *La Dolorosa,* the characters moved about in a worldly setting of trendy beaches and millionaire gardens. Intricately plotted, with pretensions of psychological depth, the opera kept the singers in a state of constant agitation, exiting and entering the stage as if moved by some locomotive force, whether it was to sing a sonnet or express an emotional state. An ending worthy of D'Annunzio had a wife committing suicide so that the husband would be forever separated from the woman that would have become his lover.

A closer look shows *La Dolorosa* as a daring work, since with this opera Sánchez de Fuentes attempted to defy the verists on their own ground. On August 8, 1911, *La Dolorosa* was premiered in the Balbo Theater in Turin, with a more than noteworthy success. Uhrbach's libretto had been transformed and rearranged, with the plot taking place in the eighteenth century. Sánchez de Fuentes, rereading the laudatory articles devoted to his work by critics in *Corriere della Sera, La Stampa,* and other Italian newspapers, could laugh at those in Havana who maliciously repeated a couplet, deriding his opera:

"¡Qué dice la Dolorosa?" (What does the Dolorosa say?)
"Siempre la misma cosa." The same thing, every day.)

La Dolorosa had been opportunely staged in Italy, since verismo had a great many practitioners. But no one asked if a Cuban composer should express himself in such an idiom. In the end, it was a repetition of Espadero's case.

With *Doreya,* premiered in February 1918, Sánchez de Fuentes returned to nationalism, but repeating an error he had made twenty years earlier: he remade *Yumurí.* Despite Hilarión Cabrisas's new libretto on the canvas of the earlier opera, it was still a return to the Indianesque cul-de-sac. Inspiring himself in the famous chronicle by Oviedo, the poet wrote a stage *areíto,* with Indians sounding drums, conch shells, and horns, dancing in an archaeologically precise way. The only thing needed — and truly the only one! — was an authentic theme from an *areíto* to sustain the scene.

El caminante, a lyric poem in one act with a text by Villaespesa (1921), is Sánchez de Fuentes's best scenic score, and musically the one presenting the least verismo influence. The religious plot and the unity of the action favored the generous melodic vein of the musician, inducing him to write pages of great tenderness. *Kabelia* (1942), composed after a long silence, in his late years, constitutes a laborious effort by the composer to bring his technique up-to-date. Unfortunately, a few new harmonic procedures did not make up for the lost emotional freshness. Furthermore, the plot was completely inadmissible: a Hindu legend, as far removed from the concerns of our epoch as the *Padmavati* by Roussel. Since the days of *The King of Lahore* by Massenet, India as a subject for Western opera is always closer to Salgari than to Tagore.

If we have dwelled in detail on the lyric work of Sánchez de Fuentes, it is because its abundance and continuity constituted an exceptional display of creative will in an era that did not count on great resources for musical performance, highlighting a series of problems whose negative solution shut out dangerous new directions. The composer also wrote an oratorio, *Navidad* [Christmas], and a ballet, *Dioné:* But his most important non-stage work was his cantata *Anacaona,* performed at the Ibero-American Symphonic Festival of 1929 in Barcelona. *Anacaona,* the name of an Indian princess from Santo Domingo, spoken of by the likes of López de Gomara, Las Casas, and Pedro Mártir de Anglería, was a true symbol. Sánchez de Fuentes refused to accept the black elements of Cuban music, in his estimation something he thought (rather simplistically) could be diassociated from "whiteness." He always insisted, on the basis of historical references, that aboriginal culture had left its imprint on Cuban music, despite the absence of a single musical text to support the affirmation. Turning a deaf ear to prudent advice, he took to working on the *Areíto de Anacaona* cited by Bachiller y Morales, disproven by new research in the field, as a representative document of primitive music of the Antilles. Even if the treatment of the *Areíto de Anacaona* had been extremely skillful, its basic theme offered nothing of true interest.

It is a shame that a succession of errors should have spoiled the greatest work of a man who had carried his musicianship for more than half a century with rare dignity. Because, in the end, aside from his lucky Italian adventure, Sánchez de Fuentes will remain, above all, a composer of habaneras and songs. In a hundred years, his Cuban melodies will occupy a place of honor in our traditions, quoted as models of certain semipopular genres that were cultivated on the island for forty years. Extremely knowledgeable about the past, Sánchez de Fuentes habitually reproduced in his songs certain forgotten rhythmic formulas, infusing them with new life. In this way, his *Cubana* reworked the rhythms of the *Sungambelo* of 1813. He gave the habanera its own stamp, freeing it from the *contradanza*. A melodist with a fine instinct when he turned to folklore, he wrote *criollas* like "La linda cubana," destined to be included in the collections of "songs from every country."

Cuba produced a surprising output of operas, in comparison with other Latin American countries. However, the successes were partial and scarce. Almost none of the scores cited would triumph if unearthed or restaged. (With Villate, the experience was conclusive.) Nonetheless, on June 6, 1921, a Cuban opera premiered in Havana, too forgotten, which belonged to that category of works that seem reborn when dressed up in fresh colors, in the light of ideas brought in by new generations: *La esclava* by José Mauri Esteve.

Accidentally born in Valencia, José Mauri (1856–1937) was self-taught but endowed with an extraordinary intuition. Too disoriented to gauge the strengths and limits of his own creativity, Mauri was always helped by a surprising musicality, evident even in his most modest efforts. For years he oscillated between religious music and zarzuela, the *danzón* and the symphonic poem (*Grandeza y locura de Don Quijote, Los gnomos del Moncayo*), squandering ideas with incredible prodigality. With *La esclava*, Mauri gave us his most interesting work, centering his roving talent on a vigorous and substantial task.

For starters, *La esclava* was an intelligently plotted opera. The libretto by Tomás Juliá unfolds in a sugar mill in Camagüey, in 1860, giving the composer the opportunity to lay hands on the folklore and rhythms that were still a living heritage on the island. A sixty-year delay was enough to give the characters a certain distant air — those troublesome costumes, always a problem on the lyric stage — but not too distant. Realistic, the plot turns on the daughter of a slave, unaware of her origins, who again becomes a salable commodity when her father dies on the eve of a financial disaster. Surrounding the main characters are blacks, *guajiros*, hunters, provincial notaries, all sorts of folks with their own language, with personalities that lend themselves to musical expression. Mauri's score, of course, could not free itself from a certain Italian style in the solely dramatic passages, but it drew constantly on popular elements. The habanera, the *criolla*, the *danzón*, and even the rumba had their assigned places in the work, and not just episodically, but as an integral part of its discourse. Mauri built a black leitmotiv around a vigorous Afro-Cuban theme. The folkloric passages, given their coloring and strength, anticipated the future handling of this material by other composers.

If *La esclava* was not a total success, it at least constituted a first document of value that would later come to light. Ignacio Cervantes used to say that José Mauri was the most important Cuban composer of his time. For the moment, he was the first to write a successful nationalist opera, able to withstand a contemporary staging. Aside from its historical interest, it contains passages that still stand on their own. In Mauri, there was a groundbreaker.

16. Afro-Cubanism

Sánchez de Fuentes's repugnance in admiting the presence of black rhythms in Cuban music can be understood as a reflection of a general outlook during the first years of the republic. Years had transpired since blacks were no longer slaves. However, in a newly conceived country that aspired to bring itself up to date with the cultural currents of the day, the authentically black cultural experience — that is, those deeply rooted and surviving African elements that remained in a pure state — was looked upon with disgust, as a kind of barbaric holdover from the past, and could only be tolerated as a necessary evil. In 1913, the traditional *comparsas* were prohibited. The religious festivities of blacks were prohibited. Undeniably, certain ritual crimes, committed by witch doctors, justified police persecution against the practices of the *babalawos* [Santeria priests]. Some street fighting between enemy *ñáñigo groups* had also logically generated repressive measures. But it should not be believed that these deeds were so frequent, nor that they reached the magnitude of the common crimes committed. It had been a long time since knife-wielders like Manuel Cañamazo, Manita en el suelo, or the black man Sucumbento were the terror of neighborhoods outside the city limits. Furthermore, if so many blacks were loitering among hoodlums with a drum on their belly, much of the blame rested with whites, who always relegated them to a marginal existence, offering them the worst jobs, except when they wanted votes, in which case they appealed to their baser qualities. The kind of politicking that went on during the first years of the republic did nothing to improve the social or cultural condition of blacks; indeed, it fueled their vices as long as blacks were useful for political ends. All these factors contributed to the attitude held by well-heeled men of mistrusting all matters black, and since they were not inclined to ask difficult questions, they did not notice that high on the scaffolds, in the heat of the foundries, under the sun of the rock quarries, or in the coachman's seat, an entire sea of humanity was on the move, a people who conserved their poetic and musical traditions, quite worthy of being studied.

Of course, these traditions offered a wide spectrum in their purity of preservation. As Ramos put it so aptly:

> In the New World, the relationships between blacks and whites brought as a corollary the subordination of one to the other, segregation and separation, and all the subsequent racial and cultural conflict (at times, acute) this subordination implied. This segregation caused the almost total disappearance, in some cases, of primitive institutions. When an individual is separated from his cultural group and placed in contact with other groups and cultures, he tends, in the second or third generation, to forget the primitive cultures and to assimilate the new cultures he has come in contact with.

This process of transculturation has happened several times in previous centuries. The "*Son* de la Má' Teodora" constitutes the most typical sixteenth-century example of this. For an Ulpiano Estrada, a Brindis de Salas, black Creoles of several generations, little was left in the nineteenth century of the primitive cultures of their grandfathers. Only an instinct survived — in this case a rhythmic instinct — of these black musicians and composers who contributed to the evolution of Cuban music in its first phase, without changing the form or the exisitng melodic sources. Nothing differentiated "the black Malibrán woman," married to an officer of the Spanish army, from any other Cuban woman of her time, except the color of her skin. This explains why so many blacks made "white music" during the nineteenth century, refusing to play the roles of "black professors," while the whites — a Bartolomé José Crespo, a Guerrero — were the ones who dressed up as blacks.

But it must not be forgotten that while the transculturation process had completed itself for certain generations, the slave ships kept bringing, with a horrendous regularity, their cargo of "ebony flesh." Thousands upon thousands of slaves kept swelling the workforces of Cuba's plantations, reinitiating a cycle of adaptation whose earlier phases were fixed in the Cuban vernacular: *bozales*, when they arrived from Africa and spoke only in their dialects; *ladinos* when they began to speak in Spanish; *criollos*, the offspring of the ladinos; and *reyoyos*, the children of the criollos. With free slaves or those recently emancipated, the process of transcultura-tion took place swiftly, since contact with the outside world was immediate. But in the slave barracks it was infinitely slower, be-cause knowledge of white culture was gleaned from what the slave could observe at a distance, when there was a party in the master's house. The slave was told to dance his native dances, because it was considered important for the preservation of his health. The slave traders had learned this much earlier than the landowners. However, there were limitations. In 1839, a circular by General Ezpeleta established that, "the slaves in the countryside should be allowed to dance their native dances known as 'with drums,' on holidays, under the vigilance of their overseers, without blacks from any other farm being present." That is, if the slaves from one farm were, in their majority, from one tribe or nation, they would not have the slightest opportunity to have contact with a neighboring workforce of different ethnic origins. The varying conservation or dilution of African traditions derives from this history, and holds true even today among Cuban blacks. Certain old men, born in cap-tivity, remember legends and songs from Africa with extraordi-nary precision. The black man Yamba, more than a hundred years old, whom I met at a farm in the remote countryside, spoke just like blacks in the work of Bartolomé José Crespo, without knowing any other type of dance than what he had seen in the slave barracks as a child. Those same dances are long gone, a tradition the black university student is unaware of, equally true for the mulatto mu-sician of a Havana swing orchestra. After severing the umbilical cord of the slave trade, Cuban blacks lost their contact with Africa, conserving an ever hazier memory of their ancestral traditions. When the *comparsas* were allowed to function again, about ten years ago [1937], they no longer had the same power; they had gained much as moving spectacle, as luxurious theater, in abundance of instruments; but they had lost authenticity. There are not many performers today who are capable of making the array of *batá* drums speak. And yet, their musical awareness is incomparably vaster than that of their grandfathers.

This might explain why certain arcane aspects of black music have taken so long to interest more "serious" composers, more directly drawn to what they immediately heard: the rhythms and singing of the *comparsas,* incorporated into the *contradanzas* in the last phase of their evolution. There was more. Much more. Without mentioning groups from long ago, like Nuestra Señora de los Remedios, founded by free blacks in Havana in 1598, nor the petition for land to establish *cabildos,* which figure in the town records of eighteenth-century Santiago, in 1796 there was already a Cabildo de Congos Reales, under the name of one of the Three Kings, Saint Melchior. The increasing black population, together with a proportionately greater manumission of slaves, made these groups proliferate. Essentially, the *cabildos* were "mutual aid societies," which prevented the ex-slave from being buried in a common grave. The following *cabildos* appeared: Arará, Apapá, Apapá Chiquito, Mandinga, Oro, Lucumí, Carabalí Ungrí, Nación Mina Popó de la Costa de Oro, Arará tres ojos, and so on. The blacks from Calabar created secret *ñáñigo* societies, whose first activities date from around 1835, when the Acabatón society appeared in Regla. Although the *cabildos* composed of offspring of the "nations"—blacks from different regions/ethnicities—endured to our times, *ñañiguismo* spread throughout Cuban society, because it had a more inclusive notion of membership. They admitted people of all races and walks of life into their ranks, as long as they observed the established rules. (Chinese, Creoles, even Spaniards were affiliated with *ñañiguismo.*) Their initiation ceremonies and the true brotherhood of those who belonged made *ñañiguismo* a true popular masonry. Around 1914, in Havana, Regla, Guanabacoa, and Matanzas, there were fifty-seven *juegos* [groups] of *ñáñigos.* Currently, even though *ñañiguismo* has lost a lot of its strength because of the previously described transculturation process, various groups still remain, strict guardians of the language and the ritual.

If the black *cabildos* were mutual aid societies, they also specified, when legally registered, that they were created for "recreational and leisurely pursuits." This authorized them to hold dances and form *comparsas* for Three Kings Day [January 6] or, after the abolition of slavery, for carnival. In different periods the *comparsas* paraded through the streets of Havana, sporting vivid names: *El gavilán, Los congos libres, El alacrán chiquito, La culebra, El pájaro lindo, Mandinga Moro Rizo, Mandinga Moro Azul, Los moros, Los peludos*. [The hawk, The free congos, The small scorpion, The snake, The pretty bird, Mandinga curly Moor, Mandinga blue Moor, The Moors, The hairy ones]. The *comparsas*, more than just a marching rhythmic collective, were like an itinerant ballet. They had their "themes." A spider or a snake, represented by a huge figure held on high by an expert dancer, served as the focal point for dancing and singing. The *comparsa* members would "kill the spider" or "kill the snake."

"Mamita, mamita,	
yen, yen, yen:	
que me mata la culebra,	(the snake's gonna kill me,)
yen, yen, yen.	
Mírale los ojo	(Look at its eyes,
que parecen candela;	they seem like fire
mírale lo diente,	look at its teeth
que parece filé (alfileres)"	they seem like needles
"Mentira, mi negra,	It's a lie, my black woman,)
yen, yen, yen;	
son juego e mi tierra,	(they are the game of my soil,)
yen, yen, yen."	

As Ramos observed referring to similar dances seen in Brazil, those figures that used to (and still do) inspire the name of certain *comparsas* undoubtedly represent a totemic survival. In the snake dance, Fernando Ortiz sees an offshoot of a Dahomey snake cult that still persists in Haiti, where a serpent of forged steel appears on all voodoo altars. As for the violent and bloody strife between *ñáñigo* groups in the nineteenth century, Vivó maintains that they reflect old intertribal rivalries from Africa. The initiation ceremony of the *ñáñigos*, which we have witnessed many times, is truly a collective spectacle, in which episodes of the same legend are mimed, danced, and sung with slight variations. Something of old funeral rites has stayed embedded in them. A government edict in 1792 prohibited that "blacks could conduct or allow others to conduct, to the *cabildos* the cadavers of blacks, in order to sing or cry as is customary in their native land." Years later, the bishop Trespalacios insisted on the point. As for the festivities with magic — a different issue altogether — their main objective continues to be a believer's possession, so thoroughly studied by Jacques Roumain in his *Le sacrifice du Tambour Assohtor*. In the commonly accepted notion, the possession by a saint or divinity in the black pantheon is syncretically represented almost always by a Catholic image. This is currently referred to in Cuba as *"bajar al santo"* [to make the saint descend] or *"subirse el santo"* [to make the saint come up through you]. But let us not linger here on matters amply dealt with by specialists in the field.

Musically, the matter is very complex. Because to say "African music" is the same as saying "medieval knights." As Ortiz has pointed out, "in studying Afro-Cuban music one has to distinguish between music descended from Dahomey, or the Yoruba, or the Carabalí and Conga." Unfortunately, a scientific work of notation, compilation, comparison, rhythmic and modal study, with its ensuing classifications, still has not been undertaken, because the task, admittedly so, is beyond the scope of one individual. In the first place, if one does not have informants who are intelligent and trustworthy, it is impossible to find out when and where a religious ceremony or a profane drumming session will be held. In the second place, because the true *ñáñigos* — that is, the most interesting ones — ascertained on many occasions, are opposed to having their musical rituals notated or taped, since they view these acts as a profanation of their secrets. In the third place, a researcher's interest quickly awakens the greed among people who do not know any better, who then scheme up some kind of charade in exchange for a few coins. Fernando Ortiz, appealing to a heroic sense of patience, is the person who has most deeply researched these matters. But he is not a musician, nor does he claim to be, and for different reasons he has been bereft of the best collaborators that he could have had in his musical research.

Let us rely, then, on certain authoritative conclusions drawn by Ortiz:

> The river peoples of the Niger, particularly the Yorubas and the Nagós, in Cuba known as *lucumís*, brought, along with their complex religious beliefs, drums, songs, and dances of their ancient rites that still resonate intact under the skies of the Americas imploring favors from their African divinities. Dahomeyan music, or of the *dajomés*, as in Cuba they have been referred to with true phonetic propriety, is almost identical to that of their neighbors, the *arará*, and both have been maintained, sheltered by *lucumí* rites. We know that the Yoruba pantheon spread among the bordering towns, especially toward the north, penetrating Dahomey and its coastal area, in the ancient Ardrá or Arará region, absorbed more than a century earlier by that very powerful kingdom. For this reason, among blacks of this region one finds an advanced theological and liturgical syncretism, and the chants, drum beats, and instruments have intermingled, where similar deities are invoked under different names. This allows us to infer, if we know beforehand the religious nomenclature of these peoples, whether a chant is Dahomeyan or Yoruba, according to the language of the prayer or name of the god being propitiated. It is easy to deduce that a chant to Shangó (deity of lightning), is from the *lucumís*, and one for Ebioso (also an igneous god) is from Dahomey or the *dajomés*. Ñañiguismo has an unmistakable musical personality; its naked simplicity sustains *carabalí* music in Cuba.

And Ortiz adds in another work:

> Here, at the core of our people, there is still much music of *bantú* or *conga* origin in the dances of our peasants; we have *gangá* music, from which the primitive rumba is derived; some bits of *arará* or *dajomé* music, called voodoo in Haiti, which here tends to mix in with *lucumí* music; and, finally, best-conserved and varied of Cuba's Afican music, the religious liturgy of the Yoruba.

Lucumí and *ñáñigo* music generally has melodies that are ample, noble, slow in contrast with the dynamism of the percussion. It is sung by the faithful, in unison or in octaves. In all of the hymns one observes an antiphonal form: a soloist and a chorus or two semichoruses, the second repeating the phrases of the first. "In Yoruba religious chants the antiphonal soloist initiates or raises the chant to a pleasing level, and the chorus, called the *ankori*, responds in the same tone as the soloist" (Ortiz). This liturgy comprises, among others, songs to Elegguá, overseer of all roads; to Ogún, blacksmith and inventor of the anvil, represented by the image of Saint Peter; to Ochosi, god of hunting and warriors (Saint Norbert); to Babalú-Ayé (Saint Lazarus); to Yemayá, goddess of the sea and cosmic mother; to Obatalá, to Ochún, to Changó, to Oyá . . . It is extremely rare to find a theme of these chants that begins on the dominant note. The elimination of the leading note is so frequent that when a popular composer wants to impart an "African air" to a melody, by instinct he suppresses or alters the seventh note. Quite frequently the hymns are based on pentatonic scales without semitones. But the use of these ranges is capricious, without obeying the rules. We will not speak of modes or particular characteristics of one or another kind of music, since the scarcity of scientifically established documents makes any analysis pointless.

As for percussion, it is simply prodigious. The Afro-Cuban drums compose an entire arsenal: the *ñáñigos,* tensed with strings and wedges, one-sided, played with two hands, designated generically with the name of *encomos,* although the family includes, as Israel Castellanos points out, the *bencomo,* the *cosilleremá,* the *llaibillembi* and the *boncó enchemillá;* the *batá* drums, "bimembraned, played on both sides, with a wooden hourglass shape, closed, permanently taut with a rope-like skin" (Ortiz), which are called, as we have seen, *okónkolo* (the smallest), *itótele* (the medium-sized one), and *iyá* (the largest), which is "the mother of the drums." In addition, one must mention the *tumba* and the *tahona,* used for profane and sacred functions. To these are usually added, although not as a rule, the *cajón,* the *marímbula,* the *güiro,* the *econes,* or the little iron bells without tongues, and the *claves.* Also used are two types of *marugas:* the one that consists of two tin cones, welded at the base and filled with little stones (what is called in other Antillean isles the *chá-chá*), and the one that consists of a cone made of laced fibers, filled with seeds or *mates,* which is shaken from the top down, and held by a ring fixed at its vertex (one of the many kinds of basket rattles known by certain indigenous peoples of the Americas).

Notice that Afro-Cuban music dispenses with any melody-making instruments. Pure singing over percussion. On the other hand, in the ceremonial rituals—the *ñáñigo* initiation, for example, or those of Santeria—one does not observe the slightest watering down of a way of singing that remains true to old African customs. Blacks who pride themselves on knowing ancestral hymns and traditions are unaware of hybrid genres, analogous to the windward *fulía,* for example, and that the *décima* derived from the *romance*—in Cuba part of the cultural patrimony of white peasants—alternated with sung and instrumental passages of purely African technique. There are cases where the *batá* drums, aided by their rich tuning and the virtuosity of their performers, play entire solo passages, eliminating the voices. Once, at a Santeria party in Regla, we heard the drummers play a "march" and a "wail" of considerable duration, which were true pieces, complete, balanced, developed within the tempo, evolving from fundamental rhythmic cells. In many cases, this prime beat flowers into a *rhythmic mode.* Really, how can we properly speak of rhythm when faced with a true phrase, composed of notes and groups of notes, that outpaces all metrical limits before acquiring a rhythmic function through sheer repetition? When this happens—and it does so frequently—we are in the presence of a rhythmic mode, with its own accents that have nothing to do with accepted notions of a strong or weak beat. The player stresses this note or another, not for scansional reasons, but because the traditional expression of the *rhythmic mode* demands it. It is not mere happenstance that blacks say that "they make the drums speak"! Now consider the disconcerting effect of movement, of internal palpitations given off by the simultaneous pacings of various rhythmic modes, which end up establishing mysterious relationships among themselves, conserving, however, a certain independence, and you will have a remote idea of the kind of bewitching effect produced by certain expressions of the *batá* drums!

On the other hand, we must not forget that in certain kinds of ceremonies the chants respond to very diverse uses and emotions. If the practice of "making the saint descend" is accompanied by a monotonous chant whose purpose is to engender an obsession, a fixed idea conducive to an ecstatic state; conversely, in the *ñáñigo* celebrations, for example, there are so many different chants and phases that accompany an intricate initiation ceremony. A true mystery play, the *juego* includes, in this case, antiphonal hymns, dances by *diablitos* [little devils], prayers for the dead, marches, processionals, and an invocation to the sun, as well as recitations of formulas "in native tongue," measured out on the skin of the drum. It is pointless to go on about the rich sonorities of these types of folkloric expression.

In 1925, Amadeo Roldán began to consciously exploit this wondrous wellspring of rhythms and melodies. However, a phenomenon prevalent in all Afro-Cuban symphonic output bears pointing out: bereft of scientific work where they can study the modal and rhythmic laws governing black music, the Cuban composer works with materials haphazardly chanced upon at a ceremony that he has personally witnessed, without really knowing the rich textures of this sonorous treasure. Although *ñáñigo* music is a branch of the *carabalí* tree, it is easy to note that, along with its basic percussion, it is unaware of the music's origins. This allows us to differentiate between what is *ñáñigo* and what is *carabalí*, an almost imperceptible difference if compared to the dissimilarities between certain expressions of Yoruba music from *lucumí* or *conga* music. Under apparent similarities, each one of these musics possesses its own sound environment, rules, ways of being. Without having to subscribe to the role of cultured composer as ethnographer when approaching the primitive soul and his music, we see how, in the work of Roldán, as well as in that of a García Caturla — when they compose girded by the document in hand — all of the elements of that vast sonority of the Afro-Cuban realm are all mixed together. And thus we find, side by side, the *lucumí* hymn, the tune of a

bembé, the *ñáñigo* invocation, as well as an array of percussion—
from the regular and symmetrical that accompanies the dance of the
diablito or *írime,* to the complex percussion of the Yoruba drums.

The Afro-Cuban music movement initiated by some composers provoked a violent reaction from those opposed to anything black.
Guajiro music was pitted against Afro-Cuban music, the former
purveyed as representative of white music, more noble, melodic,
pure. However, those who claimed to utilize *guajiro* music in larger-
scale works were surprised that after a first score nothing else was
left to be done. And this for an unforeseen reason: the *guajiro* sings
his *décimas* with the accompaniment of the *tiple* [treble guitar], but
he does not invent anything new musically.

This unique fact is explainable: when he sings, the *guajiro's* poetic invention is fitted to a traditional melodic pattern, whose roots
are steeped in the tradition of the Spanish *romance* [ballad], brought
to the island by the first colonizers. When the Cuban *guajiro* sings,
he sticks to the inherited melody with utmost fidelity. Throughout
the Cuban nineteenth century, the popular printing presses flooded
the towns and villages with reams and reams of *décimas* "to be sung
accompanied by the tiple." But all of those volumes did not inl-
cude a single bar of music. Why? The reason is simple: if it is true
that the *guajiro* was inclined to renovate the lyrics to his songs,
learning the words of others, or relying on his own inspiration, he
made no pretense of introducing the slightest variety in terms of
the tune. The *décimas* offered had to adjust to a model known by
all. Quite the poet, the *guajiro* is no musician. He does not create
melodies. Throughout the island, he sings his *décimas* over ten or
twelve fixed patterns, all similar to one another, whose original
sources can be found in any old anthology of ballads from Extremadura [Spain]. (The Venezuelan poet and folklorist Juan Lis-
cano made the same observation when studying certain popular
expressions of his country, quite rich in poetic content, but always
the same musically.) The same thing happens with the *zapateo.*
There is no such thing as different *zapateos.* There is only one, always the same, which returned after eighty years, like a classical
quote, in the works of popular Cuban composers: Anckermann,

Marín, Varona, and so on. (Formerly, there was another type of *za-pateo* that has disappeared without a trace, and it is harmonized, in published works of last century, in pure Haydnesque style.) At times, and what recently occurred with "La guantanamera," is an example, a *guajiro* singer seems to have invented a new melody. But let us not fall for the ploy. It is simply a reappearance of the ballad, whose song was conserved by those in the interior. And as for the much-heralded "total Cubanness" of the *guajira* melody, we should not have too many illusions. The *guajira* melody of Cuba is identical to that of the Venezuelan *galerón*. (The only difference between the two genres is in the type and number of verses employed.) The only thing that imbues any élan to this static folklore is the virtuosity of the performer or the inventive verve of the singer. But felicitous moments do not a tradition make. Furthermore, the song of the Cuban *guajiro* seems to have lost the luster of its grace, praised a hundred years ago by the Countess of Merlín. There is an evident impoverishment of material.

This explains why scores such as *Suite cubana* by Mario Valdés Costa (a prematurely deceased composer) or the *Capricho* for piano and orchestra by Hubert de Blanck, based on *guajiro* themes, exhausted the possibilities of a folklore after the first attempt. In mixed-blood and black music, on the other hand, if the interest in the lyrics seems scant, the sonic material is incredibly rich. This is why attempts to create a work of national expression always return, sooner or later, to Afro-Cuban and mestizo genres or rhythms.

17. Amadeo Roldán–Alejandro García Caturla

After the heat of the aborted revolution of Veterans and Patriots (1923), which was a typical example of a Latin American declaration lacking cohesion, or direction, or concrete ideology, some young writers and artists who had been involved in the movement and had drawn fruitful lessons from the dangerously futile adventure, met frequently seeking to maintain the camaraderie forged in those agitated days. This is how the Grupo Minorista was formed, without manifestos or high priests, as a meeting ground for men sharing concerns in common. Without aiming to create a movement, *minorismo* quickly became a spiritual climate. Thanks to its efforts, exhibitions, concerts, and lecture cycles were organized; magazines were published; personal contacts with intellectuals in Europe and the Americas were established, which represented new ways of thinking and seeing. In that period Picasso, Joyce, Stravinsky, Les Six, L'Esprit Nouveau, and all of the isms were "discovered." Books printed without capital letters circulated from hand to hand. It was the time of vanguards, of far-flung metaphors, of magazines with obligatory titles such as *Espiral, Proa, Vértice, Hélice* [Spiral, Bow, Vertex, Propeller], and so forth. Moreover, all Latin American youth seemed to suffer the same fever.

Nonetheless, in Cuba these spirits quieted quickly. The presence of rhythms, dances, rituals, visual-sculptural elements, traditions, that for too long had been held back because of absurd prejudices, opened up a realm of immediate action creating possibilities to struggle for goals far more significant than an atonal score or a Cubist painting. Those who already knew the score of *The Rite of Spring*—the great revolutionary banner of the day—began to notice, justifiably, that in Regla, on the other side of the bay, there were rhythms as complex and interesting as those created by Stravinsky to evoke the primitive rituals of pagan Russia. Milhaud had already been seduced by the Brazilian sambas, writing "El buey en el techo" [The ox on the roof], "L'Homme et son désir" [Man and his desire], and the famous "Saudades do Brazil," which were already being heard in Cuba. Awareness of this quickly returned the sheep to pasture. Eyes and ears opened up to what was living and all around them. On the other hand, the birth of Mexican mural painting, the work of Diego Rivera and Orozco, had impressed many Cuban intellectuals. The possibility of expressing what was local with a new conception of its values became ingrained in the minds of artists. Fernando Ortiz, despite the age difference, mixed in with these young voices. His books were read. Suddenly, blacks were at the center of everything. Because this irritated old guard intellectuals, one would go with utmost devotion to the *ñáñigo juramentos* [initiations], praising the dance of the *diablito*. Thus the Afro-Cuban tendency was born, which for more than ten years would nourish poems, novels, folkloric and sociological studies. The tendency, in many cases, remained superficial and peripheral, with the stereotype of the "black man under palm trees drunk on the sun." However, Afro-Cubanism was a necessary step in better comprehending certain poetic, musical, ethnic, and social factors that had suffused all contours of what it meant to be uniquely Cuban.

In the midst of the Afro-Cuban "discovery," Amadeo Roldán appeared.

Born in Paris in 1900, but of purely Cuban descent, Amadeo Roldán had entered the Madrid Conservatory at the age of five, and at fifteen won first prize in violin and the highly competitive Sarasate prize. After studying harmony and composition with Conrado del Campo, he came to Cuba in 1919, leading an obscure existence for a period of time, necessarily obliged to earn a living as a musician in restaurants, movie theaters, and nightclubs. In 1923, he wrote *Fiestas galantes*, for voice and piano, based on poems by Verlaine — he was under the full sway of Impressionism, as evidenced by other piano pieces of the same period — and a quartet that embodied the inevitable school exercise. In that same year, when he undertook the writing of an opera, the clarity of his artistic vision was a distant reality. It was going to be a "Gaelic opera," with a Luis Baralt libretto, titled *Deirdre*. It was a tropical throwback to César Franck's *Hulda*, to Chabrier's *Gwendoline*, to Chausson's *King Arthur*, filtered through Debussy and Dukas, of course. Roldán finished the first act and began work on the second. In a hunting scene he used augmented fifths with a scandalous lavishness. However, in this score he was already leaning toward a certain rhythmic intensity, a primitive violence that broke with Impressionist blandness. Roldán underwent slow, painful changes, full of renunciations, which would take him to the premiere of *Obertura sobre temas cubanos* [Overture on Cuban themes].

For Roldán, in those years of arduous development, the capital had made musical progress. Founded in 1922 by the maestro Gonzalo Roig, the Havana Symphony Orchestra had received the backing of Pablo Casals, who was enthusiastic about the endeavor. The Pro Arte Musical Society already existed, and organized concerts and performances featuring the most famous soloists that delighted audiences. Pedro Sanjuán Nortes, a Spanish musician, arrived in Havana in 1923, and he created a second orchestra, the Philharmonic, which survived the former and is currently directed by Erich Kleiber. The coexistence of two enemy orchestras gave way to a battle that culminated in true violence, with physical aggression between musicians. A highly beneficial situation, in sum, for Cuban culture. Trying to outdo each other, the musicians of both groups would rival each other's efforts to best perform the same score. If a work appeared in the program of the Symphony Orchestra, the Philharmonic would play it at its next concert, to prove it was a superior performance. It did not always turn out that way, but that struggle became an excellent school, since it obligated the musicians to focus thoroughly on what they were playing. Moreover, that match shook up the audience's indolence, egging it on to pick favorites. One was either a "symphonist" or a "philharmonic" fan.

From the outset, Roldán decided in favor of the Philharmonic Orchestra, becoming its concert violinist. The reasons for his preference were more aesthetic than anything else. Having come from Europe, Sanjuán was devoted to premiering in Cuba scores by Debussy, Ravel, de Falla, the Five, until then unknown to the public (remember, in those years recordings of symphonic music had just begun). In addition, Sanjuán, quite knowledgeable about orchestration, was a skillful composer who wrote scores inspired by Castilian folklore before being seduced by Afro-Cuban music. Sanjuán composed a *Liturgia negra* [Black liturgy], with folk elements, and although it did not prove anything beyond a proficient command of his métier, the result was a repetition, almost a hundred years later, of the work done by Casamitjana using *comparsa* themes heard one night in the streets of Santiago. Always alert to any expression far removed from salon formulas, then quite the rage, Sanjuán rounded out Roldán's technical training, and in 1925 he staged his *Obertura sobre temas cubanas*.

Even though it is not a completely accomplished work, one can say that the premiere of this *Obertura* constituted the most important event in Cuban musical history of the twentieth century (as of this writing), in terms of influence and implications. Despite the claim by all Cuban musicians about the musical value of popular forms, be it nourishment for all of their oeuvre (Saumell), or partially (Espadero), blacks, long exploited by the *guaracheros* of *bufo* theater, had not been part of a symphonic work. What was unique was that Roldán, when he sketched out his *Obertura*, had instinctively gone back to a type of folkloric expression captured various times in the nineteenth century: the eastern *Cocoyé*, stylized already by the likes of Casamitjana, Desvernine, Reinó, and even by Gottschalk. That is, when Roldán opened the cycle of his true work and began to find himself, he harvested a tradition that directly linked him to the first effort made in Cuba to incorporate black themes into a serious score (Casamitjana's *Cocoyé*). But, aside from its polemical and revelatory significance, Roldán's *Obertura* should be considered today simply as a document that establishes the beginning of a career. The many tentative elements of the work failed to free his persona from his own prejudices and influences. One passage must be cited, however, as a sensational innovation for 1925: the section that prepares the coda and features only percussion, mobilizing various Afro-Cuban instruments. Those bars embody a veritable declaration of principles.

The *Tres pequeños poemas* ("Oriental," "Pregón," "Fiesta negra") were premiered in 1926, immediately performed by the Cleveland Symphony Orchestra. In "Oriental," there was a renewed use of themes from the *Cocoyé*, but trimming all the orchestral fat that had tarnished the mischief and grace of the previous work. The "Pregón," inspired by a true street vendor cry, with its torpid and torrid atmosphere, was still reminiscent of Roldán's Impressionist phase. In the "Fiesta negra," on the other hand, the musician starts to experiment with themes chosen for musical reasons rather than their poetic value, or as color and ambience. The initial theme was a cell that grew and developed horizontally, with a systematic rhythmic variation within the measure until the final chords. "Fiesta negra" was the first truly accomplished work by Roldán.

It is worth noting that the composer at this stage resorted sparingly to folk elements (except for the "Pregón"). It seems he wanted to familiarize himself with all the elements that made up the Cuban musical tradition, so he worked with secondhand materials, as long as they revealed rhythms and procedures. He arranged two *Danzas cubanas* by Laureanito Fuentes, so he could study the possibilities of the *contradanza*, before composing *La rebambaramba* (1928), a colonial ballet in two scenes based on a local event. Through Cuban Romantic engravings (mostly from Mialhe), it was an attempt to evoke the ebullient popular life of 1830s Havana during a Three Kings Day celebration. The first scene takes place in the patio of an old city mansion, on the night between January 5 and 6. The characters are mulatta women, carpenters, calash drivers, black cooks, a black *curro* [dandy], a Spanish soldier. The second scene simply shows the passing of the *comparsas* in San Francisco plaza, on the way to the captain general's residence, where the slaves would receive their *aguinaldo* [Epiphany gift].

Starting with an insistent and recurring minor second, Roldán organized his rhythmic world from the beginning with schematic, dry, and free quotes of themes that would later be fully developed. The first dance, with theme fully stated, was a *contradanza*, copied from the *segunda* of the *San Pascual Bailón* (1803). At the end of the first scene, in 6/8 time, reminiscent of the French *contradanzas*, things turn gradually more African until we get to the black world of the Three Kings Day celebration. Three episodes almost totally infuse the second scene: a rhythmically unique *lucumí comparsa*, apportioned to the strings playing heavy chords; the *comparsa* or *juego de culebra* [the snake game], with the intervention of voices in the orchestra pit, singing the true verses; and a *comparsa ñáñiga* as a kind of raucous coda. Aside from a Stravinskyan flourish (the second scene), which has disappeared from the suite currently offered in symphonic concerts (five pieces), Amadeo Roldán had found his voice and the right shading for his orchestral palette. *La rebambaramba* has remained as the most famous of his scores, having been performed in Mexico, Paris, Berlin, Budapest, Los Angeles, and Bogotá.

Finished with *La rebambaramba*, the composer wanted to write a complementary ballet that would evoke the modern rural life of Cuba. Based on a Cuban text, he composed *El milagro de Anaquillé*, a choreographed one-scene mystery play (1929). The musical action develops in the confines of a sugar mill, and begins by exploiting *guajiro* themes—a *décima* and a *zapateo*—before elaborating extremely intricate themes derived from *ñáñigo* initiation ceremonies. The "black-bottom" that accompanies the dance by the North American owners of the sugar mill serves as a bridge between the "white" and "black" worlds of Cuba, in this case perfectly demarcated. When it premiered, its grimness provoked scandal. Nothing in it sought to caress or seduce the listener. Harmonically, it is one of Roldán's severest scores. Everything is angular and linear. It is possible that this ballet has a certain post–*Rite of Spring* but pre–*Pulcinella* Stravinsky influence. But the color—that color of steel, with no trace of flattery, fugacity, or haziness, reflecting a mature handling of the orchestra—belongs entirely to Roldán.

As of 1930, after having worked for a large orchestra, Roldán saw himself increasingly drawn to tackling problems of sonority, balance, and construction elicited by smaller instrumental groupings. He had already written his *Danza negra,* based on a famous poem by Luis Palés Matos, for a female voice, two clarinets, two violas, and percussion (first performed in Paris). Now he began a series of his *Rítmicas,* four of them, for flute, oboe, clarinet, bassoon, horn, and piano (1930), played in Mexico and the United States. *Rítmicas V* and *VI,* written a few months later, were conceived exclusively for folk percussion instruments.

In these works one sees a sure evolution over previous scores. Roldán, following the inevitable road that all who work within a nationalist orbit must traverse, distances himself from the true folk element (so pronounced in *La rebambaramba,* and at the end of *El milagro de Anaquillé*), to find Afro-Cuban motifs within himself. The rhythm has ceased to be a textual borrowing: it is more his own vision of the known cells — a re-creation. Roldán's work gains in profundity, looking beyond folklore to the spirit of that folklore. In the last two *Rítmicas* he achieves, with the awareness of a refined artist, a work parallel to that of the *batá* drums, ruled by instinct. More than rhythms, he produces *rhythmic modes,* entire phrases that mix together and are completed, creating periods and sequences.

With *Tres toques* ("March," "Ritual," "Dance"), written in 1931 for chamber orchestra, he introduces a series of concerns that until then made the percussive forces (drums or instruments used liked drums) the linchpin of his previous works. Here the percussive action, though not dispensed with, is much less direct and constant. The percussion intervenes in certain passages as a building block, utilized to its maximum possibilities, but without playing a major role. The *toque* [drumbeat] is produced by all of the instruments present, establishing a *summa* of the factors that characterize mestizo or Afro-Cuban music, although it is placed in an absolutely personal sonic environment. The *Tres toques* comprise, without a doubt, the greatest effort of synthesis accomplished by Amadeo Roldán, drawing close to the spiritual core of certain *Choros* by Villa-Lobos.

After writing *Curujey* (1931), using a poem by Nicolás Guillén, for chorus, two pianos, and two percussion instruments, Roldán published in New York, in 1934, his *Motivos de son,* with texts by the same poet. Eight songs for voice and eleven instruments encompass the suite, which is an in-depth exploration of the lyrical expressions of black song. In it, despite very elaborate instrumental work, the melody retains all its prerogatives. It is an angular melody, fragmented, often subjected to the tonal characteristics of the genre, but in which the black realm has become Roldán's own language, flowing from within to the outer world. Exceedingly difficult to perform, these *Motivos de son* are among the most personal scores of the composer. It would be pointless to look for a manifest influence in them, a borrowed harmonic ruse. They constitute, up to now, a unique attempt in the history of Cuban music, because of the type of sonic and expressive problems they resolved.

To this work we must add the incidental music for Evreinov's *La muerte alegre* [The happy death — 1932]; two *Canciones populares cubanas*, with a *guajiro* lilt, for cello and piano (1928); a piece for piano, *Mulato* (1934), of little interest; a *Poema negro* (1930) for string quartet — taken from material of a quartet for lutes, written for the Aguilar brothers — and two *Piezas infantiles* for piano (1937), published in New York.

Amadeo Roldán died in 1939, at thirty-eight, victim of a particularly cruel illness that slowly deformed his body, without affecting his spirit. He devoted his last energies to sketching out future compositions and to notating all of a series of songs from Cuba's eastern provinces unknown to the majority of his contemporaries. As of 1932 he was director of the Philharmonic Orchestra, exerting himself in disseminating contemporary music, without slighting his performances of classical and Romantic music. Thanks to him, Beethoven's Ninth Symphony was heard in Cuba for the first time, with the collaboration of the Choral Society of Havana, founded and directed by María Muñoz de Quevedo.

His work embodied a technical contribution that should not be forgotten: for the first time the notation of the rhythms by Cuban folk instruments was executed with precision, revealing all of their technical possibilities, and with all the obtainable sounds by percussion, friction, shaking, glissandi with the fingers over the skins, and so on. In this regard, Roldán's method of transcription constitutes a veritable methodology that Cuban and foreign composers have followed.

As contemporaries who appeared at the same time and shared similar affinities, Amadeo Roldán and Alejandro García Caturla are two inseparable figures in the history of Cuban music. However, this confluence of tendencies and chronology should not make us forget that their natures were absolutely different and that, although it is true that they worked in parallel terrains, their respective works are diametrically opposed.

A disciple of Pedro Sanjuán and later of Nadia Boulanger, Alejandro García Caturla was the richest and most generous musical temperament the island has ever known. Endowed with true genius, his creative powers were manifest from adolescence in a series of vehement, dynamic works of uncontrollable expression, like a force of nature. This refined man who looked Irish, who assimilated everything with prodigious ease, learned languages without a teacher, and completed a law degree in three years without abandoning his musical studies, had always felt a powerful attraction to black culture — and not as an aesthetic game or as a reflection of the intellectual concerns of the day. He defied the bourgeois prejudices of his well-to-do caste, and married a black woman. This was typical of a fervent independence that characterized his entire life. That same independence also cost him his life: as a provincial trial judge, he did not buckle under pressure to absolve a delinquent who had been tried. The next day he was assassinated by two shots at point-blank range, fired by the same person he was going to condemn.

There is little to be said of his life. Aside from two trips to Europe, Alejandro García Caturla lived only to create music. His compulsion to compose was so great that during his stay in Paris he barely visited a museum or frequented artistic gatherings in the cafés, even though he was greatly admired in surrealist circles. He never left the rarefied orbit of the concert hall, the Russian ballets, Nadia Boulanger's house, and his work desk. Condemned to incomprehension by the milieu of the provincial cities he was relegated to, he organized orchestras and musical groups in all of the places he worked as a judge. Born in 1906, he died in 1940. In his last letters he bitterly complained that it was not possible for him to move to Havana and be more intimately involved in a musical life.

Alejandro García Caturla was barely a child when he handed the printer his first popular compositions: a bolero, a song, and three *danzones*. In one of them, "El olvido de la canción," unique rhythms already appear, given curious treatment, a speculative beginning to his experiments from within Cuban folklore. The discovery of contemporary music — principally Milhaud, Satie, Stravinsky — astonished him. For a short time he busied himself with more or less felicitous imitations, which he tossed into the archive of useless artifacts. He was not yet twenty when he returned to his own voice, looking for his own accent linked to Cuban concerns. But from the beginning, Caturla had a unique way of feeling the island's folklore. Unlike Roldán, he did not go to it, little by little, trying to first understand and then adjust to it. Having just released himself from his European fever, he went back to the *danzones* of his adolescence, starting anew from them. Without hesitation, he began expressing himself in a musical idiom nourished by black roots, guided by a dark instinct and by the affinities eloquently manifested in his private life. On the other hand, quite impermeable to Spain's traditions — Manuel de Falla never exerted the slightest influence on him — he passionately studied the creations of nineteenth-century Cuban composers, professing a true love for Saumell and Cervantes. He was powerfully attracted to that music, made from a slow fusion of classical elements, French themes, of throwbacks to the *tonadilla*, with black rhythms forged in the Americas. The last work he left us, an admirable *Berceuse campesina* (Peasant berceuse) for piano, is a posthumous reflection of these concerns. In a composition of surprising stylistic unity, he achieves a melodic and rhythmic synthesis of *guajiro* and black music through a process of total assimilation of both types of sensibility. Because *guajiro* music is monotonous and invariable and could not offer him rich material, he built his own melody, opened over two octaves, absolutely unsingable, yet with a surprising aroma of authenticity that departs from traditional meter or rhyme. By placing a *son* rhythm under the melody, he was able to achieve a miraculous balance between two genres of music that never tolerated the slightest fusion during various centuries of coexistence.

This mixing of genres explains all of his music. Caturla never took a folkloric genre separately, writing a *danza* or a rumba for orchestra in the spirit that animated the *Batuque* by Fernández, for example, or the *Danzas africanas* by Villa-Lobos. When García Caturla composed *La rumba,* he did not want a rhythmic movement for orchestra, just any old rumba that could be the first of a series. No, in *La rumba* he thought of the spirit of the rumba, of all the rumbas heard in Cuba since the arrival of the first blacks. He did not seek to experiment with the rhythm, building a crescendo until the end, according to the much-abused formula in vogue for the last twenty years. On the contrary, right from the introduction, showing a strange confidence in the lower woodwinds, he proceeded with sudden pulsations, with violent and rapid progressions, with a sealike swelling and release, in which all the rhythms of the genre were inscribed, inverted, crushed. He was not interested in the rhythms themselves, but instead in a general trepidation, a series of sonic outbursts, which would translate the essence of the rumba into a total vision. (Quite possibly, a black man of the streets would not know what dance moves should accompany such a score, which, nevertheless, expresses his most profound instincts.) The *Bembé* for woodwinds, brass, piano, and percussion, which premiered in Paris in 1929, and in which we find the soul of Santería dancing, is of a similar order as *La rumba.*

In the brief phase that Caturla worked under the sway of Milhaud and other European composers, and the following one, in which he finds his own voice, he wrote various *Danzas* for piano visibly inspired by Ignacio Cervantes. But if it is true that the model is identifiable, the type of writing resolves a unique problem: to find a sonority that is absolutely Cuban, with harmonic procedures as audacious as the music of the time. Interestingly, even with chords all bristling with alterations and that are difficult to play and read, Caturla elicits a sound within the Cervantes tradition, without forgetting the inevitable thirds and sixths. This was always one of Caturla's skills. When, in the first of the *Dos poemas afrocubanos* (Paris, 1929), he wrote, with his own technique, an accompaniment to the *tres,* the piano sounded like a *tres* despite the dissonant intervals. Caturla not only showed a surprising power to assimilate all the ambience around him, but also an instinctive tendency to re-create the timbre of folk instruments, even within the framework of a normal orchestra. (When he did employ those traditional instruments, he was always content to use the simplest Afro-Cuban percussion, without resorting to unusual timbres.) It was enough for him to use the clarinet, and said clarinet would become rustic, acidic, as if made from the poorly varnished wood of street musician instruments.

Caturla left behind a considerable amount of work, all reflecting the same kinds of concerns: to find a synthesis of all the musical genres of the island within his own mode of expression. His oeuvre includes the following: *Tres danzas cubanas,* for orchestra (1927); *Bembé,* for brass, woodwinds, piano, and percussion (1929); *Yamba-O,* a symphonic movement (1928–31); *Primera suite cubana,* for woodwinds and piano (1931); *La rumba* (1933); *Suite para orquesta* (1938); *Obertura cubana* (1938). He wrote a great number of works for voice and piano, with poems by Nicolás Guillén and by the author of this book. Also a poem, *Sabás,* for voice, five wind instruments, and piano, on a text by Guillén, and *El caballo blanco* (1931) and *Canto de los cafetales* (1937) for a capella mixed chorus. Among his piano works, one must cite, in addition to his Cervantes-like *Danzas,* a *Son* (1930), *Comparsa* (1936), *Danza lucumí* and *Danza del tambor* (1928), *Sonata corta* (1934), and the *Berceuse campesina,* published in New York with another *Son* (1944). More fortunate than Roldán in having his work published, many of Caturla's compositions were printed by New Music Edition in New York and by Editions Maurice Senart in Paris. The Interamerican Institute of Musicology in Montevideo brought out his *Dos canciones corales.* When he died, he left an unstaged chamber opera, *Manita en el suelo,* on one of our texts [by Caturla and Carpentier], which scenically featured some characters of Cuban popular mythology: Papá Montero, Candita la Loca, Juan Odio, Juan Indio, Juan Esclavo, the Virgen de la Caridad del Cobre, the Gallo Motoriongo, the Chino de la Charada, Tata Cuñengue, and so on.

Certain scores by Caturla sin from an excessive richness. The sonic dough is kneaded with a full hand, without consideration for the performer. Once again, one can see the difference between Caturla and Roldán. In Roldán, an orchestral conductor, everything is measured, placed at the opportune time, at the mercy of a previous, sometimes cold, calculation. In Caturla, on the contrary, the orchestra can become an earthquake, but never a finely made watch. A barbarous, primitive force is brought to the terrain of civilized instruments, with all the luxuries available to a composer familiar with all the modern schools. And yet, except for some brief and fleeting Stravinsky influences (so briefly seen that they are barely noticeable), something, cleverly observed by Adolfo Salazar, contributes to distancing Caturla from any kind of harmonic atmosphere seen before: those rare scales integral to his idiom. "A turn of phrase typical of Caturla," says Salazar, "is the narrowness of the melodic ambience and the avoidance of intervals of minor seconds within it." Quite often the assimilation of black music makes him conceive his themes within the limits of the pentatonic scale. From there, if he tends to use polytonality, the character of his ideas impedes him from being boxed in by a clever formula. His themes always have the freshness of a primitive chant. The peculiar spirit that suffused Caturla's work always gave it an unmistakable character.

He seemed to be lacking something in his last years: the gift of simplification, of being able to attain with the greatest economy of means what he had achieved until now, using all of the orchestral luxuries. The *Berceuse campesina,* a posthumous work, written with a frightening simplicity, as if meant to be played by children, shows us that Caturla had finally been able to tame his temperament, putting the reins of an angel on the devil that dwelled within him.

The adversaries of nationalist tendencies that prevail today in Brazil, in Mexico, and to a greater or lesser degree in almost all of the nations of the New World, often use the following polemical argument: to gain inspiration from the music of blacks, Indians, or primitive men is no sign of progress; to cut ties with the great

European artistic tradition, subsituting the great disciplines of Western culture with voodoo, the *juego ñáñigo*, the *batuque* of the *candombe*, is equivalent to reneging on the most noble roots of our idiosyncracy, replacing a harpsichord with a drum.

However, those who reason in this fashion often forget that the Latin American composer, turning toward Europe to find aesthetic solutions to problems, has heard nothing if not about folklore, popular songs, primitive rhythms, and nationalist schools, for more than forty years. After Grieg, Dvořák, the Five Russians, who were part of his adolescent ambience, the Latin American composer gets to know Stravinsky by way of *Petrouchka*, *The Rite of Spring*, *Les Noces*, and *The Fox*. Spain arrives in the form of the voice of Albéniz and the de Falla of *El amor brujo* [Love, the sorcerer] and *El sombrero de tres picos* [The three-cornered hat]; Hungary in the form of Béla Bartók; Italy in *La giara* by Casella. He sees how Milhaud takes on Brazilian music and Cuban *danzones*,[1] introducing *güiros* and maracas into his orchestra (*The Ox on the Roof*). The North Americans Copland and Mac Bride ransacked Mexican folklore. Schoenberg offers eulogies to Gershwin and shuns North American atonalists. In Russia, regional music is exalted. Of course, along with this we have the *Concerto* by de Falla, Poulenc's *Concert champêtre*, Hindemith's *Schwanendreher*, the *Concertante Overture* by Rodolfo Halffter. But, looking closely at these works—are they not in some way an exponent of musical nationalism? Are they not responding to profound conceptions of racial genius or the expression of idiosyncracies?

The young Latin American composer turns his eyes to his own world. There, still fresh, virginal, are the themes that Milhaud has left for him; the primitive impulses that did not appear in *The Rite of Spring;* a polyrhythm in an unpolished state, which outpaces anything by the "advanced" composers of Europe. And, furthermore, what the French composer has used as an exotic, disconcerting, unexpected element is full-fledged and authentic for a Brazilian, for a Cuban, for a Mexican, who carries it deep within. In creating a nationalist work, is he not responding in full sincerity to an order of concerns that has precisely been the product of the highest European culture of the last few years?

Of course, nationalism has never been a definitive solution. The cultured music of a country cannot develop exclusively as a function of its folklore. It is a mere passage. But an inevitable passage since it was seen as a necessary step for all the musical schools of Europe. Thanks to popular song, as Boris de Schloezer once pointed out, the schools of the Old Continent acquired their own accent. This truth is so evident that it frees us from having to give examples. Surrounded by popular expressions in a continuous process of creation — not of a dying folklore as in France, where peasants sing the latest hits by Maurice Chevalier — the Latin American composer starts working with what he has at hand, looking for the characteristics that in fact belong to him. At least this is a way of evading the dangerous desire to imitate what is perfectly realized and accomplished on the other side of the Atlantic. Finding a national accent with the help of living elements of folklore — and someone like Glinka did not proceed otherwise — the musician of the New World ends up by freeing himself from folklore, finding in his own sensibility the reasons for a national idiosyncracy. When this happens you get the creation of a *Concierto para piano y orquesta* by Carlos Chávez, as the outgrowth of a natural process. The adventure we are living through now is that of all countries with a rich folklore, and whose musical consciousness has experienced, for different reasons, a late awakening.

With their probing compositions, Roldán and Caturla liberated the current generation of Cuban musicians from a good many anxieties, reducing the range of certain problems whose solution seemed overwhelming twenty years ago. For the moment, they opened good and wide pathways in the Afro-Cuban *manigua*.[2]

Notes

Introduction

1. Alejo Carpentier, *Entrevistas,* ed. Virgilio López Lemus (Havana: Editorial Letras Cubanas, 1985), 218.

2. The amount of scholarly work on rap has grown to huge proportions. A small sampling might include David Toop, *Rap Attack 2: African Rap to Global Hip Hop* (London and New York: Serpent's Tail, 1991); Nelson George, *Hip Hop America* (New York: Viking, 1998); Timothy Brennan, "Off the Gangsta Tip: A Rap Appreciation, or Forgetting about Los Angeles," *Critical Inquiry* 20 (summer 1994): 663–93; Houston A. Baker, *Black Studies, Rap and the Academy* (Chicago: University of Chicago Press, 1993).

3. Alejo Carpentier, "Sóngoro Cosongo . . . en París," in *Obras completas* (Coyoacán: Siglo veintiuno, 1985), 8:32.

4. Ibid.

5. Araceli García-Carranza, *Bibliografía de Alejo Carpentier* (Havana: Editorial Letras Cubanas, 1984), 19.

6. Carpentier, *Entrevistas,* 85.

7. Ibid., 26.

8. Ibid., 196.

9. Ibid., 238, 323.

10. Ortiz's *Africanía de la música folklórica de Cuba* would appear with the Editorial Universitaria in 1950. Ortiz, a member of the white elite educated in Spain and, later, a well-connected consular official in Genoa and Marseilles, helped found the Society of Cuban Folklore in 1923 at the age of forty-four. He went on to become the most celebrated ethnographer his country ever produced.

11. Carpentier, *Entrevistas,* 185, 226.

12. Ibid., 226.

13. Martín Casanovas, ed., *Revista de Avance* (Havana: Colección Orbite, 1965).

14. Carpentier, *Entrevistas,* 163.

15. Alejo Carpentier, "Un ballet afrocubano," *Revista Cubana* 8:22–24 (April–June 1937): 146–47.

16. Carpentier, *Entrevistas*, 249.

17. Walter Benjamin, "Surrealism: The Last Snapshot of the European Intelligentsia," in *Reflections* (New York: Schocken, 1978; essay published in 1929), 180; César Vallejo, *Autopsy on Surrealism* (Willimantic, Conn.: Curbstone, 1982).

18. Marie-Claire Dumas, *Robert Desnos ou l'exploration des limites* (Paris: Librairie Klincksieck, 1980), 136.

19. Ibid., 137.

20. Mary Ann Caws, *The Surrealist Voice of Robert Desnos* (Amherst: University of Massachusetts Press, 1977), 9.

21. Alejo Carpentier, "México, según una película europea," in *Obras completas*, 8:386.

22. Carpentier, *Entrevistas*, 176.

23. Michael Richardson, ed., *Refusal of the Shadow: Surrealism and the Caribbean* (London and New York: Verso, 1996), 205.

24. Carpentier, *Entrevistas*, 18.

25. Ibid., 19.

26. Carpentier was frustrated by the denial of Picabia's origins, a topic he returned to repeatedly. See, for example, *Sobre el surrealismo*, the documentary film he wrote in 1973 (reprinted in "Conferencias," in *Obras completas*, 14:16): "The Cubanness of Picabia").

27. Alejo Carpentier, "El cubano Picabia," in *Obras completas*, 9: 384.

28. Ibid.

29. Carpentier, *Entrevistas*, 275.

30. Alejo Carpentier, "América ante la joven literatura europea," in *Obras completas*, 9:299.

31. Alejo Carpentier, "Primer viaje a la Exposición Colonial," in ibid., 8:280; "La Exposición Internacional de París," in ibid., 9:408.

32. Carpentier, "América ante la joven literatura europea," 298.

33. Ibid., 301, 300.

34. André Breton, "Silence Is Golden," in *Music Is Dangerous*, ed. Paul Nougé (New York: Peter Garland, 1973), 3; Breton's emphasis. Breton's essay was written in 1944.

35. Richardson, *Refusal of the Shadow*, 146.

36. Carpentier, "Sóngoro Cosongo . . . en París," 323–24.

37. There are exceptions, although work on early radio in general is still tentative. See W. J. West, ed., *Orwell: The War Broadcasts* (London: Gerald Duckworth, 1985); Jeffrey Mehlman, *Walter Benjamin for Children: An Essay on His Radio Years* (Chicago: University of Chicago Press, 1993); (on

Artaud) Allen S. Weiss, *Phantasmic Radio* (Durham, N.C.: Duke University Press, 1995).

38. Anton Kaes, Martin Jay, and Edward Dimendberg, eds., *The Weimar Republic Sourcebook* (Berkeley: University of California Press, 1994), 595.

39. Ibid., 597.

40. Carpentier, "Sóngoro Cosongo... en París," 323–24.

41. Alejo Carpentier, "Rita Montaner," in *Obras completas,* 10:403–4.

42. Alejo Carpentier, "La radio y sus nuevas posibilidades," in *Obras completas,* 9:392; Carpentier's emphasis.

43. Carpentier, *Entrevistas,* 201.

44. Dumas, *Robert Desnos ou l'exploration des limites,* 215.

45. Denis Maréchal, *Radio Luxembourg 1933–1993* (Nancy: Presses Universitaires de Nancy, 1994), 70.

46. Dumas, *Robert Desnos ou l'exploration des limites,* 210.

47. The Spanish term Carpentier uses is *"bufo."* I have rendered it here with its original spelling rather than anglicize it ("buffo") in order to distinguish it from the so-called opera buffa of Europe. In *Music in Cuba,* Carpentier describes at length the *zarzuela,* a small-scale operatic form borrowed from Spain that Cubans filled with serious social content during the Afro-Cuban period. The "mulata" was one of the stock characters of this musical/social genre. The *bufo* contains features similar to the *zarzuela* in its ribald, satirical, "low" comedic manifestations. The *teatro vernáculo* and traveling comedy troupes found the "negrito" character prominent, and it is this kind of genre Carpentier has in mind when he writes about the *"bufo."*

48. For a better reading of this form, see Robin Moore, *Nationalizing Blackness* (Pittsburgh: Pittsburgh University Press, 1997), 132–46.

49. Klaus Mueller-Bergh, ed., "Corrientes vanguardistas y surrealismo en la obra de Alejo Carpentier," in *Asedios a Carpentier* (Santiago: Editorial Universitaria, 1972), 20.

50. Carpentier *Entrevistas,* 230. Subsequent references will be given in the text.

51. García-Carranza, *Bibliografía de Alejo Carpentier,* 18.

52. Joan Dayan, "Preface" to René Depestre, *A Rainbow for the Christian West* (Amherst: University of Massachusetts, 1977), 48.

53. Milton Meltzer, *Langston Hughes: A Biography* (New York: Thomas Y. Crowell, 1968), 148–49.

54. Langston Hughes, *The Big Sea: An Autobiography* (New York and London: Alfred A. Knopf, 1940), 249.

55. Edward J. Mullen, ed., *Langston Hughes in the Hispanic World and Haiti* (Hamden, Conn.: Archon Books, 1977), 25.

56. Ibid., 324.

57. Langston Hughes, *Ask Your Mama: 12 Moods for Jazz* (New York: Alfred A. Knopf, 1961), 50–51.

58. Edouard Glissant, *Caribbean Discourse* (Charlottesville: University Press of Virginia, 1989), 111.

59. James Weldon Johnson, *Autobiography of an Ex-Colored Man* (New York: Vintage Books, 1989; first published in 1927), xi.

60. Leo Brouwer, *La música, lo cubano y la innovación* (Havana: Editorial Letras Cubanas, 1982), 18.

61. See, for example, Alejo Carpentier, "Abuso de la palabra folklore," in *Obras completas*, 11:195.

62. Carpentier, *Entrevistas*, 99.

63. Eduardo Sánchez de Fuentes, "Influencia de los ritmos africanos en nuestro cancionero," in *Evolución de la cultura cubana 1608–1927*, ed. José Manuel Carbonell (Havana: Imprenta El Siglo XX, 1928), 155–202; and "La Música cubana y sus orígenes, *Boletín Latino-Americano de música* (Bogotá) 4 (October 1938): 177–82.

64. Carpentier, *Entrevistas*, 22. Subsequent references will be given in the text.

65. Theodor Adorno, "Why Still Philosophy" and "Philosophy and Teachers," in *Critical Models: Interventions and Catchwords*, trans. Henry W. Pickford (New York: Columbia University Press, 1998); and "Skoteinos, or How to Read Hegel," in *Hegel: Three Studies*, trans. Shierry Weber Nicholsen (Cambridge: MIT Press), 89–148.

66. Carpentier, *Entrevistas*, 183.

67. Rolf Wiggershaus, *The Frankfurt School: Its History, Theories, and Political Significance*, trans. Michael Robertson (Cambridge: MIT Press, 1994), 70.

68. Carpentier, *Entrevistas*, 43.

69. Alejo Carpentier, "El jazz y los jóvenes," in *Obras completas*, 11:163.

70. Ibid.

71. Alejo Carpentier, "Moisés Simons y el piano Luis XV de Josephine Baker," in *Obras completas*, 9:322.

72. Alejo Carpentier, "El jazz y la música culta," in *Obras completas*, 11:166.

73. Alejo Carpentier, "Don Azpiazu en París," in *Obras completas*, 8:302–3.

74. Carpentier, *Entrevistas*, 34.

75. Ibid.

76. Ibid., 33.

77. Ibid., 357.

78. Theodor Adorno, *The Philosophy of Modern Music* (New York: Seabury Press, 1980), 138.

79. A very good, but I think finally failed, attempt to do so can be found in Thomas Y. Levin's "For the Record: Adorno on Music," *October* 55 (winter 1990):23–47. Levin tends to mix together several controversies surrounding Adorno, defending him against the antitechnological bias found in his writing on film and the phonograph, at the same time that he defends him on "popular music and jazz" (23). The combined defense eases his standards of proof. He expertly defends Adorno's views on technology but says nothing new to defend him on popular music — an aspect that gets lost in the larger argument. I believe that Adorno's contributions to the critique of modern culture are unrivaled, but it would be a mistake to temporize about his theories of black culture in the Americas. He quite literally did not know what he was talking about. To argue, as some have, that when he said "jazz," he meant white big-band music (Paul Whiteman, Benny Goodman) is unconvincing, in part because he lived into the post–bebop era and never revised his comments.

80. See, for example, Ben Watson, *Frank Zappa: The Negative Dialectics of Poodle Play* (London: Quartet Books, 1994), 4–10, 46–48.

81. See Ronald Radano, *New Musical Figurations: Anthony Braxton's Cultural Critique* (Chicago: University of Chicago Press, 1993), 230.

82. To take only two recent examples, Elena Pérez Sanjurjo's *Historia de la música cubana* (Miami: Moderna Poesía, 1986) is thoroughly dependent on the information and organization of Carpentier's book, but seeks to hide the fact by failing even to list him in her bibliography, much less emphasize his importance. Robin Moore's *Nationalizing Blackness* (Pittsburgh: University of Pittsburgh Press, 1997) does indeed cite Carpentier, but begrudgingly and misleadingly. It goes out of its way to give the impression that Carpentier's influence is minor (at times quoting other Cuban writers who themselves borrowed freely from *Music in Cuba*). Although Moore's book goes beyond Carpentier's in its treatment of the *bufo* form, he — like Sanjurjo — repeats Carpentier's insights without crediting him. In Cuba itself, Carpentier has prompted a more forthright following. Among those nodding in his direction are José Ardévol, Carmen Valdés, Gloria Antolitia, and Zoila Lapique Becali. Musicologists such as Leonardo Acosta, Harold Gramatges, Argeliers Leon, and María Teresa Linares have all benefited from the book, while remaining original scholars in their own right. They represent the wave of Cuban scholarship and musical theory that the book, as it were, announced.

83. Odilio Urfé, "Factores que integran la música cubana," *Islas* 2 (September–December 1959):7–21; and Alberto Muguercia y Muguercia, "Teodora Ginés: mito o realidad histórica?" *Revista de la Biblioteca Nacional José Martí* 8 (September–December 1971):53–85.

84. Carpentier, *Entrevistas*, 239.

Preface

1. One exception must be made: the well-documented study by Edwin Tolón and Jorge Antonio González, *Óperas cubanas y sus autores*.

1. The Sixteenth Century

1. José Manuel Ximeno, *Obispos de Cuba* [Bishops of Cuba].
2. Undoubtedly, this refers to a panpipe or a reed flute.

2. The Seventeenth Century

1. Gabriel Saldívar, *Historia de la música en México*, 1934.

3. Esteban Salas

1. Although we have more than enough reason to believe that it is in a private library not willing to reveal how it was acquired.
2. Burial records, Number 7, Folio 25, Verso #50, Cathedral of Santiago, Cuba.

4. Salon and Theater at the End of the Eighteenth Century

1. That is, the impresario, or director of the company.
2. Don Juan Manuel Mármol, a builder of clavichords and pianos, moved to Mexico shortly afterward.

6. Introduction to the *Contradanza*

1. Wimpfen, *Voyage a St. Domingue*, 1797.
2. Quoted by Pérez de la Riva.

7. Blacks in Cuba

1. [A type of fish. — *Trans.*]
2. [A mountain song. — *Trans.*]
3. It is important to point out here the inexplicable error of Sánchez de Fuentes, a statement that has surprised eminent Latin American musicologists. After, reading in an old chronicle that "the class of mulatas was what distinguished itself at these dances," Sánchez de Fuentes arrived at the unique conclusion that the "mulatas" were a type of dance. The truth is that in Cuba there never was a dance with that kind of name.
4. This fact was unearthed by Herminio Portell Vilá.

9. Antonio Raffelin–Juan París

1. See the correspondence of Domingo del Monte.
2. What is most surprising is that this affirmation comes from Laureano Fuentes, who was, to a certain extent, a disciple of París.

10. Saumell and Nationalism

1. It is curious that Sánchez de Fuentes is the author of this generally admitted statement, when in one of his essays he refers to a contest of *danzones* given in Havana a year earlier.

12. Ignacio Cervantes

1. [*Manigua* means "bush," a remote area with dense vegetation. Many runaway slaves started a new life in the *manigua* and the phrase *irse a la manigna* (go to the *manigna*) in the nineteenth century meant to take up arms against Spanish colonialism. More than a locale with lush vegetation, the word *manigua* carries a profound symbolic weight that resonates with Cuba's racial dilemmas, identity, and history. — *Trans.*]
2. The statement is by Serafín Ramírez, a close family member of the composer and a very esteemed critic of his time.

13. Cuban *Bufos*

1. We have found the original manuscripts.
2. I am referring to the most typical example of this drum, which consisted at first of one percussive surface. After an absurd prohibition that banished its use in popular groups for a while, it reappeared coupled with a twin drum, higher pitched, displacing the *timbales* or *timbalitos*, taking over its function. Nowadays, popular musicians designate it with the name of *bongoses,* and not *bongó.*

15. A Transition Period

1. A fact discovered by Joaquín Argote.

17. Amadeo Roldán–Alejandro García Caturla

1. The overture that opens up his orchestral version of the *Saudades do Brazil* is written over a *danzón* by Antonio María Romeu, *Triunfadores,* heard by Milhaud in Puerto Rico, according to a personal conversation with Milhaud.
2. [See note 1 in chapter 12. — *Trans.*]

Bibliography

Manuscripts

Actas Capitulares del Ayuntamiento de Santiago de Cuba.
Actas Capitulares de la Catedral de La Habana.
Actas Capitulares de la Catedral de Santiago de Cuba.
Capilla de Música, Cajón sin número, Catedral de La Habana.
Capilla de Música, Cajón sin número, Catedral de Santiago de Cuba.
Cartas de Ignacio Cervantes, Archivo de los herederos del compositor.
Carta de Alejandro García Caturla, Archivo de Alejo Carpentier.
Fondo Guillermo Tomás, Biblioteca Nacional, La Habana.
Fondo Gaspar Villante, Biblioteca de la Sociedad Económica de Amigos del País, La Habana.
Libro de Entierros, núm. 7, Folio 25 vuelto, núm. 50, Catedral de Santiago de Cuba.

Cuban Periodicals

Apolo Habanero, El, 1836.
Archivo del Folklore, La Habana, 1924 *ss.*
Aviso, El, La Habana, 1805.
Cartera Cubana, La, La Habana, 1838.
Cuba y América, New York, 1897 *ss.* (La Habana).
Cuba Musical, La Habana, 1882.
Curioso Americano, El, La Habana, 1892.
Diario del Gobierno de La Habana, 1812–20.
Diario de La Habana, 1810–12.
Don Juñipero, 1862 *ss.*
Figaro, El, La Habana, 1888 *ss.*
Guirnalda Cubana, La, 1854.
Lucero de La Habana, El, 1831–32.
Moda o Recreo Semanal del Bello Sexo, La, La Habana, 1892.
Musicalia, La Habana, 1928 *ss.*

Noticioso y Lucero de La Habana, El, 1832.
Papel Periódico de La Habana, 1790–1805.
Plantel, El, La Habana, 1833.
Regañón de La Habana, El, 1800.
Revista Cubana, La Habana, 1935 ss.
Revista de Estudios Afrocubanos, La Habana, 1937.
Revista Musical, Artística y Literaria de La Habana, 1883.
Revue Musicale, La, París, 1922 ss.
Semanario Cubano, El, Santiago de Cuba, 1851.

General Sources

Abbad y Lasierra, Iñigo. *Historia geográfica, civil y natural de la isla de San Juan Bautista de Puerto Rico* [1782], Puerto Rico: Impr. y Librería de Acosta, 1866.

Abbot, Abiel. *Letters Written in the Interior of Cuba, between the Mountain of Arcana, to the East, and of Cusco, to the West, in the Months of February, March, April and May*. Boston: Bowles and Dearborn, 1829.

Andueza, *La isla de Cuba pintoresca*. Madrid, 1841.

Arrate, José Martín Félix de. *Llave del Nuevo Mundo, antemural de las Indias Occidentales. La Habana descripta: Noticias de su fundación, aumentos y estados* [1761]. La Habana, 1876.

Arrom, José Juan. *Historia de la literatura dramática cubana*, New Haven: Yale University Press, 1944.

Azcuy Alón, Fanny. *Psicografía y supervivencia de los aborígenes de Cuba*. La Habana: Ediciones Revista de Educación, 1941.

Bacardí Moreau, Emilio. *Crónicas de Santiago de Cuba*. 10 vols. Santiago de Cuba: Arroyo Hermanos, 1929.

Bachiller y Morales, Antonio. *Apuntes para la historia de las leyes y la instrucción pública de la isla de Cuba*. 3 vols. La Habana: Impr. De P. Massana, 1859–61.

———. *Cuba: monografía histórica que comprende desde la pérdida de La Habana hasta la restauración española*. La Habana, Librería Miguel de Villa, 1883.

———. *Cuba primitiva. Origen, lenguas, tradiciones e historia de los indios de las Antillas Mayores y las Lucayas*. 2d. ed. La Habana: Librería Miguel de Villa, 1883.

———. *Los negros*. Barcelona: Gorgas, 1887; Colección facticia Vidal Morales.

Cabrera, Lidia. *Cuentos negros de Cuba*. Prólogo de Fernando Ortiz. La Habana: La Verónica, 1940.

Calcagno, Francisco. *Diccionario biográfico cubano*, New York: Imprenta y Librería de Néstor Ponce de León, 1878 [hasta la p. 120]; La Habana: Librería e Imprenta de Elías Fernández, 1885–86.

Calendario manual y Guía de forastero de la Isla de Cuba para el año de 1798. La Habana: Imprenta de la Capitanía General, 1798.

Campos, Rubén. *El folklore y la música mexicana; investigación acerca de la cultura musical en México (1525–1925).* México: Secretaría de Educación Pública, 1928.

————. *El folklore musical de las ciudades.* México, 1930.

Castellanos, Israel. *Instrumentos musicales de los afrocubanos.* La Habana: Imprenta El Siglo XX, 1927.

Cernicchiaro, Vincenzo. *Storia della musica nel Brasille, Dai Tempi Coloniali sino ai nostri giorni (1549–1925).* Milán: Stab. Edit. Fratelli Riccioni, 1926.

Colección de documentos inéditos relativos al descubrimiento, conquista y organización de las antiguas posesiones de Ultramar. secunda serie, vol. 6. Madrid: Real Academia de la Historia, 1891.

Cotarelo y Mori, Emilio. *Colección de entremeses, loas, jácaras y mojigangas desde fines del siglo XVI a mediados del XVIII.* Madrid: Bailly-Baillière, 1911.

Crespo y Borbón, Bartolomé José. *Un ajiaco o La boda de Pancha Jutía y Canuto Raspadura; juguete cómico por Creto Gangá.* La Habana: Impr. de Oliva, 1847.

Chacón y Calvo, José María. *Romances tradicionales de Cuba.* La Habana: El Siglo XX, 1914.

Chase, Gilbert. *La música de España,* Buenos Aires: Librería Hachette, 1943.

Dantés Bellegarde. *La nation haïtienne.* París, 1938.

Díaz del Castillo, Bernal. *Historia verdadera de la conquista de la Nueva España.* París: Louis-Michaud, 1837.

Diccionario de Autoridades, de la Real Academia.

Fernández de Castro, José Antonio. *Medio siglo de historia colonial de Cuba. Cartas a José Antonio Saco ordenadas y comentadas (1823 a 1879).* La Habana: R. Veloso, 1923.

Fernández de Oviedo, Gonzalo. *Historia general y natural de las Indias, Islas y tierra-firme del Mar Océano.* 4 vols. Madrid: Impr. de la Real Academia de la Historia, 1851–55.

Ford, Jeremiah, D. M. and Raphael I. Maxwell. *A Bibliography of Cuban Belles-Lettres,* Cambridge: Harvard University Press, 1933.

Fors, Luis Ricardo. *Gottschalk.* La Habana: La Propaganda Literaria, 1880.

Fuentes Matons, Laureano. *Las artes en Santiago de Cuba.* Santiago de Cuba: Imprenta Ravelo, 1893.

González, Enrique. *Discours sur la musique.* La Habana, 1853.

Grenet, Emilio. *Música popular cubana.* La Habana: Secretaría de Agricultura, 1939.

Guerra y Sánchez, Ramiro. *Manual de historia de Cuba* (económica, social y política). La Habana: Cultural S. A., 1938.

Guillén, Nicolás. *Claudio José Domingo Brindis de Salas, el rey de las octavas*. La Habana: Municipio de La Habana, 1935.

Guiteras, Pedro José. *Historia de las Isla de Cuba*. 3 vols. La Habana: Cultural S. A., 1927–28.

Iraizoz, Antonio. *Lecturas cubanas*. La Habana: Editorial Hermes, 1939.

Las Casas, Bartolomé de. *Historia de las Indias*. Madrid: Imp. De M. Ginesta, 1875–76.

López Chavarri, Eduardo. *Música popular española*. Barcelona: Editorial Labor, 1927.

Mayer-Serra, Otto. *Panorama de la música mexicana; desde la independencia hasta la actualidad*. México: El Colegio de México, 1941.

Mendoza, Vicente T. *El romance español y el corrido mexicano, estudio comparativo*. México: Eds. de la Universidad Nacional Autónoma, 1939.

Mitjans, Aurelio. *Estudio sobre el movimiento científico y literario en Cuba* [obra editada póstumamente]. La Habana: Impr. de A. Álvarez, 1890.

Morell de Santa Cruz, Pedro Agustín. *Relación histórica de los primeros obispos y gobernadores de Cuba*. La Habana, 1841.

———. *Historia de la isla y catedral de Cuba*. La Habana: Imprenta Cuba Intelectual, 1929.

Ortiz, Fernando. *Los negros brujos*. Madrid, 1906.

———. *Los negros esclavos; estudio sociológico y de derecho público*. La Habana: Bimestre Cubana, 1916.

———. *Los cabildos afrocubanos*. La Habana: Imprenta La Universal, 1921.

———. *La fiesta afrocubana del día de Reyes*. La Habana, 1926.

———. *La clave xilofónica de la música cubana, Ensayo Etnográfico*. La Habana: Tipografía Molina y Cía., 1935.

Ortiz Oderigo, Néstor R. *Panorama de la música afroamericana*. Buenos Aires: Editorial Claridad, 1944.

Pérez de la Riva y Pons, Francisco. *El café; historia de su cultivo y explotación en Cuba*. La Habana: J. Montero, 1944.

Pezuela, Jacobo de la. *Ensayo histórico de la Isla de Cuba*. New York: Impr. Española R. Rafael, 1842.

Portell Vilá, Herminio. *Histora de Cuba en sus relaciones con los Estados Unidos y España*. La Habana, 1938.

Ramírez, Serafín. *La Habana artística. Apuntes históricos*. La Habana: Imprenta del E. M. de la Capitanía General, 1891.

Ramos, Arthur. *Las culturas negras en el Nueva Mundo*. México: Fondo de Cultura Económica, 1943.

———. *Las poblaciones del Brasil*. México: Fondo de Cultura Económica, 1944.

Roig de Leuchsenring, Emilio. *Historia de La Habana: I, desde sus primeros días hasta 1595*. La Habana: Municipio de La Habana, 1938.

Rosain, Domingo. *Necrópolis de La Habana. Historia de los cementerios de esta ciudad con multitud de noticias interesantes.* La Habana: Impr. El Trabajao, 1875.

Roumain, Jacques. *Le Sacrifice du Tambour Assohtor.* Puerto Príncipe, 1943.

Sachs, Curt. *The History of Musical Instruments.* New York: W. W. Norton, 1940.

———. *Historia de la danza.* Buenos Aires, 1945.

Saco, José Antonio. *Memoria sobre la vagancia en la isla de Cuba.* La Habana, 1832.

Salazar, Adolfo. "La obra musical de Alejandro García Caturla." *Revista Cubana,* vol. XI, núm. 31, La Habana, enero de 1938.

Sánchez de Fuente, Eduardo. *El folklore en la música cubana.* La Habana: Imprenta El Siglo XX, 1923.

———. *Folklorismo.* La Habana: Imp. Molina y Compañía, 1928.

Seabrok, William. *The Magic Island.* New York, 1929.

Subirá, José. *La tonadilla escénica.* 3 vols. Madrid: Tipografía de Archivo, Publicaciones de la Real Academia Española, 1928–30.

Tolón, Edwin T., and Jorge Antonio González. *Óperas cubanas y sus autores.* La Habana: Ucar García, 1943.

Torre y de la Torre, José María de la. *Lo que fuimos y lo que somos, La Habana antigua y moderna.* La Habana: Impr. Spencer y Cía., 1857.

Trelles, Carlos Manuel. *Bibliografía histórica cubana.* 3 vols. Matanzas: Imprenta de Quirós y Estrada, 1911–17.

Urrutia, José Ignacio de. *Teatro histórico, jurídico y político de la isla Fernandina y principalmente de su capital La Habana.* 2 vols. La Habana: Imprenta El Siglo XX, A. Muñiz y Hno., 1931.

Vaissière, Pierre de. *Saint-Domingue; la société et la vie créole sous l'ancien régime (1629–1789).* París: Perrim, 1909.

Vega, Carlos. *Danzas y canciones argentinas.* Buenos Aires, 1936.

Villaverde, Cirilo. *Cecilia Valdés o La loma del Ángel.* New York: Impr. de El Espejo, 1882.

Wimpfen, Barón de. *Voyage à Saint Domingue.* Paris, 1797.

Wright, Irene. *Historia documentada de San Cristóbal de La Habana en el siglo XVI, basada en los documentos originales existentes en el Archivo general de Indias en Sevilla* [vol. 1 siglo XVI; vol. 2 siglo XVII]. La Habana: Emprenta El Siglo XX, 1927–30.

Ximeno, José Manuel. *Obispos de Cuba.*

Zaldívar, Gabriel. *Historia de la música en México.* México, 1934.

Index

Compiled by Alan West-Durán

Alejo Carpentier (1904–80), Cuban novelist, essayist, and musicologist, first published *Music of Cuba* in 1946. His novels include *Explosion in a Cathedral*, *The Chase*, and *The Lost Steps*, all published by the University of Minnesota Press, and *The Kingdom of This World*.

Timothy Brennan has written on popular music, race, cultural theory, imperial politics, and minority fiction for a variety of publications, including *Transition*, *Public Culture*, *South Atlantic Quarterly*, and *Critical Inquiry*. His reviews and feature articles have appeared in *The Nation*, the *Times Literary Supplement*, and the *Minneapolis Star Tribune*. He is a former radio journalist in Central America and the author of *At Home in the World: Cosmopolitanism Now* and *Salman Rushdie and the Third World: Myths of the Nation*. He is now at work on a book on Havana and New York Bohemia.

Alan West-Durán was awarded the Latino Literature Prize in Poetry in 1996. He is the author of *Tropics of History: Cuba Imagined*, a book of essays, and he has translated writing by Rosario Ferré, Luis Rafael Sánchez, Cristina García, Dulce María Loynaz, and Nancy Morejón. He teaches at Northeastern University.